Prentice-Hall
Contemporary Topics in Accounting Series

ALFRED RAPPAPORT, SERIES EDITOR

REPLACEMENT COST ACCOUNTING

REPLACEMENT COST ACCOUNTING

LAWRENCE REVSINE

Graduate School of Management, Northwestern University

PRENTICE-HALL, INC., ENGLEWOOD CLIFFS, NEW JERSEY

Library of Congress Cataloging in Publication Data

REVSINE, LAWRENCE.
    Replacement cost accounting.

    Includes bibliographical references.
    1. Cost accounting.   2. Replacement of industrial
equipment.   I. Title.
HF5686.C8R43   657'.42   73-1709
ISBN 0-13-773648-7
ISBN 0-13-773630-4 (pbk)

PRINTED IN THE UNITED STATES OF AMERICA

10 9 8 7 6 5 4 3 2 1

Prentice-Hall International, Inc., LONDON
Prentice-Hall of Australia, Pty. Ltd., SYDNEY
Prentice-Hall of Canada, Ltd., TORONTO
Prentice-Hall of India Private Limited, NEW DELHI
Prentice-Hall of Japan, Inc., TOKYO

Contents

vii

Foreword

Accounting, broadly conceived as the measurement and communication of economic information relevant to decision makers, has undergone dramatic changes during the past decade. Recent advances in quantitative methods, the behavioral sciences, and information technology are influencing current thinking in financial as well as managerial accounting. Leasing, pension plans, the use of convertible securities and warrants in mergers and acquisitions, inflation, and corporate diversification are but a few of the challenging problems facing the accountant.

These developments and the very pervasiveness of accounting activity make it difficult for teachers, students, public accountants, and financial executives to gain convenient access to current thinking on key topics in the field. Journal articles, while current, must often of necessity give only cursory treatment or present a single point of view. Many of the important developments in the field have not crystalized to a point where they can be easily incorporated into textbooks. Further, because textbooks must necessarily limit the space devoted to any one topic, key topics often do not get the attention they properly deserve.

The Contemporary Topics series attempts to fill this gap by covering significant contemporary developments in accounting through brief, but self-contained, studies. These independent studies provide the reader with up-to-date coverage of key topics. For the practitioner, the series offers a succinct overview of developments in research and practice in areas of special interest to him. The series enables the teacher to design courses with maximum flexibility and to expose his students to authoritative analysis of controversial problems.

ALFRED RAPPAPORT

Preface

This study is not designed to advocate either corporate reporting of market value measures in general, or replacement costs in particular. Instead, its main effort is directed toward developing a theoretical basis for replacement cost accounting. We believe that an analysis of the utility of any accounting measurement system involves three distinct steps. Initially, one must derive the theoretical basis underlying the purported advantages of a given measurement system. Next one must assess the relative importance of these advantages to the decision makers for whom the information is intended. (It is conceivable that some measurement systems may possess "advantages" that are of incidental concern to the users of the information.) Once the theoretical benefits are identified and established, it is then necessary to test whether they do, in fact, arise under real-world conditions.

The literature currently lacks a clear expression of the theoretical basis for using replacement cost accounting in external reports. This absence of objectives for replacement costing (indeed, for financial reporting in general) means that there are no guidelines for empirical research. That is, since there is no clear specification of what theoretical benefits and limitations exist, there is little to test. To alleviate this deficiency, the objective of this study is to develop a theoretical basis that provides direction for needed empirical research. That is, this study is a first step in a much longer research process. The hope, of course, is that this foundation will hasten the process of accumulating evidence needed to make informed choices among measurement alternatives.

The basic approach of this study is influenced by several premises and beliefs, which are examined in Chapters 1 and 2. We will introduce only the most important of these premises here. First, much of the inquiry examines the potential ability of replacement cost income to predict future events. It is possible, of course, that the Securities and Exchange Commission may eventually *require* direct predictions of future earnings and/or cash flows in all filings with the Commission. Even if the Commission were to do this, external users would still require information to use in generating their own predictions of future events. These self-generated predictions would be needed for comparison with the direct predictions supplied by management in an attempt to corroborate the reasonableness of the direct forecasts. Thus, the potential predictive advantages of replacement costing would still be useful even in an environment in which direct management forecasts were made available externally.

A second underlying assumption of this study is that there is no a priori reason to believe that the information generated by a single measurement method is necessarily relevant to a wide variety of external users. Instead, it seems necessary to examine the correspondence between the data provided by a given method and the information needs of a single category of user. This is precisely what is done when our theoretical model and subsequent analysis is directed toward the normative information needs of long-term equity investors. Accordingly, this study is not intended to be a universal analysis of replacement costing; it concentrates on the specific needs of a single group.

Our final major assumption is that any attempt to design an improved external reporting system should utilize the simplest possible means for satisfying perceived information requirements. Although a highly complex, multifaceted report could conceivably incorporate a wealth of analytical data, it is possible that such reports might be cumbersome, and, under the circumstances discussed in Chapter 1, lead to less effective decision-making. Thus, this study analyzes only a single measurement method—replacement cost accounting. Although it might be possible to satisfy long-term investors' information requirements with some combination of measurement methods, predictions, and so forth, efficiency considerations suggest that a simpler approach (i.e., the relevance of a *single* measurement basis) be investigated first.

The major portion of this analysis examines the predictive ability of replacement cost accounting. At the market level, such predictions are obviously necessary in order to generate security prices. That is, the "market as a whole" would quickly evaluate accounting data as it becomes available in order to predict variables of interest. These predictions would then be used as an input to security valuation models in order to generate security prices. Whether this approach is also useful to *individual* investors is a controversial issue. Those who believe in market efficiency deem the search for undervalued securities on the part of individual investors to be fruitless since publicly available information is thought to be already impounded in securities' prices. In contrast, older theories suggest that individual investors might also generate predictions, and resultant "intrinsic values," in an effort to discover undervalued securities. While available evidence is in accord with the market efficiency position, we introduce this controversy only to emphasize that predictions would be needed under either view. Thus, our examination of the predictive ability of replacement cost data is relevant in either context.

One reason for examining the theoretical foundation for an accounting measurement system is that this process identifies the conditions that must exist if the system is to operate as intended. Our analysis reveals that there are several assumptions regarding the behavior of prices and other economic conditions that are implicit to the reputed predictive ability of replacement cost accounting. To cite one important example, theoretically if replacement cost information is to provide a predictive basis for external investors, there must be high covariance between changes in asset prices and changes in an individual firm's operating flow potential. Realistically, this condition is so stringent that we would not expect to find it satisfied precisely in an actual environment. In light of this expectation, the empirical research question becomes: How well does this stringent condition approximate real-world conditions? If empirical research reveals that some approximate relationship does exist, then replacement costing may provide a useful predictive basis even though this specific stringent condition is not met precisely. Alternatively, if the required condition is greatly at variance with observed real-world conditions, then the theoretical predictive potential of replacement costing would not exist in practice. Obviously, empirical research is needed to answer this question. Although prior beliefs may cause us to question the actual performance of the measurement model, we must remember that the severe conditions isolated herein need not be met precisely. A reasonable surrogate relationship may be adequate. Hopefully, this study will provide an impetus for gathering the evidence needed to assess the performance of replacement costing.

While our primary emphasis is directed toward the development and analysis of a theoretical model, we do introduce suggestions for needed empirical tests as well. Indeed, where the means for gathering the required evidence are not straightforward, we briefly discuss some methods which might be employed to accumulate the necessary information (see especially pp. 140-42 and related footnotes).

This book can be used in several different ways. It can be assigned in an undergraduate accounting theory course or graduate seminar to provide an intensive examination of the theory underlying replacement cost accounting; or, alternatively, it can be used as a supplementary text in an intermediate or advanced accounting course to provide a strong conceptual flavor. For example, the first several chapters of the study introduce issues that are relevant to an analysis of *any* financial reporting framework. The foundation provided by these chapters is then used to evaluate replacement cost accounting, but could easily be used to evaluate historical cost reporting as well. When used in this manner, the book may enhance students' understanding of the advantages and deficiencies of generally accepted accounting reports as a means for satisfying users' information needs.

The author was fortunate in having the benefits of many useful comments and criticisms from colleagues and graduate students. Frederick L. Neumann and James C. McKeown, my former colleagues at the University of Illinois, acted as a sounding-board for some earlier articles on this subject. Professor Kermit Larson of the University of Texas read the entire study and made many valuable suggestions. Earlier drafts of the manuscript were read and carefully critiqued by Shane Moriarity (University of Kansas) and John Cumming (University of Minnesota). Their comments were of great help in improving the exposition and in sharpening the logical development. Peter Chant helped put the references and citations in proper form. The editor of this series, my colleague Alfred Rappaport, made numerous important suggestions regarding content and style and helped improve the end product. To all of these people, I express my gratitude and appreciation. The reader must understand, of course, that any deficiencies are the sole responsibility of the author and are probably occasioned by his failure to heed the advice offered.

One final acknowledgment is appropriate. Unquestionably, my greatest debt is owed to a nonaccountant—my wife Barbara. It was her patient understanding and encouragement that made the completion of this book possible.

Evanston, Illinois   LAWRENCE REVSINE

CHAPTER ONE

Methodological Considerations

Replacement cost accounting is a system that uses current market price data to reflect the performance of various entities. In contrast, traditional historical costing employs past transaction costs to generate reports on enterprise results. Replacement costing and historical costing thus represent different approaches to measuring performance. Each may therefore be called a measurement process.[1]

The replacement cost measurement process (or more simply, replacement costing) has received much attention in the accounting literature. Many contemporary writers believe that replacement cost financial statements are superior to traditional, historical cost statements. The primary purpose of this book is to evaluate these beliefs by investigating the usefulness of replacement cost data.

---

[1] By "measurement process" we mean simply the rules for assigning numbers to events that have occurred. For example, when a sale is made, the cost of the sale is also computed. In an accounting sense, some dollar value must be assigned to "cost of goods sold." One measurement process might employ the historical cost of what was sold as the cost of the sales. Another measurement rule might reflect the cost of the sale in terms of the prevailing current market cost of the goods at the time of sale. Under normal circumstances, each of these two accounting rules would assign a different dollar measure to cost of goods sold. In this sense, each rule measures cost of goods sold differently. Each such rule (or set of rules) thus constitutes a measurement process.

There are several approaches that could be employed to evaluate the usefulness of a measurement process like replacement costing. Generally, these approaches can be classified as either empirical or normative. In the sections that follow we will briefly examine these methodological approaches and explore the advantages and deficiencies of each as a means for evaluating accounting measures. After completing this analysis, it will then be possible to select and defend the methodology that will be used in this book to evaluate replacement costing.

METHODOLOGICAL APPROACHES FOR
EVALUATING ACCOUNTING MEASUREMENTS

Empirical approaches

One methodology that might be used to evaluate the usefulness of accounting measurements is the *empirical approach*. Empirical research uses actual data to rigorously test some proposition or belief. In this approach, the issue to be investigated must be developed into a testable hypothesis. Once the testable hypothesis is developed, data that are relevant to the hypothesis are collected. These data are then processed in some experimental framework and the results evaluated. If the results of the experiment are in accord with the hypothesis, the hypothesis is said to be affirmed. If the results of the experiment are in opposition to the hypothesis, the hypothesis is denied.[2]

The empirical research approach has been employed with increasing frequency in recent accounting investigations. This approach is used because empirical evidence can transform interesting speculation into demonstrable fact. In other words, the empirical approach is one important component of a two-stage total research process. In the first stage, logical analysis is used to develop some testable propositions or rudimentary theories. In the second stage, these theories are tested in order to determine their ability to explain observable phenomena.[3] Generally, then, empirical testing requires a well-developed theoretical

[2] Since the research process is continuous, the results of a single experiment or test are seldom conclusive. Replication is usually needed to confirm the findings of previous efforts. In this view, hypotheses are never "affirmed," although they may be denied. To deny a hypothesis one need discover only a single instance in which it fails to apply. But to theoretically confirm a hypothesis it must perform as predicted in every conceivable environment. In practice, once a hypothesis has been upheld in many different tests, one might say that the hypothesis has been affirmed.

[3] The temporal sequence of the two stages may sometimes be reversed. For instance, previously developed empirical results may stimulate theoretical efforts to explain those phenomena. Thus, theory may be used to explain already known behavior rather than to predict expected response.

foundation. Furthermore, this theoretical foundation must be formulated in a manner that allows its hypotheses to be tested.

On balance, the theoretical literature in the replacement cost area does not conform to these specifications. The supposed advantages of replacement costing are often developed in a cryptic fashion. Furthermore, many of these reputed advantages cannot be tested. Thus it is not yet possible to use an empirical approach to evaluate the usefulness of replacement cost measurement procedures. Before the empirical approach can be employed, several crucial issues must be resolved. First, we must select some operationally workable definition of usefulness. Usefulness alone is a vague and untestable attribute. Second, we must be able to identify the group(s) for whom the measures are intended to be useful. Unless the audience is known, detailed testing is difficult. Third, we must be able to specify the objective(s) of the intended audience. Usefulness is definable only in relation to some objective; unless this objective is known, usefulness is untestable.

In summary, empirical evidence is an important component of the total research process. In the replacement cost area, however, there is no underlying theoretical base to guide empirical tests. Without this base, empirical tests are likely to be disjointed. Much effort would be wasted in attempting to discover what might later prove to be irrelevant data. In the long run it would seem to be far more efficient if the needed theoretical foundation were developed first. Then, with this foundation to guide later testing of the theory, empirical progress would be expedited.

Accordingly, our approach in this book will be to develop a theoretical structure that explains the *potential* usefulness of replacement costing. If successful, this theory would then form the basis for later empirical testing of the *actual* usefulness of replacement costing.

Normative theory approaches

Another methodology that could be used to evaluate the usefulness of accounting measures is called the normative theory approach. A normative theory examines characteristics, relationships, and actions that "ought to" exist. The important point is that normative theories are not necessarily empirically based. Rather, such theories rely on deductively plausible analyses of human behavior and/or expected consequences of actions. To illustrate, a normative theory of the investment tax credit would attempt to explain how total business investment *ought* to respond to a tax credit. Because of errors in the theory or changes in circumstances, actual business investment may not correspond to the predictions of the normative theory.

Despite certain limitations, the normative theory approach is often a useful method for examining a problem, particularly when knowledge about the underlying environment is limited and direct empirical tests are not feasible. In such circumstances a normative approach provides a useful starting point for developing what may later prove to be a testable hypothesis.

In examining accounting measurement issues, there are several different levels at which the normative approach may be employed. Since we will be using a normative approach to examine the utility of replacement costing, a brief discussion of various normative options is necessary. This discussion will identify the strengths and weaknesses of the various methods and will explain our choice of the specific normative approach that will be used in this book.

GENERAL PURPOSE APPROACH [4]

One normative method that has been widely used to evaluate alternative accounting methods is the general purpose (or universal) approach. In this approach, a measurement method such as replacement costing is analyzed in order to determine its relevance to a wide variety of users. The focus is not on any single user group; instead, the analysis centers on the utility of the data to the entire financial community.

The popularity of this general purpose approach for evaluating accounting measures is easy to explain. Traditional accounting theory suggests that a single set of financial statements is simultaneously relevant to the general information needs of many user groups.[5] This firmly entrenched principle goes by the name *general purpose reporting*. Since accounting reports are supposedly relevant to a wide audience, it is not surprising that alternative accounting measures are often evaluated in terms of this same broad audience.

However, there are serious questions concerning the validity of the general purpose reporting philosophy. That is, there is some reason to question whether accountants can simultaneously satisfy the information needs of the entire financial community with a single set of general purpose reports. For this same reason, the validity of the general purpose

[4] The material in this section is adapted from Lawrence Revsine, "General Purpose Reports and Users' Data Needs," *Financial Analysts Journal*, 25 (September–October, 1969), 37–46. It is reproduced with permission of the Editor of the *Financial Analysts Journal*.

[5] Accounting Principles Board Statement No. 4, *Basic Concepts and Accounting Principles Underlying Financial Statements of Business Enterprises* (New York: American Institute of Certified Public Accountants, Inc., 1970), pp. 19–20.

approach to evaluating alternative accounting measurement systems also can be questioned. We now turn to an examination of some of the weaknesses that are inherent in the general purpose, or universal, approach.

Decision model determines needed data inputs. Whenever a decision is made, some decision rule or decision model is used in reaching that decision. The actual model used may be simple or complex. The model may or may not be well suited to the problem faced. The model may be carefully formulated or may be applied on an *ad hoc* basis. It may or may not lead to the desired outcome. But as long as the decision maker selects a course of action, he is using some sort of model to reach that decision.

In order to reach a decision, the decision maker also needs information.[6] The information that he needs is that information required by his decision model. In other words, the relevance of a given bit of data is a function of the decision model employed.[7] Insofar as certain data are required as an input to a decision model, such information is relevant and useful to the decision maker. Notice, however, that employing "useful information" does not necessarily guarantee that the decision will lead to the desired consequences. This will happen only if the model itself is consistent with the decision maker's preferences.

Decision models may vary between users. The potential users of accounting reports are quite diverse. This group includes investors, credit grantors, customers, labor unions, and even the general public, which might use accounting data to evaluate an entity's social performance. While the specific decision models used by each of these groups are not known, there is little evidence to suggest that each of these categories of users employs the same basic type of decision model. On the contrary, given the diversity among these potential users, it would be unusual if their individual objectives would simultaneously be satisfied by a single, general decision model. Pending additional evidence, it seems more reasonable to suggest that the decision models

---

[6] We do not use the terms "information" and "data" interchangeably. Data will be used when we refer to inputs that have not been evaluated by the decision maker. By contrast, information is either evaluated data, or data intended for a specified use. See Alfred Rappaport, *Information for Decision Making: Quantitative and Behavioral Dimensions* (Englewood Cliffs, N.J.: Prentice-Hall, Inc., 1970), p. 54.

[7] This is the ideal situation. That is, the decision model is first specified and then the data is evaluated in light of that model. In a constrained environment it is possible for the reverse sequence to exist; i.e., the nature of the information actually available may dictate the decision model to be used. For example, a theoretically "ideal" model may be impractical because the information needed to operate the model is unavailable. A data deficiency may thus necessitate the use of a sub-optimal model.

used by each group are likely to vary. These variations could potentially be significant.

Diversity in decision models implies diversity in needed information. To the extent that the decision models employed by each user group differ, it is also possible that the information required by each individual model may vary from group to group. Two categories of divergence are possible. First, the *type* of information needed to operate each model may vary. Second, the *amount* of information necessary for informed decision making may differ. We will examine each of these possibilities in turn.

Differences in Type of Information. In referring to differences in the type of information needed for decision making, two possibilities exist. The first is that the nature of the information required may vary. For example, assume that a seller of raw materials is anxious to avoid extending excessive trade credit to his customers. His decision rule is to extend credit to a customer only if the customer has exhibited a past ability and willingness to pay obligations within the discount period. To satisfy the information requirements of this decision model, the supplier would need to know about the past credit performance of his potential customer. This data is certainly different from that likely to be used by a wage review board in determining productivity increases.

A second possible reason for differences in the type of information needed is that the measurement rules applied to the data must differ. To illustrate, we will examine and contrast the needs of both the equity investor and creditor for profit data. An equity investor chooses an investment because of its future profit potential. He attempts to assess the performance of each investment relative to available alternatives. He should want to know whether any portion of a firm's reported earnings are nominal "paper profits" that have been eroded by price increases, because by distributing such artificial gains, a firm pays a liquidating dividend and reduces its future real earnings potential.[8] This reduced real earnings potential makes the firm a less attractive investment opportunity. Thus, an investor would seemingly desire an earnings report based on real—rather than nominal—dollars.

A creditor is also interested in the profit performance of a company to which he extends credit. The safety of his claim is a function of the ability of the firm to maintain or improve its net asset position. But the creditor's potential return is fixed. Irrespective of the extraordinary profitability of the firm, the lender will receive only the agreed

---

[8] Until Chapter 3, where we advance a more rigorous definition of real earnings, we will use the term to mean earnings adjusted for price changes.

on interest and the principal repayment. The lender should have already adjusted for anticipated inflation in setting his required interest rate.[9] Thus, his prime concern is whether the firm can maintain or improve its existing *nominal* dollar position. If it can, payment of both principal and interest is likely. If it cannot, payment is jeopardized. Notice that the creditor is not harmed by a weakening in the firm's real net asset position so long as the nominal net asset position is maintained.

It is possible, then, that investors and creditors might each prefer different measurement rules for computing earnings. As we have suggested, an investor probably prefers an earnings report based on real dollars. In contrast, a creditor concerned with repayment of his nominal dollar loan might find it easier to judge the safety of his claim if earnings are measured in nominal dollars. Thus, the *type* of earnings figure required by each may vary.

There is another dimension to the problem of providing data in a form that is simultaneously relevant to a wide range of users. It is possible that there is not only divergence of information needs *between* user groups, but also divergence *among* users within a single, broadly-defined group. Consider the fact that the investor category can be further subdivided; e.g., there are individual investors, mutual funds, insurance companies, and pension funds. It would not be surprising to discover that many of these investor sub-categories rely on basically dissimilar decision models and thus require essentially different information inputs. Furthermore, within each of these sub-categories various institutional and psychological considerations could cause still more divergence among decision models. It is conceivable that the "psychological set" of individual investors (attitude toward risk, aspiration levels, tolerance for ambiguity, and so on) might cause great differences in investment objectives and consequently alter the set of information relevant for decision making. Accordingly, it seems quite possible that users' information needs could vary even more dramatically than the preceding analysis indicated.

Differences in Amount of Information. Differences in the objectives and interests of each user group cause differences in the importance attached to various elements of operating performance and financial position. It seems plausible to suggest that the greater the emphasis one places on a given aspect of performance or position, the more diverse and detailed is the amount of information required in that area. Since areas of emphasis will vary among user groups, the

---

[9] For example, if the normal rate of return on loans of a given risk class is 5 percent, and if a 2 percent rate of inflation is forecast, then the interest rate charged should be 7 percent.

amount of information needed in each statement section is also likely to vary among users.[10]

Summary. If there is variation in the decision models employed by statement readers, then it is likely that the type and amount of financial information needed will also vary among users. *This suggests that universally relevant accounting measurements may not exist.* Instead, relevance may vary from group to group. Accounting reports prepared using one measurement method may be highly relevant to one category of users and irrelevant to another. The existence of this possibility has caused some writers to question the utility of the general purpose reporting philosophy.[11] Furthermore, this possibility negates the usefulness of a general purpose approach for evaluating alternative accounting measures. No single measure is necessarily relevant for all conceivable users. For this reason, the general purpose evaluative approach will not be used in this book. We will make no attempt to analyze the universal relevance of replacement costing.

DATA EXPANSION APPROACH

Another normative method for analyzing the utility of an accounting measurement system might be called the data expansion approach. The objective of data expansion is to make more information available to the statement reader. Proponents of this approach suggest that the data contained in traditional reports should be increased in scope and quantity.

Proposals to increase the range of data reported to users immediately raise questions regarding the data to be added and the process by which these data are to be selected. Later in this chapter we will

[10] The issue of how much accounting detail should be provided in financial statements is commonly called the "aggregation problem." Above we argue that the appropriate level of aggregation is a function of the role of the statement items in a particular user's model. Applying information theory concepts to the aggregation problem allows the development of other rules that do not presuppose knowledge about the intended use of the information. For a development of this approach, see Baruch Lev, "The Aggregation Problem in Financial Statements: An Informational Approach," *Journal of Accounting Research,* 6 (Autumn, 1968), 247–61; and "The Informational Approach to Aggregation in Financial Statements: Extensions," *Journal of Accounting Research,* 8 (Spring, 1970), 78–94.

[11] See, for example, Revsine, "General Purpose Reports,"; Morton Backer, "Accounting Theory and Multiple Reporting Objectives," in *Modern Accounting Theory,* ed. Morton Backer (Englewood Cliffs, N.J.: Prentice-Hall, Inc., 1966), pp. 439–63; and Charles C. Hornbostel "A View From a Corporate Financial Executive," *Corporate Financial Reporting: The Issues, The Objectives and Some New Proposals,* eds. Alfred Rappaport and Lawrence Revsine (Chicago: Commerce Clearing House, Inc., 1972). Some empirical evidence which questions the utility of general purpose reports is contained in Vincent C. Brenner, "Financial Statement Users' Views of the Desirability of Reporting Current Cost Information," *Journal of Accounting Research,* 8 (Autumn, 1970), 159–66.

explain in detail how the data expansion approach would be used to answer these questions. For now, we can briefly summarize the approach as follows: To implement data expansion, one would need to evaluate each bit of supplementary data that has been proposed for inclusion in accounting reports. The objective is to determine the relevance of these data to a broadly defined audience. Those data that appear to provide useful information would be included in an expanded report and those that do not would be excluded.

This data expansion approach is motivated by certain unresolved controversies regarding the appropriate means for improving external reports. To fully understand the logic of the data expansion approach, it is first necessary to understand the causes for the basic controversy. Accordingly, we will briefly explore this external reporting controversy in the following sections. This digression will serve to explain the rationale underlying the data expansion approach.

Perceived deficiencies of historical cost reports. Many accountants question the interpretation and usefulness of historical cost balance sheet figures. They point out that amounts recorded for various asset categories do not represent the current cost to the firm of duplicating these service capabilities (replacement costs); nor do they represent the cash that a firm would collect for its assets should it decide to dispose of them (net realizable values); nor, finally, do these amounts represent the subjective profit generating capabilities of the assets to the firm (discounted service potential). Since some accountants contend that any or all of these three valuation devices are preferable to historical costs, there is considerable support for an alternative balance sheet treatment.

Critics further contend that the traditional income figure and its sub-components are apt to be misleading. During periods of fluctuating prices, the difference between realized revenues and expired historical costs will not necessarily represent the real change in net assets over the preceding period. (That is, some portion of this margin may be needed for reinvestment in order to maintain the prior level of operating activity.) Thus, the resultant income figure may not provide an adequate basis for dividend determination purposes. Furthermore, because the income computation does not incorporate specific price changes for certain assets, the historical income figure may be a poor estimator of the firm's expected future profit generating capabilities. Finally, there is no basis for subdividing the traditional income figure into components that separately reflect the success of management's operating activities and its asset holding activities.

Alternative measurement models. Several external reporting models that incorporate other measurement bases have been proposed to alleviate some or all of these deficiencies. For example, Edwards and

Bell recommend a system in which asset values would be shown at their current replacement cost. Cost expirations would similarly be measured using the prevailing market price at the time of asset disposition. Consequently, balance sheets would reflect the current replacement costs of all items, and the income statement operating margin would reflect the excess of realized revenues over the expired current costs of asset services. A separate component, realizable cost savings, would contain the impact of specific price changes on assets held by the enterprise.[12]

Chambers proposes a measurement system that stresses what he calls the current cash equivalent of financial items. In this framework all balance sheet accounts are valued at net realizable value, or some approximation thereof. Income in this system is the excess of realized revenues over expired disposition values of assets at the time of their severance.[13]

Bedford developed an essentially hybrid system that incorporates replacement costs, net realizable values, and subjective values. The resultant income figure can be broken into sub-components; each of these sub-components corresponds roughly to some classified operation(s) of the entity from which income emerges. Thus, this concept would be most useful in evaluating the effectiveness of management in several distinct income generating activities.[14]

Causes for continuing disagreement. [15] Judging from comments that have appeared in recent accounting literature, many accounting practitioners and academicians accede to the deficiencies of historical cost reports that these alternative measurement theories are designed to remedy. Since recognition of the existence of a problem is one of the important prerequisites for its solution, one might think that an acceptable, improved reporting framework is close at hand. Here this is not the case. The relative advantages of the different measurement bases have been earnestly and, at times, bitterly debated in the accounting literature. It would seem that advocates of change are united only by their dissatisfaction with the existing historical cost model. How can we explain this continuing debate regarding alternative measurement models?

[12] Edgar O. Edwards and Philip W. Bell, *The Theory and Measurement of Business Income* (Berkeley and Los Angeles: The University of California Press, 1961).

[13] Raymond J. Chambers, *Accounting, Evaluation and Economic Behavior* (Englewood Cliffs, N. J.: Prentice-Hall, Inc., 1966).

[14] Norton M. Bedford, *Income Determination Theory: An Accounting Framework* (Reading, Mass.: Addison-Wesley Publishing Company, Inc., 1966).

[15] This discussion (through p. 14) is adapted from Lawrence Revsine, "Data Expansion and Conceptual Structure," *The Accounting Review*, 45 (October, 1970), 704–11. It is reproduced with the permission of the Editor of *The Accounting Review*.

A plausible explanation for this dispute relates to the linkage between users' information needs and the data provided to them through accounting reports. Specifically, accountants believe that the data generated by the accounting process ought to correspond to the information required by users' decision models. But notice that there are differences in the form and content of the data generated by various measurement models. The output of certain measurement models will conform to the information required by certain decision models. When this correspondence between data output and information needs occurs, the measurement model satisfies the information needs of users. In practice, some measurement models are more effective than others in satisfying the information needs of certain decision models. If the information generated by a given measurement model is deemed irrelevant to the actual information needs of the group of users toward whom the model is directed, then the measurement model will likely be rejected. Thus, for a measurement model to gain wide acceptance, its output must be viewed as relevant for the information needs of its intended audience. But, as we pointed out earlier in the chapter, it can reasonably be presumed that financial statement users' decision models differ. Therefore, the output of a single measurement model is not likely to be viewed as universally relevant for a wide range of decision models.

Another cause for the debate regarding alternative measurement models relates to the profession's inability to isolate users' decision models. Such decision models must be identified if we are to assess the correspondence between data supplied by various measurement models and information required to operate the decision model. At present, it is only possible to make certain very abstract observations about the nature of a particular decision process and thereby develop some general notions concerning the appropriateness of a given accounting measurement model. Such vague but intuitive observations are useful as negative screening criteria; that is, they are adequate as a basis for disqualifying certain measurement models because of their obvious irrelevance. But, logically, it is often far easier to say what something *is not,* than to describe what it *is*.[16] For example, it is possible that statement users' evaluations of management performance require that such performance be separated into controllable and non-controllable elements; one could contend that traditional historical cost reports violate this requirement by commingling external and internal events. But after making this general observation, it is difficult to specify which particular types of controllable activities merit isolation. Since we lack this detailed empirical knowledge about users' information needs, it is not surprising that proposed alternative

---

[16] Morris R. Cohen and Ernest Nagel, *An Introduction to Logic and Scientific Method* (New York: Harcourt, Brace and Company, Inc., 1934), p. 240.

models have failed to gain wide acceptance. Each accounting model generates a somewhat different kind of data output. Since most data are best suited to satisfying particular information needs, each accounting measurement model has imbedded within it specific assumptions regarding which user data needs are "appropriate." Notice, however, that without empirical evidence, such models are based solely on subjective, and hence, arguable, premises. As one accountant stated:

> . . . the . . . proposals put forth by R. [J.] Chambers, Edwards and Bell, and others are merely untested hypotheses. While these are logical structures, persuasively presented, they are founded wholly upon assumptions as with respect to the kinds of data their proponents think statement users ought to need or want.[17]

There is yet another explanation for the controversy regarding alternative measurement models. Even if accountants were somehow able to agree that a particular type of information is unquestionably relevant to a given user category, certain measurement controversies would remain. For purposes of illustration, assume that everyone agrees that income should be subdivided into components that separately reflect operating activities and holding activities. Despite this general agreement, there may be several alternative methods for effecting this separation. Each of these methods may use different measurement modes (e.g., holding gains measured on a replacement cost basis versus a net realizable value basis). Then, despite the general agreement, there might still be controversy concerning the ability of a particular measurement method to generate data that accurately reflects the desired separation of income components. Certainly a portion of the disagreement that exists in the literature regarding alternative measurement models is attributable to this general phenomenon.[18]

A compromise. We can summarize our digression regarding the external reporting controversy as follows:

Accountants are well aware of many of the deficiencies inherent in the existing reporting model. However, the absence of detailed information regarding explicit user needs severely limits progress. It is impossible to reach agreement on an alternative reporting framework while

[17] Walter B. McFarland, "Letters to the Editor," *Financial Analysts Journal*, 26 (January–February, 1970), 123.

[18] See, for example, David F. Drake and Nicholas Dopuch, "On the Case for Dichotomizing Income," *Journal of Accounting Research*, 3 (Autumn, 1965), 192–205; Kermit Larson and R. W. Schattke, "Current Cash Equivalent, Additivity, and Financial Action," *The Accounting Review*, 41 (October, 1966), 634–41; and George J. Staubus, "Current Cash Equivalent for Assets: A Dissent," *The Accounting Review*, 42 (October, 1967), 650–61.

we are still unsure of the needs that this framework must satisfy. Furthermore, even if users' needs were clearly identified, many would still argue about the relative abilities of different accounting measures in satisfying these needs.

Because of this apparent impasse, several accounting theorists have been led to propose what appears to be a means for escaping the current dilemma. The route they have taken is an intuitively pleasing one. Proponents of this approach point out that different users apparently require different data inputs to satisfy their decision needs; but they also point out that accountants have been unable to specify what these information needs are. This has led to seemingly endless debate among advocates of different measurement models. To end this debate, they suggest that external reports be expanded to accommodate several measurement bases. This data expansion approach would allow the decision maker to determine for himself what data are relevant to his needs. In the words of Sorter, one proponent of data expansion:

> Instead of producing input values for unknown and perhaps unknowable decision models directly, accounting . . . [would provide] . . . information about relevant economic events that allows individual users to generate their own input values for their own individual decision models. . . .
>
> . . . the real difference between . . . [this approach and traditional accounting reports] lies in what level of aggregation and valuation is appropriate in accounting reports and who is to be the aggregator and evaluator.[19]

Sorter's data expansion proposal, which he calls the "events approach," in essence suggests that accountants expand the amount of valuation data provided in reports by limiting each account classification to a single type of event (e.g., disaggregate the traditional plant and equipment account into components that separately reflect a beginning value, acquisitions during the period, and dispositions).

A slightly different approach to data expansion was proposed in *A Statement of Basic Accounting Theory*.[20] The authors of that monograph suggest that traditional external reports be transformed into multiple-column, multiple-valuation reports. For the present, the Committee suggests that such reports contain two parallel columns, one prepared using the historical cost measurement mode, the other prepared using current cost as a measurement basis. Eventually, they suggest, this

[19] George H. Sorter, "An 'Events' Approach to Basic Accounting Theory," *The Accounting Review*, 44 (January, 1969), 13–14.

[20] Committee to Prepare a Statement of Basic Accounting Theory, *A Statement of Basic Accounting Theory* (Evanston, Ill.: American Accounting Association, 1966).

report format can be further expanded to incorporate other measurements.[21]

It is not difficult to understand the motivations that prompted these data expansion proposals. Data expansion is viewed as a means for overcoming limitations of contemporary reports without requiring currently unavailable knowledge regarding users' decision models.[22] Furthermore, a proposal to expand external reports is more palatable than a proposal to substitute one measurement basis for another; conceivably relevant data are added through expansion but no data are discarded.

The data expansion criterion. Having developed the apparent rationale for data expansion, it is now necessary to discuss how the data expansion approach might be used as a normative criterion for evaluating accounting measures.

In practice, the data expansion criterion is merely a variant of the general purpose or universal criterion that we have already discussed. The primary difference between the two approaches is quite simple. The universal approach assumes that the measurement method being evaluated will be the only one reported. As such, it must be relevant to the widest possible audience. The data expansion approach, on the other hand, assumes that the measurement method under analysis will be added to those methods already reported. Accordingly, the criterion for acceptance is whether the *incremental* data added by this method are conceivably relevant to some non-trivial (but broadly defined) number of users. To quote Sorter:

> . . . it is only necessary to decide that information about . . . [various financial and operating events] are relevant to a host of decision models for such information to be included in accounting reports.[23]

Using this criterion, if the added data are deemed to be relevant to a large number of users, they would be reported. The problem with this approach is in determining when to stop expanding. Obviously, unlimited data expansion is neither feasible nor desirable. Yet this approach provides no guidelines for choosing among alternative measurements. As long as every proposed addition is thought to be relevant to some users, all such methods would be reported. Since most data could be defended as relevant to some class of users, the end result of these broad guidelines would necessitate reporting all conceivable data using all known measurement approaches.

[21] *Ibid.,* p. 65.
[22] *Ibid.,* p. 20; and Sorter, "An 'Events' Approach," 13–14.
[23] Sorter, "An 'Events' Approach," 14.

Obviously, advocates of data expansion would contend that more stringent guidelines could be developed for choosing among potential supplementary measurements. Such an improved approach would, in some way, measure the marginal contribution from reporting each new type of data. Only those measurements that promise the highest marginal contributions would be chosen for inclusion in expanded reports. Proponents contend that these more stringent guidelines would prevent indiscriminate expansion.[24]

Limitations of the data expansion approach. The data expansion approach suffers from certain deficiencies. The most obvious deficiency is that unlimited data expansion is likely to lead to information overload.[25] Under such circumstances, the decision maker is so overburdened with data that his decision effectiveness either remains constant or decreases. Rather than serving to improve the users' performance, the added information is, at best, discarded. This reaction arises from physiological causes. Humans have limited capabilities for processing data. Beyond some point it becomes physically impossible to assimilate and react to incremental messages. As we have already indicated, proponents of data expansion are well aware of this difficulty and do not themselves propose to inundate the user with data. Instead, they envision only a modest expansion in the data provided.

It appears, however, that even a modest expansion in the amount of data provided could worsen decision effectiveness. The cause for this decline is not physiological, but is instead psychological. That is, there seem to be cognitive limits on decision making that arise even from modest increases in the amount of data provided. The reasoning that supports this position is rather complex. Only the highlights of the argument will be explored here. A more detailed analysis is presented in the Appendix to Chapter 1.

To explain why cognitive limits on decision making are relevant to data expansion proposals, we will review some recent empirical evidence gathered by social psychologists. This evidence suggests that there is a curvilinear relationship between environmental complexity and the conceptual level achieved by decision makers. The nature of this relationship is depicted in Figure 1–1.[26] In this context conceptual

24 Cf. Joel S. Demski, "Decision-Performance Control," *The Accounting Review,* 44 (October, 1969), 677.

25 For a discussion of information overload, see Daniel Katz and Robert L. Kahn, *The Social Psychology of Organizations* (New York: John Wiley & Sons, Inc., 1966), pp. 229–35.

26 This illustration relies on the findings of Harold M. Schroder, Michael J. Driver, and Siegfried Streufert, *Human Information Processing* (New York: Holt, Rinehart and Winston, Inc., 1967).

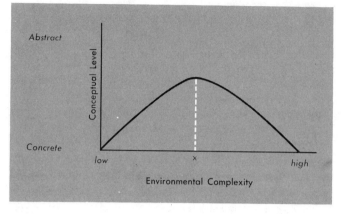

FIGURE 1-1

level is defined by the amount of abstract reasoning ability displayed by decision makers. Abstractness is a function of both (1) the number of dimensions that decision makers recognize in a problem, and (2) the complexity of the decision rules used in interrelating these different dimensions of the problem. At one extreme, concrete decision makers are able to recognize only a few aspects of a problem and employ simple cause-and-effect rules in analyzing these data. At the other extreme, abstract decision makers perceive many more dimensions to the problem and integrate these data using relatively sophisticated analytical techniques.

Figure 1-1 shows that the conceptual level of a decision maker is not necessarily invariant. Instead, the degree of conceptual abstractness that he achieves is a function of the complexity of the environment in which he operates. At very low levels of environmental complexity, there is little need for sophisticated decision making. As the environment becomes successively more complex, this growing complexity motivates the individual to develop the more complex decision rules that he needs to perform effectively. Beyond some point, however, increases in environmental complexity cause the decision maker to revert to more concrete decision rules. The reason for this regression in conceptual level is straightforward. As the environment becomes more complex, it becomes increasingly difficult for the decision maker to mentally manipulate the additional data. The potential interaction among bits of data increase geometrically with each increase in complexity. At some point, the decision maker is no longer able to integrate new data with existing knowledge in any kind of complex fashion. Instead he reverts to more concrete decision rules and treats each new bit of data in iso-

16

lation. (Simple "if *A,* then *B*" kinds of rules become operative at this point.)

This phenomenon seems to be quite relevant to the issue of data expansion. When the range of data provided to financial statement readers is expanded, new dimensions are introduced into the perceived financial environment. Each new bit of data either (1) separately reflects previously aggregated variables, (2) reports previously known variables using a new measurement process, or (3) introduces entirely new variables. In every case, however, the new data were previously not available to the decision maker. *Once available, these new data serve to increase the perceived complexity of the financial environment.* This increase in perceived environmental complexity occurs in two ways. First, new dimensions are introduced into the environment. Second, the number and variety of possible interrelations among the variables are increased.

Conceivably, data expansion could increase perceived environmental complexity beyond optimum levels (e.g., beyond point *x* in Figure 1–1). This increase in complexity could cause decision makers to revert to simpler conceptual levels. Insofar as the underlying relationships in the financial environment are complex, this regression to concrete conceptual levels might lower the quality and effectiveness of decision making.[27]

The relationship between environmental complexity and conceptual level has been subjected to many empirical tests, which have invariably supported the curvilinear relationship.[28] Thus, the process depicted in Figure 1–1 has a strong empirical foundation. We must emphasize, however, that this relationship has yet to be tested in an accounting environment. Accordingly, it is premature to conclude that data expansion will positively lead to less effective financial decisions. Nevertheless, there is a strong possibility that data expansion could become dysfunctional.

One point merits special emphasis. The curvilinear model suggests that dysfunctional consequences are possible even if the data expansion is of modest proportions. This would be the case if present reports are at or near optimum levels of complexity. Even a modest increase could

[27] This suggests that complex decision models will outperform concrete models in a complex environment. Indeed, there is empirical support for this belief. Available evidence suggests that decision effectiveness is highest when there is a match between environmental complexity and conceptual level. That is, concrete conceptual models outperform abstract models if the environment is inherently simple. Similarly, abstract conceptual models outperform concrete models if the environment is inherently complex. See Michael J. Driver and Siegfried Streufert, "Integrative Complexity: An Approach to Individuals and Groups as Information-Processing Systems," *Administrative Science Quarterly,* 14 (June, 1969), 280.

[28] For a listing of these tests, see footnote 42 in the Appendix to this chapter.

then place the expanded reports in the downward sloping portion of the curve. Because of this possibility, data expansion proposals are premature. Before expansion can be safely attempted, more must be learned about the perceived complexity of present external reports.[29]

We conclude that the data expansion approach for evaluating alternative measurement methods is not yet operational because this approach provides no criteria for selecting among competing measurement possibilities. Preliminary evidence from the behavioral sciences suggests that, at best, only moderate data increases are possible. That is, expansion possibilities are constrained by users' processing capabilities. If further research indicates that a certain amount of additional data can be reported, the best possible data must be selected from the competing sources available. This necessitates detailed knowledge about the characteristics and performance of the alternative measurement methods. The best means for developing this knowledge is to analyze

[29] An important question is whether the curvilinear relationship between environmental complexity and conceptual level varies among individuals. Of particular interest is whether the curve "peaks" at the same level of environmental complexity across individuals. If it does not, then the notion of an optimal level of environmental complexity is highly individualistic. One level of complexity might be excessive for one individual and overly simple for another.

The available evidence on this point is fragmentary. However, early evidence indicates that differential peaking does not occur. That is, individuals' curves all tend to reach a peak at the same level of environmental complexity. The height of the curve varies between innately abstract and innately concrete persons, but the peak occurs at the same environmental complexity level. This condition is illustrated by the following diagram:

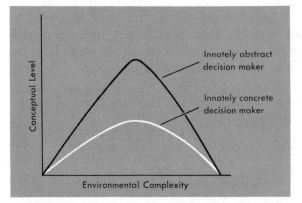

Source: Schroder, et al., *Human Information Processing.* Copyright © 1967 by Holt, Rinehart and Winston, Inc. Adapted and reprinted by permission of Holt, Rinehart and Winston, Inc.

For a discussion of these findings see Schroder *et al., Human Information Processing,* pp. 149–54. Driver and Streufert suggest that the issue merits further research since differential peaking is still a real possibility. (See Driver and Streufert, "Integrative Complexity," pp. 277–81.)

the most promising measurement methods in some detail. Unfortunately, the data expansion approach provides no guidelines or criteria to facilitate this analysis.

SPECIFIC USER APPROACH

Each of the preceding normative approaches for evaluating the relevance of accounting measures has been found to be deficient. Accordingly, neither the universal approach nor the data expansion approach will be used in this book. Instead, we will employ another normative method, the *specific user approach*. The purpose of this section is to introduce this technique and to outline its essential characteristics.

The specific user approach rests on the belief that no one measurement system is necessarily relevant to a wide range of decision makers. Since financial decision makers are a heterogeneous group, possessing potentially diverse decision models, the information relevant to one group may be irrelevant to another. Accordingly, the usefulness of a measurement basis like replacement costing must be determined sequentially for each major category of statement user.

This is the approach that will be followed here in analyzing replacement costing. We will not attempt to determine the universal relevance of replacement cost measurement methods. Instead, we will explore the ability of replacement costing to satisfy the *presumed* information needs of a *single* group. This concentration on one user group is the essence of the specific user approach. The user group that we have selected is long-term equity investors. In Chapter 2 we will both explain this choice and develop a normative model of equity investors' information needs. This normative model will then become the reference point for evaluating the relevance of replacement cost reports to equity investors.

Obviously, it would be preferable to base our analysis on actual investor information needs rather than on presumed needs. Unfortunately, little is currently known about the detailed information needs of various categories of users. Investors' information needs are no exception; therefore, we are forced to rely on a normative model of investors' information requirements. This does not mean that the results of this inquiry will be less meaningful. If the normative model is judiciously selected and if the analysis is carefully performed, long-term benefits will result. Hopefully, other studies will eventually isolate investors' actual needs. Once these empirically derived needs are known, they can be compared with the user needs presumed in this study. If no disparities exist, then the foundation for our analysis of the relevance of replacement costing survives. If serious discrepancies between presumed and actual needs are found, then the *methodology* used here must be redirected towards those alternative, actual needs. That is, one would replicate this analysis and examine the ability of replacement costing in satisfying these empirically derived information needs of investors. In either case, the methodological approach used in this study promises eventual progress toward the development of accounting outputs that are consistent with user requirements.

Furthermore, there is another reason for choosing this particular normative framework. As we will discuss in the Appendix to Chapter 2, there is reason to believe that a detailed empirical specification of information needs is a practical impossibility. If this is indeed true, then the only feasible means for linking accounting outputs with user requirements is to use a normative specification of information needs.

SUMMARY

In this chapter we have reviewed several methods that might be used to evaluate the relevance of replacement costing. We concluded that an empirical approach is not feasible at present. Our reason was that empirical tests require a well-developed theory that identifies the characteristics that need to be tested. Since no such theory now exists, empirical testing seems premature.

Since meaningful empirical research is not yet feasible, we concluded that some normative approach must be used to evaluate replacement costing. Three normative approaches were considered: the general purpose approach, the data expansion approach, and the specific user approach.

The general purpose approach, which examines the universal relevance of a measurement model, was rejected. This rejection was based on the belief that no single information model is necessarily relevant to all interested user groups. Since decision models probably vary from group to group, the information requirements probably vary also. Therefore, it is not fruitful to examine the simultaneous relevance of a measurement model to a diverse audience.

The data expansion approach was also rejected. We contended that the data expansion approach ignores the constraint of limited human cognitive abilities. If we introduce this constraint, some criteria are needed in order to select those data that merit inclusion in an expanded report. Since no such criteria currently exist, this approach is not yet operational.

The specific user approach was selected as the technique to be used in evaluating the utility of replacement costing. This approach recognizes from the beginning that no measurement system is necessarily relevant to a wide range of users employing diverse decision models. In recognition of this possibility, the specific user approach does not attempt to ascertain the universal relevance of a measurement method. Instead, a single user category is selected. Then, the measurement method (in this case, replacement costing) is analyzed to determine its relevance to the selected user category. (It is possible that after employing the specific user approach in many different contexts, we might observe that most information needs are common to several user groups. If this commonality does, in fact, exist, then it would not be necessary to prepare a different type of accounting report for each of these groups. But in contrast to the general purpose approach, the specific user approach does not *assume* commonality. That is, the same type of report would be directed to different user groups only after commonality was found to exist among user needs.)

We emphasized that little is now known about the actual decision models used. Thus, it is necessary to presume a decision model in order to apply the specific user approach. This will in fact be done in Chapter 2. There, a normative model of investor data needs will be developed. This model will be used as the basis for analyzing the relevance of replacement cost reports to investors.

APPENDIX TO CHAPTER 1 [30]

This chapter included a discussion of some possible adverse effects of data expansion. That discussion was unavoidably brief. In this Appendix we will present a more detailed analysis of the behavioral issues that might arise from data expansion in order to clarify the potential hazards.

Actual environmental complexity

Complexity and multidimensionality are prime features of the economic data contained in external reports. Financial performance data are subject to many different interpretations; environmental and contextual factors that must be considered are numerous and varied. Take the simple example of a decline in advertising expenditures for a given product from one year to the next. There may be various explanations for a decline. Perhaps management has developed a less costly

[30] This Appendix is a condensation of Revsine, "Data Expansion and Conceptual Structure," 704–11. It is reproduced with the permission of the Editor of *The Accounting Review*.

media-mix that maintains effective product exposure at former levels. Alternatively, perhaps market research revealed that the product did not appeal to one category of potential customers, and media designed to reach this class have been deleted. Or, the decline in advertising expenditure could reflect a shift in relative marketing effort to more profitable products.

Notice that an external user's overall assessment of periodic enterprise performance necessitates similar analyses of many economic variables. Seldom is an unequivocal interpretation of an observed variable value possible in the extant financial environment; rather, the economic significance of a given measurement varies depending on the context in which it arises. A decision-making environment that requires integration of multiple dimensions and in which simple conclusions based on straightforward cause-and-effect relationships are generally inappropriate, will be defined as "complex." [31]

It must be emphasized that our ability to simplify the actual, complex business environment through the use of surrogates in financial reports is limited. No surrogate framework yet proposed is able to incorporate the diverse factor interrelationships deemed necessary for effective action without discarding potentially important data.[32] In the absence of such surrogates, we must conclude that accounting is currently of limited aid in simplifying the basic complexity of the environment actually confronting the user.

Conceptual structure

Social psychologists differentiate human information processing structures by their degree of concreteness:

> Concrete conceptual systems are characterized by a relatively small number of judgmental dimensions and an inflexible, hierarchical organization among the schemata which govern the use of these dimensions. Information tends to be mapped according to a fixed set of rules, and conflict or ambiguity is difficult to resolve except by excluding some of the available information from consideration. Such systems are rigid and highly de-

[31] See Schroder, Driver, and Streufert, *Human Information Processing*, pp. 31–32. Others have specifically categorized the financial environment as complex; however, not all of these writers have simultaneously stressed both the multidimensionality *and* variable interaction facets of our definition of environmental complexity. See Harold J. Leavitt, *Managerial Psychology*, (2nd ed.) (Chicago and London: The University of Chicago Press, 1964), pp. 352–54; Yuji Ijiri, *The Foundations of Accounting Measurement: A Mathematical, Economic, and Behavioral Inquiry* (Englewood Cliffs, N. J.: Prentice-Hall, Inc., 1967), pp. 157–64; Demski, "Decision-Performance Control," 669–79; and John P. Fertakis, "On Communication, Understanding, and Relevance in Accounting Reporting," *The Accounting Review*, 44 (October, 1969), 688.

[32] Indeed, the absence of such surrogates has been the primary impetus for data expansion in external reports.

pendent upon external referents. Towards the abstract side of the continuum, the conceptual structure becomes capable of more varied differentiations, finer discriminations along each dimension, and eventually of organizing, combining, and comparing items of information in accordance with complex, flexible schemata.[33]

Stated in another way, we can say that abstract conceptual structures, or decision models, differ from more concrete structures in at least two ways: (1) abstract structures can generate a greater number of dimensional units of information from perceived stimuli (termed "differentiation") and (2) abstract structures are capable of more intricate combination and interconnection of differentiated data bits (termed "integrative complexity").

It was suggested earlier that the actual financial environment confronting the statement user is complex. Such inherent complexity necessitates simultaneous analysis of many variables in order to establish the expected future financial impact of a given series of observed events. This kind of financial analysis requires that the user be capable of somewhat complex differentiation and integration of data. Since these processes are attributes of abstract conceptual structures, we can say that in a complex environment, the more abstract the conceptual structure, the greater the effectiveness of resultant decisions.[34]

Perceived environmental complexity

Financial decision makers have access to a wide range of data. Government and business periodicals provide an abundance of information regarding macro-environmental events such as the state of the economy and factors relevant at an industry-wide level. Similarly, certain kinds of micro-environmental events that affect an individual firm are widely available. However, the preponderance of disseminated micro-environmental data is contained in, or derived from, traditional accounting reports. It follows, then, that accounting reports constitute a primary source for users' perceptions regarding the quantified financial elements in a firm's micro-environment.[35]

---

[33] Peter Suedfeld, "Attitude Manipulation in Restricted Environments: I. Conceptual Structure and Response to Propaganda," *Journal of Abnormal and Social Psychology*, 68 (March, 1964), 242.

[34] See Driver and Streufert, "Integrative Complexity," p. 280.

[35] Recent empirical evidence supports this statement, at least for one important category of users; statement data are apparently a significant source of information for financial analysts. See R. K. Mautz, *Financial Reporting by Diversified Companies* (New York: Financial Executives Research Foundation, 1968), pp. 294–99; and T. R. Dyckman, *Investment Analysis and General Price-Level Adjustments*, Studies in Accounting Research #1 (Evanston, Ill.: American Accounting Association, 1969), pp. 28–30. However, it is doubtful that such data are as important a *direct* source for small, individual investors.

The range of data contained in an accounting report can, of course, be expanded. For example, we can prepare multiple column, multiple valuation reports or incorporate completely new data such as opportunity costs. Strong theoretical arguments can be made supporting the relevance of such additional data. Despite their conceivable relevance, these additional data, if not available to the user, cannot enter his decision process. Once available, these additional data might be used in conjunction with traditionally reported information in making economic decisions. If the new data incorporated into expanded external reports provide information regarding previously ignored elements of the financial environment, then the expanded reports are dimensionally richer than traditional reports.

We mentioned that accounting information forms the basis for a user's perception of the quantified financial environment of a firm. Now, if the new data are perceived as relevant by the user, it follows that by expanding the dimensionality of accounting reports we have increased the complexity of the quantified financial environment in which the user operates.[36] It would appear, then, that whenever accountants expand reports to incorporate new, relevant information, this expansion increases perceived environmental complexity.

Summarizing:

1. Economic occurrences are the result of complex phenomena. The interpretation of a given event can vary depending on the context in which it arises. By definition, a multidimensional environment of this type is deemed "complex."

2. Given the complexity of the financial environment, statement users require somewhat abstract conceptual skills in order to perceive and develop the complex relationships among variables necessary for effective decision making.

3. A primary means by which external users perceive the quantified financial micro-environment of the firm is through prepared accounting reports.

4. The augmentation of traditional historical cost reports with new, *relevant* information injects more dimensions into the financial environment and by definition increases perceived environmental complexity.

Variability of conceptual level

If users' conceptual levels were invariant, there would be no particular accounting problem with the data expansion approach. Naturally, some statement readers would possess abstract conceptual ability whereas others would think in more concrete terms. Those who were abstract

---

[36] Ijiri, *Foundations of Accounting Measurement*, p. 157.

would, in a complex environment, tend to outperform those who were not. Data expansion would provide some benefit to the more abstract decision makers and, at a minimum, would not harm those with more concrete conceptual structures.

However, recent evidence indicates that we are generally mistaken in viewing conceptual level as invariant. Innate conceptual abstractness does vary *among individuals,* but more important, certain factors can influence the level of information processing actually achieved by a *given individual.* Within limits, a decision maker's conceptual level is apparently responsive to environmental changes.[37] That is, a "concrete" individual, given appropriate environmental stimuli, can achieve somewhat "abstract" processing levels.[38] Since we shall see that one stimulus that influences processing ability is environmental complexity, and since the perceived complexity of the financial statement reader's environment is a function of the data provided in accounting reports, it seems that accountants cannot avoid influencing users' conceptual levels.

This ability to influence conceptual levels has generally been ignored in the accounting literature. Since this influence has important implications for report design, in the next section we examine a conceivable impact of expanding external reports.

Environmental complextity and abstractness of conceptual level

Schroder, Driver, and Streufert have formulated and tested a theory that relates changes in certain environmental variables to decision makers' conceptual levels.[39] They theorized that environmental complexity, noxity (perceived severity of the adverse consequences of behavior), and eucity (perceived reward or promise furnished by an environment) are individually (and additively) related in a curvilinear fashion to abstractness of information processing. Since our primary concern centers on the impact of information load and information diversity on users' decision models, we will illustrate the hypothesized relationship using the primary variable of environmental complexity.

Figure 1–1 illustrates the basic curvilinear relationship between environmental complexity and conceptual level. Conceptual level is assumed to reach maximum abstractness at some intermediate level of environmental complexity (point x in Figure 1–1). To the left of that

---

37 Empirical evidence to support this position is presented in footnote 42 below.

38 However, even at optimum levels for these environmental stimuli, such an individual's integrative complexity will be below that of a basically "abstract" individual subject to similar, optimum, stimuli levels.

39 Schroder, Driver, and Streufert, *Human Information Processing.* As set forth, this model applies to both individual and group information processing.

point, conceptual level is lower, since "overly simple environments, which fail to present sufficiently diverse and/or numerous dimensional units of information, fail to stimulate the processes of integration—that is, simple [conceptual] structures are sufficient for coping with such environments." [40] Conceptual level also diminishes when environmental complexity is to the right of point x. "Overly complex environments, which provide excessively diverse and/or numerous dimensional units of information, reduce the generation of integratively complex rules for processing information and also reduce the levels of differentiation and integration involved." [41] Empirical evidence supports the Figure 1–1 relationship between environmental complexity and conceptual level.[42]

This conceptual structure model has yet to be tested in an accounting environment. Thus, any conclusions based on this evidence must be tentative. However, our analysis does suggest that increases in perceived financial environmental complexity (which can be accomplished through increases in the amount and diversity of relevant information provided), could affect the abstractness of financial statement users' decision processes. Given the inherent complexity of the actual financial environment, changes in conceptual abstractness could have an important bearing on the effectiveness of resultant decisions. If empirical testing indicates that the Schroder *et al.* model is relevant in an accounting environment, then data expansion could affect users' conceptual levels. In terms of Figure 1–1, the direction of the change precipitated by data expansion would depend on whether the environmental complexity inherent in extant reports is to the left or right of point x. For example, if the environmental complexity communicated in contemporary reports is optimum or nearly optimum,[43] broadening the scope of such

[40] *Ibid.*, p. 31.

[41] *Ibid.* This "information overload" phenomenon has been frequently observed and reported in the literature; e.g., Katz and Kahn, *Social Psychology of Organizations;* and Russell L. Ackoff, "Management Misinformation Systems," *Management Science,* 14 (December, 1967), B-147–B-149. The unique contribution of the Schroder *et al.,* hypothesis relates to its ability to explain the underlying conceptual processes that precipitate the decline in decision quality and the circumstances in which such a decline may be expected to occur. See Driver and Streufert, "Integrative Complexity," pp. 273–75.

[42] Schroder, Driver, and Streufert, *Human Information Processing,* pp. 54–66; Siegfried Streufert and H. M. Schroder, "Conceptual Structure, Environmental Complexity and Task Performance," *Journal of Experimental Research in Personality,* 1 (October, 1965), 132–37; also, Suedfeld, "Attitude Manipulation," 242–47; Siegfried Streufert and Michael J. Driver, "Conceptual Structure, Information Load and Perceptual Complexity," *Psychonomic Science,* 3 (September 15, 1965), 249–50; and Siegfried Streufert, Peter Suedfeld, and Michael J. Driver, "Conceptual Structure, Information Search, and Information Utilization," *Journal of Personality and Social Psychology,* 2 (November, 1965), 736–40.

[43] Notice we refer to the complexity as being nearly optimum, not the relevance of the data.

reports could lower users' conceptual levels. Insofar as this decline leads to a more simplistic view of the environment, and insofar as we can agree that economic phenomena are essentially complex and subject to diverse interpretation, then it is *per se* undesirable to precipitate more concrete processing models.

Sorter has contended that:

> . . . it is only necessary to decide that information about . . . [various financial and operating events] . . . are relevant to a host of decision models for such information to be included in accounting reports. It is unnecessary to justify how, if at all, this information should be weighted in an income valuation model.[44]

This approach tacitly assumes that the quantity of information can be expanded without cost. But this "costless expansion" position runs counter to available empirical evidence. We have cited studies that suggest that *beyond some point, additional information, no matter how relevant, reduces rather than enhances conceptual abstractness.* Insofar as abstract conceptualization is important for financial decision making, data expansion could conceivably reduce the effectiveness of decisions.[45]

In summary, the data expansion approach seemingly presumes that present statement complexity is less than optimum and that expansion is accordingly "costless." Since we do not know the position of current statements along the complexity continuum, such proposals are premature. Conceivably, if complexity is already at or near optimum levels, new information should not be introduced indiscriminately. Knowledge that a particular kind of data is relevant could not be the sole criterion for admissability since there are numerous bits of potentially relevant information. In such circumstances reported information might have to be limited to some sub-set of relevant information that promises the highest "weighted marginal knowledge contribution." [46]

[44] Sorter, "An 'Events' Approach," 14.

[45] Cf. Fertakis, "Relevance in Accounting Reporting," 689.

[46] Cf. Alfred Rappaport, "Management Misinformation Systems—Another Perspective," Letters to the Editor, *Management Science*, 15 (December, 1968), B–134.

CHAPTER TWO

A Normative
Development of Investors'
Information Needs

There are two basic sets of unknowns in the contemporary external reporting environment: (1) the general information needs of various user groups (information needs), and (2) the relative ability of different measurement models to satisfy these information needs (model utility). Ideally, research in the second area—model utility—should begin after users' information needs have been empirically specified. Unfortunately, little is presently known about users' information needs. Furthermore, there are serious theoretical and practical obstacles that diminish the prospects for empirically isolating users' needs in the near future. For these reasons we are compelled to use normative information needs as the benchmark for assessing the usefulness of replacement costing. (The Appendix to this chapter explores some of the difficulties that confront those who wish to empirically derive information needs and the likelihood for eventually overcoming these obstacles.)

Our normative analysis of the utility of replacement cost financial information will proceed as follows. First, we will select a single user group as the focus for the analysis. This, of course, is in accordance with the specific user approach introduced in Chapter 1. Second, we will identify a decision model for this user group that appears to have a dominant normative appeal. Third, we will specify the information required by this normative decision model. Finally, we will analyze the ability of replacement costing to generate output relevant to these information needs.

We have chosen long-term equity investors [1] as the specific user group whose information needs will provide the basis for evaluating the usefulness of replacement costing. In this chapter we will develop a normative decision model for long-term equity investors and derive the information requirements of that decision model. Later chapters will use these information needs as a benchmark in analyzing the relevance of replacement costing to the long-term equity investor group.

There are three reasons for choosing to base this analysis on investors' decision needs. First, investors are generally presumed to be the most important of the many readers of external reports, both in terms of number and magnitude of transactions. Second, investors must rely more extensively than other users on external financial reports for the information they receive. This makes the issue of relevance especially important to this category of users. Third, at a general level there is agreement that long-term investors' information needs are oriented toward predictive data. While subtle differences may exist regarding the precise object of prediction, nevertheless, the predictive issues examined herein are generally believed to be important for long-term equity investors.

The advantage of a normative approach is that it allows research in the areas of model utility and information needs to proceed simultaneously. [2] We must reiterate that this approach is not intended to evaluate the universal utility of replacement cost reports. Rather, it is

---

[1] Our reason for specifying "long-term" equity investors is best explained by quoting a recent American Accounting Association Committee report:

. . . short-term investors are generally more interested in changes in security prices than in cash distributions by the firm; and short-term fluctuations in security prices are frequently more closely related to external factors in the economy than to expectations regarding the individual firm. This condition makes accounting data of less assistance to short-term investors than to those interested in taking a long-term position in corporate securities.

See 1966–68 Committee on External Reporting, "An Evaluation of External Reporting Practices," *Committee Reports,* Supplement to Vol. 44, *The Accounting Review* (1969), 80.

[2] As is true with most research, the use of a normative specification of information needs makes our findings regarding the utility of replacement costing subject to reexamination when and if empirically derived investor decision models are identified. To the extent that this empirically based model is inconsistent with some aspect of the normative model, then, the analysis would have to be repeated by substituting the new empirical findings for the erroneous normative component. Despite this possibility, the normative approach facilitates the accumulation of valuable insights regarding the ability of accounting measurement models to generate data relevant to various types of information needs.

directed toward the needs of a single group, long-term equity investors. A universal evaluation of the relevance of replacement costing would require a similar development of normative decision models for many other user groups. Then, the information needs implied by each of these decision models would have to be compared with the output generated by the replacement cost measurement process.

NORMATIVE INVESTOR MODEL

In this section we will identify a widely cited normative decision model for long-term investors. In the interests of simplicity, our analysis focuses on a decision model for selecting individual securities. The issues that arise in choosing and monitoring a portfolio of many securities are beyond the intended scope of this book.[3] However, in some respects the information requirements of the portfolio problem are similar to those of the single security case. If information requirements do differ for the portfolio decision, we will disclose the nature of these differences by using footnote references.

Overview:
primacy of cash flow potential data

It is generally agreed that investors are not interested in historical financial data *per se*. No rational investor purchases stock in a company because of the firm's past profit performance; rather, it is the prospects for future profitability that induce investment. Past financial data are potentially relevant to the external user either as a basis for predicting future events or as corroborating evidence in support of previously developed predictions.[4]

The accounting literature is filled with statements which recognize that investors' data needs are oriented toward the future. In this regard Staubus writes:

[3] For an excellent survey of this topic see William F. Sharpe, *Portfolio Theory and Capital Markets* (New York: McGraw-Hill Book Company, Inc., 1970).

[4] See, for example, Benjamin Graham, "Two Illustrative Approaches to Formula Valuations of Common Stocks," *Financial Analysis Journal*, 13 (November, 1957), 11, reprinted in *Readings in Financial Analysis and Investment Management,* ed. Eugene M. Lerner (Homewood, Ill.: Richard D. Irwin, Inc., 1963), pp. 289–90; Robert T. Sprouse, "The Measurement of Financial Position and Income: Purpose and Procedure," in *Research in Accounting Measurement,* eds. Robert K. Jaedicke, Yuji Ijiri, and Oswald Nielsen (Menasha, Wis.: American Accounting Association, 1966); The Committee to Prepare a Statement of Basic Accounting Theory, pp. 5–6, 23–26; and Jean St. G. Kerr, "Expectations and Realization as Bases for the Determination of Profit," in *The Accounting Frontier,* eds. R. J. Chambers, L. Goldberg, and R. L. Mathews (Melbourne, Australia: F. W. Cheshire, 1965), pp. 50–51.

We must never lose sight of the fact that investment decisions require judgments regarding the future. Investors rely on the amount of the residual equity and changes therein as a partial basis for making such judgments; they are most concerned with those aspects of past events that portend some part of the future.[5]

Vatter alludes to the same phenomenon:

. . . to make a forecast of future expectations (as present or prospective investors must do in making their decisions). . . .[6]

Sprouse states:

The primary purpose of the measurement of last year's income reported to investors is to provide a basis for predicting future years' income. Such predictions have obvious relevance to all investors—to current and prospective preferred stockholders and bondholders, as well as to current and prospective common stockholders.[7]

Finally, the Committee to Prepare a Statement of Basic Accounting Theory declared:

Almost all external users of financial information reported by a profit-oriented firm are involved in efforts to predict the earnings of the firm for some future period. Such predictions are most crucial in the case of present and prospective equity investors and their representatives—considered by many to be the most important of the user groups.[8]

Precisely what is it about the future that is of such interest to investors? A model of investor behavior that is quite pervasive in the literature of economics and finance provides a normative answer to this question. Essentially, this model suggests that investors are primarily concerned with the level and timing of future cash inflows. One of the earliest proponents of this model stated that:

. . . *the proper price of any security, whether a stock or bond, is the sum of all future income payments discounted at the current rate of interest in order to arrive at the present value.*[9] (Emphasis in original.)

[5] George J. Staubus, *A Theory of Accounting to Investors* (Berkeley and Los Angeles: The University of California Press, 1961), p. 50.

[6] William J. Vatter, *The Fund Theory of Accounting and Its Implications for Financial Reports* (Chicago: The University of Chicago Press, 1947), p. 72.

[7] Sprouse, "The Measurement of Financial Position," 106.

[8] *A Statement of Basic Accounting Theory*, p. 23.

[9] Robert G. Weise, "Investing for True Values," *Barron's* (September 8, 1930), 5. Weise was, of course, simply formulating a specific application of the work of Irving Fisher in *The Nature of Capital and Income* (New York: The Macmillan Company, 1906).

This concept of investment worth was popularized several years later by Williams:

> Let us define the investment value of a stock as the present worth of all the dividends to be paid upon it. . . . To appraise the investment value, then, it is necessary to estimate the future payments.[10]

A quote from a contemporary security analysis textbook gives some idea of the extent to which this concept has been accepted:

> The *standard method* of valuation of individual enterprises, consists of capitalizing the expected future earnings and/or dividends at an appropriate rate of return.[11] (Emphasis supplied.)

This investor decision framework has been the subject of many journal articles.[12] Furthermore, several models of the firm's investment financing process and strategy have also incorporated this concept.[13] Accounting authors have not ignored this future flows concept or its possible implication for financial reporting:

> At this juncture we should point out that, so far as is known today, if investors (both potential and actual and both owners and creditors) could predict the amount and timing of future cash receipts from their investments then according to many theorists they should need little else in the way of information.[14]

From this line of reasoning we can derive the following normative decision model for long-term equity investors: The selection of an in-

[10] John Burr Williams, *The Theory of Investment Value* (Cambridge, Mass.: Harvard University Press, 1938), p. 55.

[11] Benjamin Graham, David L. Dodd, and Sidney Cottle, *Security Analysis: Principles and Technique* (4th ed.) (New York: McGraw-Hill Book Company, Inc., 1962), p. 435.

[12] See, for example, Myron J. Gordon and Eli Shapiro, "Capital Equipment Analysis: The Required Rate of Profit," *Management Science,* 3 (October, 1956), 102–10; Nicholas Molodovsky, "Valuation of Common Stocks," *Financial Analysts Journal,* 15 (February, 1959), 23–27, 84–99; Diran Bodenhorn, "A Cash-Flow Concept of Profit," *Journal of Finance,* 19 (March, 1964), 16–31; and 1966–68 Committee on External Reporting, "External Reporting Practices," 78–123.

[13] Examples of this usage may be found in Myron J. Gordon, *The Investment, Financing and Valuation of the Corporation* (Homewood, Ill.: Richard D. Irwin, Inc., 1962); Ezra Solomon, *The Theory of Financial Management* (New York: Columbia University Press, 1963); Eugene M. Lerner and Willard T. Carleton, *A Theory of Financial Analysis* (New York: Harcourt, Brace and World, Inc., 1966); and Alexander A. Robichek and Steward C. Myers, *Optimal Financing Decisions* (Englewood Cliffs, N. J.: Prentice-Hall, Inc., 1965).

[14] *A Statement of Basic Accounting Theory,* p. 23n. The Committee contends, however, that such future cash flow information is an "unattainable ideal." For a similar view, also see Stephen N. Penman, "What Net Asset Value?—An Extension of a Familiar Debate," *The Accounting Review,* 40 (April, 1970), 338.

vestment security from available investment options is basically a resource allocation decision. The strategy is to select that security which promises the highest attainable return commensurate with an acceptable degree of risk. This choice should be governed primarily by the potentialities confronting the various firms whose securities are under consideration, rather than the actualities (past events).[15] In order to be relevant to this decision model, accounting data must afford investors some reasonable basis for estimating future returns and their variability.

Investors' normative information needs

The normative cash flow model already introduced can be expressed symbolically in the following fashion.[16]

$$V_o = \sum_{i=1}^{n} \frac{D_i \alpha_i}{(1+\beta)^i} + \frac{I_n \alpha_n}{(1+\beta)^n} - I_o$$

where:

V_o = the subjective net present value from purchasing one share of a given security at time period (o) at its market price I_o

D_i = per share dividend expected during period (i)

α_i = certainty equivalent factor that makes the investor indifferent between D_i and a totally riskless cash flow of the amount $D_i \alpha_i$; if the investor is risk averse, $0 < \alpha_i < 1$

β = opportunity rate for a riskless investment (assumed, for ease of exposition, to be constant over the foreseeable horizon)

I_n = expected market price at the end of the holding period (n)

This model (which, for simplicity, ignores income taxes) states that an investor is primarily interested in (1) estimating the future dividend flows expected from an investment and (2) the risk inherent to those flows. To be relevant for the information needs of this model, accounting measurements ought to facilitate estimates of such flows and their associated risk.[17] *These constitute the primary criteria by which the relevance of replacement costing to investors is to be judged.*

Obviously, there are many factors that collectively determine an

15 Revsine, "General Purpose Reports," 38.

16 This model format is based on a report of the 1966–68 Committee on External Reporting, "External Reporting Practices," 79–123. Notice that certainty equivalents might, alternatively, be incorporated in the discount rate.

17 The measure of risk that is appropriate for evaluating an individual security differs from the risk measure that should be used when a security is being considered for inclusion in a portfolio. These differences will be discussed in footnote 36, *infra*.

enterprise's ability to pay dividends. The Committee on External Reporting suggested that dividend payments are a function of several variables. Their list included:

1. Net operating flows
2. Net nonoperating flows
3. Investment and disinvestment by stockholders and creditors
4. Flows from investment and disinvestment in assets
5. Flows from random events
6. Management's dividend policy.[18]

Many of these sub-components are erratic or otherwise unpredictable, and some of them are material only when aggregated. Thus, it is difficult to design a forecast system that predicts total dividend flows. However, net operating flows—the single most important long-run component of total enterprise flows—are generally considered more stable, and hence, predictable. Therefore, although it may not be possible to predict future dividend flows directly, it does seem theoretically possible to use accounting data to predict future net operating flows.

We observe that corporate managers attempt to avoid decreases in the prevailing dividend rate because such action is thought to adversely affect stock price. Since, in the long run, net operating flows generate the bulk of the total resource flows needed to pay dividends, management's desire to maintain dividend levels immediately translates into a desire to (at least) maintain net operating flow levels.

Future net operating flow levels are determined by (1) the physical level of future operations and (2) future input and output prices. Future price levels are usually a function of events external to the firm. Accordingly, in striving to maintain net operating flow levels, management's real controllable variable is to maintain the existing physical level of operations.

We will define that portion of net operating flows that can be distributed as a dividend without reducing the level of future physical operations as the "distributable operating flow" of the firm.[19] Given management's aversion to dividend reductions, future distributable operating flow is accordingly a prime determinant of future dividend levels. Insofar as an investor is able to predict distributable operating flows accurately, his ability to predict future dividends is similarly enhanced. *Accordingly, when we evaluate the predictive ability of replacement*

---

[18] 1966–68 Committee on External Reporting, 83–88.

[19] Distributable operating flows will be defined more rigorously in Chapter 4. In the remainder of this study, when we use the terms "operating flows," or "future flows," we mean distributable operating flows.

costing, we will examine its utility as a predictor of the distributable operating flows component of total resource flows.

MARKET EFFICIENCY: A DIGRESSION

The preceding discussion implied that the appropriate objective of external reporting is to satisfy the information needs of *individual* investors. Although preoccupation with individual investor needs represents the traditional view, recent evidence suggests that this emphasis may be misdirected. This evidence is based on tests of what is popularly known as the "efficient markets hypothesis," which states that capital markets are efficient in the sense that security prices fully reflect publicly available information in an unbiased and almost instantaneous fashion. This means that at any point in time market prices incorporate all available information regarding firms, their industries, and the economy as a whole.[20] If true, this implies that individual securities are always appropriately priced relative to other securities, i.e., there is no such thing as an overvalued or undervalued security.[21] (Of course, this does not mean that the prices prevailing at one point in time are necessarily correct reflections of those future events that give rise to security values. Later events may show that the information used by the market—although the best then available—may have been faulty. When this new information becomes available, the market will again react in an instantaneous and unbiased manner. That is, subsequent price corrections will ensue in order to reflect this latest available information.)

Empirical tests have strongly supported this hypothesis regarding market efficiency.[22] These findings lend credence to the proposition that, in a relative sense, securities are always appropriately priced. If true, the existence of market efficiency would have important implications for external reporting. Traditionally, accountants have believed that their reports allow the investor to "play a game" against the market. That is, through informed study of periodic reports, shrewd investors were thought able to systematically outguess the market. But if the efficient market hypothesis is in fact correct, all publicly available information would already be impounded in market prices, and accounting reports could

[20] See Nicholas J. Gonedes, "Efficient Capital Markets and External Accounting," *The Accounting Review*, 47 (January, 1972), 11–21.

[21] William H. Beaver, "The Behavior of Security Prices and Its Implication for Accounting Research (Methods)," Chapter II in "Report of the Committee on Research Methodology in Accounting," *Committee Reports* Supplement to Volume 47, *The Accounting Review* (1972), 407–37.

[22] A synthesis of this literature is contained in Eugene F. Fama, "Efficient Capital Markets: A Review of Theory and Empirical Work," *Journal of Finance* (May, 1970), 383–417.

not help the individual investor recognize undervalued securities or otherwise outguess the market.[23]

Therefore, those who believe in market efficiency see a slightly different role for accounting information. In their view, accounting information is of little use to the individual investor. Instead, accounting should provide information that will allow the market to generate "valid" prices for securities (in the sense that the need for subsequent price corrections is minimized) and thus facilitate efficient resource allocation.

Our reason for introducing this controversy is to emphasize that accounting data are needed for purposes of prediction under either view. Following the individual investor approach, accounting-based predictions supposedly help these individuals outguess the market. Following the efficient markets approach, predictions based on accounting data are used by the market in generating security prices. If the reported accounting data provide a good basis for predictions, the resultant prices will require fewer corrections and will facilitate efficient allocation of capital. Accordingly, predictions of distributable operating flows are required under either alternative. Thus, it seems appropriate to analyze the predictive ability of replacement costing irrespective of which view of market behavior we embrace. In subsequent sections where we employ the term "investors," readers may consequently interpret the term to correspond with their own beliefs regarding external reporting. To traditionalists, "investors" will mean individuals attempting to discover undervalued securities; to advocates of market efficiency, "investors" will mean the entire market quickly impounding reported information in order to generate market prices. Since both groups would have a similar need for predictions, we need not choose between these approaches in order to evaluate the predictive ability of replacement costing.

SATISFYING THE NORMATIVE MODEL'S INFORMATION NEEDS

Means for providing predictive information

In a normative sense, information regarding future dividend flows constitutes the primary information need of investors. But we contended that dividends themselves are difficult to predict directly. However, distributable operating flows—the prime determinant of long-run dividend potential—are more stable and hence more predictable. In this view, replacement costing will be relevant to investors insofar as the financial

23 Beaver, "Behavior of Security Prices."

information it generates is useful as a basis for predicting future distributable operating flows. Thus, predictive ability becomes the focus of analysis.

There are potentially two methods by which accountants might provide needed information regarding future events.[24] The first method would necessitate reporting predictions of those future variables deemed relevant to investors' decisions. The familiar budget information is illustrative of this type of data. Information of this genre will be referred to as *direct predictive information*. A second approach is less direct, but still basically useful for prediction. Here, information regarding past events is communicated to users because it is believed that these events are indirect indicators of relevant future events. For example, one accounting procedure might be selected in preference to available alternatives because this procedure is presumed to provide users with the best basis for building their own predictions. We will designate this type of data as *information for predictions*. The difference between the two approaches is a function of who makes the predictions. In the direct prediction approach, predictions are made by management and communicated to users. In the second approach, users must generate their own predictions. To facilitate this, they are provided with information for predictions.

We will now briefly examine these alternative means for providing users with information regarding future events.

DIRECT PREDICTIVE INFORMATION

Since a reliable basis for estimating future flows constitutes the primary information need of investors, some means for satisfying this need is necessary if accounting data are to be useful in decision making. One method for providing forecast data is to incorporate budgetary projections into the formal, external reports. That is, *direct predictions* of future events could be provided. Understandably, accountants themselves are reluctant to communicate direct predictive information to investors. Many would contend that such projections are beyond the legitimate scope of the accounting profession. For example:

> Accountants generally refrain from reporting budgets relating to future periods to external users, on the ground that the information is not sufficiently verifiable, although it might be highly relevant to external [users'] needs. Failure to observe the standard of verifiability to a minimum degree

---

24 An essentially similar view was adopted by the 1970–71 Committee on Corporate Financial Reporting, of which the author was a member. See "Report of the Committee on Corporate Financial Reporting," *Committee Reports,* Supplement to Vol. 47, *The Accounting Review* (1972), 525–28.

would place the accountant, in some cases, in the role of forecaster and would reduce the confidence of the user and thereby diminish the usefulness of accounting reports.[25]

However, budgetary disclosure need not invariably necessitate predictions by the external accountant himself. Instead, the firm's own budget projections, which are prepared internally to facilitate planning, might be incorporated into the external statements.[26] Thus, the external accountant's responsibility in this area could be limited to attesting to the reasonableness and consistency of the procedures used by management in generating budget estimates.[27]

If management's own budget estimates are included in accounting reports, then one of the primary objections to reporting direct predictions is intensified. Specifically, the reliability of the resultant figures would be open to question. It could occasionally be in management's best interest to provide unrealistically generous estimates of expected future events. Cooper, Dopuch, and Keller accede to this possibility but suggest that in the long run, *ex post* comparisons between management's previous budget estimates and actual realized events would tend to deter deliberate error.[28] That is, management would eventually be obliged to explain significant deviations from planned performance. Furthermore, users would be able to evaluate management's forecasting ability by analyzing the frequency, magnitude, and direction of differences between planned and realized events.

The problems involved in implementing the direct prediction approach are formidable. First, there is likely to be resistance from business enterprises, motivated, in part, by the fear that budget disclosure could provide competitors with damaging information regarding future plans.[29] Second, the forecasting procedures necessary to develop reasonable estimates and the budget-audit procedures necessary to monitor these fore-

[25] *A Statement of Basic Accounting Theory,* p. 27.

[26] W. W. Cooper, N. Dopuch, and T. F. Keller, "Budgetary Disclosure and Other Suggestions for Improving Accounting Reports," *The Accounting Review,* 43 (October, 1968), 640–48. In addition, SEC Chairman William J. Casey recently discussed the possibility of presenting forecast data in prospectuses and other documents filed with the Commission. See "Casey Finds Review on Disclosures Needed So Forecasts Can Accompany Stock Filing," *The Wall Street Journal* (Friday, November 19, 1971), 6.

[27] See Yuri Ijiri, "On Budgeting Principles and Budget-Auditing Standards," *The Accounting Review,* 43 (October, 1968), 664–66. In this article Ijiri identifies two separate types of budget preparation procedures that must be audited: (1) those relating to the prediction of events themselves, and (2) those relating to the procedures for recording the predicted events.

[28] Cooper *et al.,* 645–46.

[29] See, for example, K. Fred Skousen, Robert A. Sharp, and Russell K. Tolman, "Corporate Disclosure of Budgetary Data," *Journal of Accountancy,* 133 (May, 1972), 50–57.

casts do not exist at present. Finally, the notion of reporting expectations is contrary to prevailing practice and current legal considerations.[30]

In light of these institutional and technological limitations, it is doubtful whether direct prediction provides a workable method for satisfying the forecast needs of investors unless such predictions are *required* by some regulatory group, such as the Securities and Exchange Commission. That is, statement users have a continuous need for future oriented data in order to assess the investment potential of alternative securities. But if we adopt a *voluntary* direct prediction approach as a means for satisfying their needs, such forecasts will not be continuously available. Instead, direct predictions will be available to users only if both of the following conditions are met:

1. Management must perceive that the firm will not be harmed by the disclosures contained in the forecast, and
2. The assumptions underlying the projection must be so reasonable and determinable that the auditor will not object to having his name associated with the forecast.

Since each of these conditions is frequently absent (and since *both* conditions must be present for a voluntary direct forecast to appear), direct forecasts would be available only occasionally. Thus, this voluntary approach is not a suitable means for satisfying the continuous forecast needs of users. Instead, direct predictions would be useful primarily for special, one-time predictive needs such as those involving new security issues or take-over bids.

It is conceivable that direct forecasts may eventually be *required* by the SEC for all public filings. This, of course, would eliminate the institutional objections associated with a *voluntary* direct forecast approach. However, even if direct forecasts are eventually required, accounting data regarding past events would still be needed for forecast purposes. That is, management would need some basis on which to build its direct predictions of future performance. Furthermore, an investor may desire to corroborate the reasonableness of a direct forecast provided by management. Both objectives could be satisfied by forecasts generated from accounting reports of past performance.

Thus, predictions generated from verifiable past data would still be needed even if direct forecasts eventually are required in public filings. Furthermore, if direct forecasts are not made mandatory, then the resultant occasional voluntary forecasts are not likely to be adequate for the continuous forecast needs of users. Under these conditions, the pri-

---

30 For a discussion of these issues see *Corporate Financial Reporting*, eds. Rappaport and Revsine, pp. 162–66.

mary basis for predictions would have to be provided by reported past data. For both of these reasons our attention in this study will be directed towards the predictive basis provided by accounting reports of past events. In other words, we will analyze the *information for predictions* provided by accounting reports in order to assess its utility in satisfying investors' needs for continuous predictive data. Direct prediction will not receive further consideration.

INFORMATION FOR PREDICTIONS

Making predictions for the user is currently deemed to be outside the scope of the accountant's reporting function. However, many accountants believe that some attempt must nevertheless be made to satisfy users' predictive needs. One means for attempting to satisfy these needs is to provide users with information about past events which is useful in generating *their own* forecasts of future flows. Acceptance of this position has given rise to the predictive ability criterion that is increasingly advocated in contemporary accounting literature.[31] Supporters of this criterion suggest that the primary aim of external reporting research should be to discover and develop reporting bases that are good predictors of various financial events. Providing users with performance data that have been shown to be a reasonable predictor of relevant future events facilitates prediction of these events by users themselves. Such information is relevant to users' requirements for distributable operating flow forecasts, but does not require the accountant to make such forecasts himself. *Information for predictions* thus represents the traditional accounting approach to satisfying users' needs for future oriented data. Accordingly, this approach will be given careful attention in this study.

There are two methods by which accounting data regarding past events can provide information for predictions:

1. The information provided by a particular measurement system could afford the user an opportunity to *discern trends* of past data, *and/or extrapolate* contemporaneous data into the future.
2. A measurement system may incorporate, either explicitly or implicitly, certain external events that are *lead indicators;* that is, detailed analysis of current data could provide information to the user regarding emerging forces that are expected to affect the firm.

We will refer to the first possibility as the *extrapolation method* and the second will be called the *lead-indicator method.* Since both of these approaches will be examined in somewhat greater detail in Chap-

31 Most notably, William H. Beaver, John W. Kennelly, and William M. Voss, "Predictive Ability as a Criterion for the Evaluation of Accounting Data," *The Accounting Review,* 43 (October, 1968), 675–83.

ters 4 and 5, the discussion that follows is intended only as a brief introduction to each.

Of the two approaches to providing information for predictions,
the extrapolation method (or some variant thereof) has received by far
the greater attention in the research literature. The predictive ability
test conducted by Frank is typical of this approach.[32] Frank attempted
to determine the relative predictive ability of two different income measures. The ability of each concept to predict itself in the following year
constituted one part of this test. Frank used actual income data for a
series of years. The income figure derived using one set of measurement
methods for 19x1 was then used to generate an income *estimate* under
this same measurement basis for 19x2. This 19x2 estimate was then compared with the *actual* 19x2 income amount. The percentage forecast
errors of many such estimates were used to assess the relative ability of
each measurement concept to predict its own future values.

In Chapter 5 we will examine the ability of replacement cost income
to generate extrapolations of future distributable operating flows. One
of the primary limitations inherent in the extrapolation approach is that
the resultant forecast is wholly dependent on the observed past relationship between the independent variable(s) and the dependent variable.
In a dynamic environment, these past relationships can shift suddenly and dramatically. Such shifts are called turning points. Because
the extrapolation approach relies entirely on past observations, it cannot
predict these turning points. Unfortunately, turning points probably constitute the single most important class of events of relevance to decision
makers. Since the extrapolation method is not likely to provide an effective means for anticipating such changes, this method would seemingly
be a reasonable forecasting tool only in a stable environment. However,
relationships do not change in a stable environment and there would
accordingly be little need for forecasts under these circumstances.

Thus, at the outset of this analysis, we must be realistic in our
expectations regarding the accuracy of users' own predictions. It is likely
that past data will often provide a disappointing basis on which to base
predictions. Rather than a deficiency of the accounting reporting process,
we must view this as a realistic and unavoidable characteristic of forecasts in general.

The lead-indicator method, the second approach to providing information for predictions, has heretofore received little attention in the
accounting literature.[33] Essentially, a lead indicator is also an indepen-

[32] Werner Frank, "A Study of the Predictive Significance of Two Income Measures," *Journal of Accounting Research*, 7 (Spring, 1969), 123–36.

[33] For one exception, see Lawrence Revsine, "On the Correspondence Between
Replacement Cost Income and Economic Income," *The Accounting Review*, 45 (July,
1970), 513–23.

dent variable that is thought to be related to the variable for which a prediction is desired. However, there is one crucial difference between this approach and the extrapolation method discussed earlier. If a lead indicator is truly effective, then changes in this variable precede changes in the dependent variable. The relative advantage of this prediction device, vis-à-vis simple extrapolation, is that an effective lead indicator will give forewarning of an impending change in the level of the dependent variable. Theoretically, this forecasting device is not subject to one deficiency which plagues simple extrapolation, i.e., the inability to anticipate turning points.[34]

In the lead-indicator approach, the research process is transformed from one of examining trends in financial measures to one of searching for effective lead indicators. Realistically, of course, the inherent complexity of the business environment, coupled with our generally incomplete understanding of the interrelationships operative therein, may make it difficult to isolate lead indicators that are sufficiently precise to be of real benefit to the user. Indeed, there is the possibility that such indicators may not even exist. Nonetheless, future flow data are important inputs to users' decision models and accountants have a responsibility for providing relevant information to decision makers. Thus, the relevance of forecast information to users requires accounting researchers to explore predictive possibilities. This is so despite the fact that the probability of the effort being totally successful may be small. Accordingly, Chapter 4 will explore the ability of replacement cost income to serve as a lead indicator of anticipated changes in distributable operating flows.

In concluding this discussion, we should reiterate the complexity of the problems confronting those who wish to enhance the relevance of external reports through improved predictive ability. Our purpose in doing so is to present a realistic picture of some of the difficulties inherent in the predictive ability notion. Prediction is a difficult area; in accounting it is doubly so, since users must rely on indirect data regarding past events in order to generate their own predictions. These difficulties suggest that one may never be totally satisfied with the predictive ability of any indirect concept. The disadvantages and problems inherent to direct prediction must be viewed as an environmental constraint. The preceding analysis suggests that accountants must search for the most

---

[34] However, the lead-indicator method *is* vulnerable to the other deficiency of the extrapolation approach. That is, lead indicators are also identified by observing past relationships between independent and dependent variables. Environmental changes can introduce new interdependencies and thus destroy previously reliable lead-lag relationships without warning.

effective predictors subject to this constraint.[35] Thus, Chapters 4 and 5 will explore the utility of replacement cost income as both an extrapolation basis and as a lead indicator for future distributable operating flows.

Means for providing information about risk

The normative cash flow model introduced earlier presumes that investors are concerned not only with flow levels but also with the risk associated with expected flows. Indeed, the certainty equivalent adjustment factor is derived by relating the investor's innate risk averseness to the expected variability of the future flows. To facilitate such adjustments, accounting data must provide the user with a means for estimating the risk associated with the forecasted flows. For simplicity, we will concentrate on the analysis of risk for an individual security. By doing so, we avoid the complexities of portfolio theory, which are beyond the intended scope of this book. But we must emphasize that the evaluation of risk for a portfolio of many securities is potentially different from the evaluation of risk for a single security.[36]

[35] Kenneth E. Boulding, *Conflict and Defense* (New York: Harper & Brothers, 1962), p. 95, provides a rather pessimistic view of the present or future utility of accounting reports:

. . . the basic problems of the accountant are fundamentally insoluble, as they involve information about the future that is not accessible to him.

[36] The appropriate measure of the riskiness of the expected flows depends on two factors: (1) whether we are dealing with individual securities or a portfolio of many securities, and (2) the characteristics of the investor's utility function.

The risk associated with ownership of a *single* security is a function of the variability of the expected flows from that security. However, when the security is being evaluated for inclusion in a portfolio of *many* securities, then the riskiness of the security is a function of the covariance of its expected returns with those of other securities in the portfolio. (For an excellent summary of portfolio theory, see Ray Ball and Philip Brown, "Portfolio Theory and Accounting," *Journal of Accounting Research*, 7 (Autumn, 1969), 300–23.)

The reason for this difference is that the risk resulting from the variability of the flows from any individual security (termed "individualistic risk") can be removed by diversification, i.e., by constructing a portfolio of many securities. The covariance is called systematic risk and this risk cannot be removed by diversification. (See Sharpe, *Portfolio Theory*, pp. 91–98.)

Another point that merits mention regarding the portfolio theory model relates to the appropriate measure of dispersion that should be used to represent portfolio risk. Many competing alternative measures might, of course, be employed. Previous research indicates, however, that the appropriate representation of risk depends on the investor's utility function. If investors are risk averse and prefer more wealth to less wealth, then the variance is the appropriate measure of risk. (See, for example, William Beaver, Paul Kettler, and Myron Scholes, "The Association Between Market Determined and Accounting Determined Risk Measures," *The Accounting Review*, 45 (October, 1970), 655–59.)

The central question becomes: How can accounting information aid the user in estimating the risk inherent in forecasted flows? We are, in essence, searching for accounting measures of risk.

Previous studies have indicated that the use of accounting *ratios* can be helpful in predicting the risk inherent in business enterprises. One recent study used accounting ratios as the independent variables in a multivariate model to predict corporate bond ratings, which are a surrogate for credit worthiness, or risk. The finding of the study was that financial ratios were useful in predicting bond ratings.[37] Another study used univariate analytical techniques to assess the ability of financial ratios as predictors. In this study, the object of prediction was the failure of the firm. Although this second study found considerable differences among ratios, the general conclusion was that "ratio analysis can be useful in the prediction of failure." [38]

Both of these studies thus indicate that financial ratios can be useful in assessing risk. Furthermore, these studies are in accord with the findings of earlier studies regarding the predictive ability of financial ratios. This evidence suggests that financial ratios might similarly provide a useful basis for predicting the variability (or riskiness) of the expected flows to investors. Although there is no *direct* empirical evidence to support this extension, it does appear to be quite reasonable in light of related evidence. Therefore, in developing our theoretical model of the utility of accounting measures, we will assume that financial ratios are *potentially* useful as indicators of the risk associated with expected flows. Then we will examine the ability of replacement costing to generate ratios that provide a basis for such assessments.

Obviously, this analysis of replacement cost ratios is exploratory and must be considered a prelude to later testing. Our purpose is to explore the general association between replacement cost ratios and the risk inherent in future flows. Hopefully, this will provide the theoretical basis for subsequent empirical tests. Later tests must not only explore the predictive ability of accounting ratios but also develop some index to reflect alternative levels of risk.

(Although our analysis of accounting ratios will focus on measuring the risk associated with individual securities, there is reason to believe that accounting ratios may also be of some use in evaluating

37 James O. Horrigan, "The Determination of Long-Term Credit Standing with Financial Ratios," *Empirical Research in Accounting: Selected Studies, 1966,* Supplement to Volume 4, *Journal of Accounting Research,* 44–62.

38 William H. Beaver, "Financial Ratios as Predictors of Failure," *Empirical Research in Accounting: Selected Studies, 1966,* Supplement to Volume 4, *Journal of Accounting Research,* 71–111, at 102.

portfolio risk.[39] Thus, our examination of risk may be relevant to both the portfolio case and the individual security case. But there is no assurance that the same ratios that are relevant for assessing risk in individual securities are necessarily the ones that are relevant for portfolio considerations.)

In order to evaluate the usefulness of accounting ratios as an indicator of the riskiness of expected flows, we must specify some transformation that links these ratios to investors' future flows. That is, we must specify how accounting ratios are related to the variability of expected flows. Unfortunately, empirical evidence is not available in this area either. Accordingly, we must rely on accepted normative judgments in selecting the desired relationships.

Many accountants believe that there are two general categories of information that are particularly useful in evaluating the potential riskiness of enterprise flows. These categories are:

1. Information that reflects a firm's liquidity-solvency position, and
2. Information that reflects a firm's profit generating potential.

Obviously, these two categories of information do not represent an exhaustive enumeration of the data useful in assessing the riskiness of enterprise flows. However, they are reasonably representative of the type of data that might prove useful. Accordingly, these two categories should provide an adequate basis for illustrating how one can begin to assess the relevance of the financial ratios generated by an accounting measurement system.[40]

LIQUIDITY-SOLVENCY POSITION

The liquid position of a firm is generally considered to be a measure of the firm's ability to pay its liabilities as they become due while

[39] Traditional accounting ratios are thought to reflect the individualistic risk of a security. However, if individualistic risk and systematic risk are themselves positively correlated, then accounting ratios may also be a surrogate for systematic risk. Indeed, this surrogate relationship is consistent with available evidence. (See Beaver, Kettler, and Scholes, "Market and Accounting Risk Measures," 654–82.) Similarly, if changes in individualistic risk elements (which are presumably captured by accounting ratios) influence systematic risk, then accounting ratios would again be relevant for assessing portfolio risk.

[40] We should emphasize that accounting ratios constitute a highly imperfect assessment basis. Their simplicity makes them subject to serious deficiencies and they must be interpreted with extreme caution. (See Alfred Rappaport, "A Capital Budgeting Approach to Divisional Planning and Control," *Financial Executive* (October, 1968), 47–63.) But despite these very real deficiencies, ratio analysis is still potentially useful in certain situations if it is applied cautiously and with awareness of its deficiencies.

providing sufficient working capital and other assets to carry on normal operating activities. Solvency represents the continuing facility with which obligations can be satisfied in the intermediate term.[41] These measures are of concern to equity holders for one important reason. No matter how favorable the long-run earnings possibilities appear to be, a firm is a risky investment if an inadequate liquidity base makes its chances for short-term survival hazardous. Thus, the theoretical relationship between liquidity-solvency and the riskiness of future flows is rather direct. In Chapter 7 we will examine the theoretical utility of several replacement cost liquidity-solvency ratios.

PROFIT GENERATING POTENTIAL

The relationship between profit generating potential and the risk associated with future flows is also quite direct. The stronger and more diversified the operating base of a given firm, the less the expected variability of its future flows. Here, too, several replacement cost financial ratios are of potential benefit and will be analyzed in Chapter 7.[42]

OVERVIEW OF THE REMAINING CHAPTERS

Briefly, our plan for the remainder of the book is as follows. In Chapter 3 we will review the fundamental characteristics of replacement cost accounting. There we will discuss the reputed advantages of this measurement method, illustrate its application, and discuss its feasibility. With this background, we begin to evaluate the relevance of replacement costing to the normative information needs of equity investors. This analysis starts with an examination of the ability of the replacement cost concept to generate information for predictions. In Chapter 4 we consider the lead-indicator method; in Chapter 5 the extrapolation approach is analyzed. Chapter 6 continues the discussion of information for predictions. There, attention is focused on several deficiencies inherent in replacement costing and some means for overcoming these limitations.

---

41 See, for example, Homer A. Black, John E. Champion, and R. Gene Brown, *Accounting in Business Decisions: Theory, Method, and Use* (2nd ed.) (Englewood Cliffs, N. J.: Prentice-Hall, Inc., 1967), pp. 331–32, or any other standard introductory text.

42 We should point out that the financial ratios that will be examined in Chapter 7 are not necessarily the same ones that were found to have the greatest predictive capacity in earlier studies. There are two reasons for this. First, we have based our selections largely on the popularity of certain ratios in the literature. Second, we are concerned with the variability of residual flows to equity investors. Since previous studies examined other flows, there is no necessary exact correspondence between their findings and the ratios best suited for our purpose.

Finally, Chapter 7 evaluates the relevance of the financial ratios generated by replacement costing. Our objective, of course, is to determine whether this information is useful in estimating the risk associated with future flows.

Although empirical evidence will be introduced where appropriate and available, the reader is reminded that our analysis is essentially normative. The objective is to provide a theoretical foundation for later tests of the relevance of replacement costing. Thus, our findings are intended to be logically compelling, *but they cannot be conclusive*. This study is thus the first stage in a longer research process that must culminate in empirical testing.

SUMMARY

In Chapter 1 we suggested that users' information needs probably vary greatly among groups. Because of this heterogeneity of information needs, a universally relevant measurement concept is not likely to exist. Accordingly, if one wishes to evaluate the relevance of an accounting measurement process like replacement costing, the analysis must be performed on a user category-by-category basis.

This is the approach that is being followed in this study. A particular user group—long-term equity investors—was selected as the focal point of the analysis. This group was selected both for its economic importance and its heavy dependence on external reports for information. In order to evaluate the relevance of a measurement process, we must identify the purpose for which the generated data are needed. Accordingly, a very general normative decision model for the investor group was introduced. Given this decision model, we observed that the primary and overriding single need of this group is for information regarding the amount and variability of future enterprise dividend flows. This information is needed to afford investors a means for evaluating their prospective rate of return and the associated risk.

Observation suggests that managers strive to avoid decreasing the established dividend rate. To achieve this end, one of management's controllable variables is to maintain the existing physical level of operations (i.e., the number of machines in use, the amount of inventory employed, etc.). We defined that portion of net operating flows which can be distributed to owners without reducing future physical operating levels as the "distributable operating flow" of the firm. We further suggested that accounting data are potentially useful in generating forecasts of distributable operating flows. Since these operating flows represent a major portion of total enterprise flows, they constitute a prime determinant of future dividends. Investors desirous of estimating future dividend flows (which are difficult to predict directly) can facilitate such estimates by generating predictions of future distributable operating flows. Thus, our examination of the predictive ability of replacement costing will focus on the ability of this concept to predict distributable operating flows.

Because the investor group needs information to facilitate forecasts of distributable operating flows, we discussed the various means by which accounting reports could provide such data. Two distinct methods for providing forecast information were introduced. Specifically, accounting data could provide direct predictive information, or information for predictions. We argued that direct predictive information would be made available to users only if (1) corporate management felt that such disclosure would not be harmful, and (2) the assumptions underlying the forecast were so determinable that the auditor would accede to its publication. Since these conditions will often be absent, direct forecasts would seldom be available continuously, as needed. This means that investors' needs for anticipatory information must be satisfied by information that provides them with a basis for generating their own predictions.

Information for prediction provides the user with data for making quantitative estimates of the level of future distributable operating flows. There are two distinct methods by which information for prediction could facilitate such forecasts. First, the information generated by a measurement system may, through the vehicle of trend analysis, allow the user to extrapolate past data and generate future flow estimates. Alternatively, the measurement basis may incorporate certain external events that are lead indicators and thus forewarn the user of emerging forces that are expected to affect the firm's operating flow stream. In either event, if the indirect predictive information generated by a given measurement model is to be relevant to the normative requirements of investors, it must provide them with some basis for developing quantitative estimates of future distributable operating flows.

Information regarding the variability of operating flows is also required by the normative decision model. Recent evidence indicates that financial ratios are potentially useful as indicators of risk, or variability. We selected two categories of ratios that are thought to be potentially useful as risk indicators. These are (1) liquidity-solvency ratios, and (2) profitability ratios. We intend to examine the ability of replacement costing to generate these ratios in a form that is useful for evaluating the variability of expected operating flows.

To summarize, this chapter has developed two criteria that can be used to evaluate the relevance of replacement cost reports to investors.

These criteria relate to the ability of replacement cost measures in predicting (1) the level of future distributable operating flows, and (2) the variability of these flows.

APPENDIX TO CHAPTER 2

Until user data needs are empirically specified, external reporting research must be limited, in large part, to certain basic explorations intended to disclose the behavior and characteristics of various income measurement models. This approach necessitates simultaneous experimentation with many broadly defined normative information needs and alternative means (reporting models) for satisfying these needs. In the body of this chapter, it was suggested that this "normative needs" approach is an interim solution. It facilitates progress regarding the relevance of accounting measures to various types of user needs. If empirical research eventually discloses disparities between actual and normative user needs, we can discard the empirically repudiated normative models. Those normative models that can be empirically supported will provide the foundation for coordinating accounting data with user decision needs.

In the final analysis, this may be the manner in which external reporting theory develops. However, some factors suggest that a normative approach to isolating user needs may not be an interim solution at all. Instead, it may be the most defensible means of approaching the issue and thus may represent a final, rather than an interim, solution. We will develop this argument in two stages. The first stage will describe some of the difficulties that would be encountered in attempting a basically empirical specification of decision models. The second stage will outline some of the advantages inherent in a normative specification of decision needs.

Difficulties with the empirical approach

Initially, the problem of identifying and specifying users' decision needs might appear to be quite simple. By questioning statement users and observing their decision processes, the decision models used—and thus the information needed to satisfy these models—would seemingly become apparent. Repeated surveys, interviews, and observations across a broad spectrum of reader categories would seemingly isolate the information requirements to which external reports must be directed. Why, then, is the absence of knowledge about needed information inputs viewed as a severe impediment to progress; would not a concerted expenditure of time and effort amass the required empirical evidence concerning user data needs?

Unfortunately, the answer to this question appears to be "not necessarily." The key to the problem requires a distinction between information that decision makers *are using* and information that they *should be using*. Clearly, even the most carefully designed analyses of actual decisions and decision processes can reveal only those information inputs that users currently employ. This information, of course, must be a subset of the type of accounting data currently available, either from periodic financial reports or from other sources. Thus, if users make the best of a bad situation, they will be forced to use currently provided information even though it may be deficient in some respect (e.g., inappropriate as to type and/or quantity). Therefore, with a given, constrained reporting environment, there may be great disparities between the information that we observe in actual use and the information that ought to be used but is unavailable.

Perhaps, then, empirical studies should not attempt to discover how *available* information is utilized. Instead, one might suggest that these studies should attempt to isolate the kind of information users would like to have available if they had their choice. Regrettably, this approach is also somewhat deficient. As Sterling says:

> . . . communications are not neutral; instead they are educational. Comparative sociologists have often pointed out that our taste in "news," "literature," "music," etc. is largely determined by what was previously communicated to us. If the newscasters poll the populace today they will find that present tastes place football scores high on the list and cricket scores low. However, the very transmission of football scores reinforces this taste and is a major factor in determining the tastes of the coming generation. The accountant is in the same position. He cannot be neutral because his transmissions will be a major factor in determining what the future generations consider relevant. The very definition of information is dependent upon previous information; it is a cause of desires in an ongoing process as well as an effect of the present desires.[43]

Because of this conditioning process, Sterling feels that a poll of users is unlikely to prove effective as a means for determining the kind of information desired.[44]

The process by which users may be conditioned to the data that they receive could occur in at least two ways. First, as students in business training curricula, the prospective users are introduced to generally accepted accounting principles and the financial statements that result from the application of these principles and their derivative procedures.

[43] Robert R. Sterling, "A Statement of Basic Accounting Theory: A Review Article," *Journal of Accounting Research*, 5 (Spring, 1967), 106.

[44] *Ibid.*, 106–7.

Furthermore, they are taught manipulative operations and techniques such as ratio and funds flow analysis that utilize accounting data as a means for evaluating enterprise performance and prospects. In short, users are generally indoctrinated concerning the relevance and utility of traditionally disseminated information. Second, this formal conditioning is continuously reinforced by each external report that users receive. The type of data that was painstakingly programmed into their emerging decision models is constantly made available. Even if short-run pressures do not preclude the external user from formulating innovative non-traditional models, the absence of data necessary to implement these models will likely discourage or abort such creative efforts. In short, the typical user's training has probably desensitized him to alternative information possibilities; day-to-day operating pressures and traditional reporting procedures further discourage reflection and experimentation. In the face of such conditioning, a survey to discover the average user's data preferences would likely prove disappointing. It would, many believe, be influenced and constrained by current reporting practices, since previous stimuli are so crucial to people's attitudes and beliefs.

It is apparent that the problems that confront those who wish to discover users' decision needs are not easy to solve. We cannot attempt to isolate decision models by simply observing "users in action" since their actions are seemingly constrained and directed by the limited financial data at their disposal. Furthermore, we probably cannot discern meaningful data needs by simply asking users to identify the kind of information they would like to have; their response would be conditioned largely by past and present experiences.

Although these are serious impediments to the feasibility of isolating decision models, there is yet another difficulty inherent to the empirical approach. There is reason to believe that even if accounting researchers were magically able to identify useful decision models, the information requirements for the identified models would still be unclear.[45] The reasoning that supports this position proceeds as follows. The kinds of analyses required of external users are often quite complex. So many variables may be involved in one facet of a decision that there may be no *formalized* decision rule or process sufficiently powerful to lead to an acceptable solution. The informal search procedures that are necessary to reach a final decision in such circumstances are called *heuristic decision processes*. As Demski states:

> . . . even when a decision model is employed, many facets of the decision process are heuristic in nature. As a consequence, the accountant can

45 For a detailed development of this position see Demski, "Decision-Performance Control," 669–79.

neither objectively specify the precise information requirements of the system nor objectively evaluate the effectiveness of any specific set of information provided to the system.[46]

If external users' decision models do contain heuristic elements, it may be impossible for the accountant to specify a complete set of relevant variables or their importance in any given application of the model. However, this issue is far from settled; one author suggests that it is possible to isolate some general characteristics common to many heuristic problem-solving processes and to use these characteristics to further refine the data inputs to the model.[47] Irrespective of the final resolution of the issue, at this juncture it seems fair to say that the mere isolation of users' decision models may be insufficient to specify the data needs implied by a model. Furthermore, it may not even be feasible, given the current state of knowledge, to specify what decision models are appropriate.

If empirical analysis is likely to prove fruitless at present, how then might we begin to assess the ability of various reporting proposals to satisfy users' data needs? At the start of this chapter we suggested that one means of working toward a solution would be to select some presumed information needs for various user categories; simultaneously, we would also select a measurement model for testing to determine its ability to provide output that is meaningful and relevant to the selected normative requirements. If the performance of several models was studied under various environmental conditions, the results of such simulations would reflect both general model behavior and the correspondence between the output generated by each model and normative user needs. In this fashion we can eventually develop a "catalogue" of those models that seem best suited to particular information needs.

Chapter 2 advanced this normative needs approach as an interim solution pending discovery of actual needs. In light of our observations in this section, we will argue for the long-term validity of this essentially normative approach to the selection of user decision models. In part this position is a pragmatic one—there is simply no other meaningful method for approaching the user needs (and thus the relevance) question; additionally, however, it is also a conceptually supportable approach.

A recent report of the Committee on External Reporting of the American Accounting Association employed this normative approach. In support of their methodology, they stated:

[46] *Ibid.*, 676.

[47] See Samuel G. Trull, "Some Factors Involved in Determining Total Decision Success," *Management Science*, 12 (February, 1966), B-270–B-280.

By choice and by necessity our general method is based on normative concepts. We start with normative investor's and creditor's valuation models and a normative dividend prediction model. These models are necessarily based upon observations regarding economic and social behavior of investors and creditors in the valuation process and of managers and directors in the dividend process and supported by the writings of researchers in the areas of economics and finance. Our procedure is, therefore, subject (as any normative model) to refutation or change as more is known about the actual goals of the decision makers and how the decisions are actually made. *This is not meant to imply, however, that the models should eventually be descriptively derived.* Decision makers may continue to utilize what appears to be irrelevant or misleading information. Such information should be brought into the models only when and if further research finds it to be, in fact, relevant in the decision process to meet the real or apparent goals of the decision makers. *Note that we are not interested so much in how investors and creditors use accounting information in their decision processes as we are in what information they should be using to meet their goals.*[48] (Emphasis supplied.)

Rationale for a normative approach

In the discipline of operations research, the basic objective is to develop and refine improved methods for making a wide variety of decisions. One text defines the operations research approach as the process of:

1. Formulating the problem
2. Constructing the model
3. Deriving a solution
4. Testing the model and evaluating the solution
5. Implementing and maintaining the solution.[49]

As this formulation of the process indicates, operations researchers adopt an essentially "activist" approach to decision problems. Their continuing objective is the development of new models to supplant or improve existing ones. The fact that a particular decision area may already have a functioning, accepted model does not preclude experimentation intended to broaden its applicability and/or remove certain restrictions. That discipline does not passively interpret the existence of accepted decision procedures or data in any area as an indication that new models are unwarranted, or as an intrusion on the decision prerogatives of the user. Operations researchers view their legitimate function to be the im-

---

[48] Committee on External Reporting, "Evaluation of External Reporting," 79–80.

[49] Russell L. Ackoff and Maurice W. Sasieni, *Fundamentals of Operations Research* (New York: John Wiley & Sons, Inc., 1968), p. 11.

provement of decision tools in whichever areas such progress is possible. Furthermore, publication of newly developed techniques constitutes an effort to "sell" the resultant fruits of their labors to a wide variety of potential users.

Although it would be difficult to cite authoritative, corroborating evidence, one senses that many accountants do not share these "activist" views of operations researchers. Many accountants would contend that accounting's only role is that of a neutral measuring device. That is, given the decision model apparently in use, it is the responsibility of the profession to generate data relevant to that model. This viewpoint would be maintained even in the face of general agreement about the inefficiency of the decision model actually in use. Proponents of the "neutral measuring device" notion would consider attempts to influence users' decision models as exceeding the legitimate purview of the accounting profession.

In our view this position is predicated on a false presumption; furthermore, it is costly for the economy as a whole. The false presumption relates to the supposed neutrality of accounting information. In reality, disseminated information acts as a stimulus to the recipient, and there are few neutral stimuli. As accountants we may be oblivious to the differential impact of one or another report format or terminology set, but there is evidence to suggest that, under certain conditions, the choice of one from among several alternative accounting procedures may have a unique effect on *individual* statement users.[50] We may not know precisely what that effect is, but choices between LIFO versus FIFO, or accelerated versus straight-line depreciation, apparently could affect certain individuals. Whether accounting should strive to eliminate this possible reaction is a controversial issue. But the ability to influence individual decisions through the selection of alternative accounting principles prompts

---

[50] This observation must be interpreted cautiously. Notice that our statement relates only to individual decision makers. To suggest that the market as a whole will be misled by alternative accounting treatments implies market inefficiency. This is not our intention. On the contrary, available evidence suggests that the market as a whole is efficient. Efficiency in this context means that market prices are not influenced irrationally by the mere choice of accounting methods. (For a review of this literature and a description of a related test, see Francis A. Mlynarczyk, Jr., "An Empirical Study of Accounting Methods and Stock Prices," *Empirical Research in Accounting: Selected Studies 1969*, Supplement to Volume 7, *Journal of Accounting Research*, 63–80.)

These issues are still somewhat unsettled. Tentatively, however, known evidence can be summarized as follows. Although the market as a whole generally processes accounting data efficiently, individual investors can be misled. Whether accountants can and/or should somehow attempt to protect individual users from possible error is a controversial issue. Furthermore, it is not yet clear whether insufficient disclosure may hide data from the market and thus hinder efficient processing at the market level.

reasonable speculation regarding the actual "neutrality" of accounting messages.[51]

Another reason for questioning the acceptance of existing, but deficient, decision models involves the cost implicit in this philosophy. Accounting is intended to be utilitarian. Information is collected and reported in order to improve the effectiveness of decision makers. In the case of external users, these decisions largely involve resource allocations. (Should a given fund of dollars be invested in stock A or stock B?) Society as a whole benefits directly from each increase in the effectiveness of capital resource allocation decisions. Improving these decisions assures a steady flow of dollar resources to those firms that tend to contribute most to consumer satisfaction. But better information (more timely reports, and improved organization and presentation) is only one means for increasing decision effectiveness and thereby promoting more efficient resource allocation. Increased effectiveness can also be achieved by directly influencing users' decision models. That is, if and when the accounting community perceives that users are employing an inadequate decision model that generates correct solutions only occasionally, or by chance, or both, then accounting can serve an important educational function. The profession can alert users to the inadequacies of currently employed models and actively promote an improved, alternative model. If a serious attempt is made to educate users to the advantages of the improved model, and if information relevant and necessary to this model is provided to users, then eventual adoption of the model is likely. In this regard, Sterling contends:

> . . . the accounting profession ought to devote some of its effort and resources to the education of the receivers. The profession ought to tell the receivers which decision theories are correct and then supply the data specified by those theories. Other professions have done this, e.g., the medical profession has gone to some lengths to convince the population that the germ theory of medicine is correct and that the demon theory of medicine is incorrect. In one sense this is a normative, as opposed to a positive, position. It results in an ought statement. The medical profession is saying, in effect, that the population ought to apply the germ theory. However, in another sense it is a positive position. The medical profession is not dictating the goal that the population ought to seek; instead it is informing them of the best method of achieving *any* health goal. . . . Accounting can take a similar position. A theory that allows one to maximize profits can also be used to minimize profits, satisfice profits, earn

---

[51] We would hope that freedom from overt bias would exist (i.e., premeditated attempts to systematically prejudice the decision maker in a particular, known direction), but lack of bias is not synonomous with neutrality.

a certain rate or amount, etc. On the other hand, an erroneous theory will not permit the achievement of any of those goals.[52]

This suggests, of course, that accountants adopt a more activist approach. Obviously, this type of change would necessitate a redefinition of the scope of the accounting function in the external reporting area. Since no other professional group has the interest or inclination to explore and effect improvements in external reports,[53] the responsibility for initiating such changes must either rest with accountants or remain undone; since the societal costs of inaction are high (i.e., inefficient allocation of capital resources), we would opt for the first alternative.

Thus, in this Appendix, it has been suggested that the normative approach is perhaps more than a temporary expedient adopted in the absence of knowledge regarding users' decision models. Rather, this methodology offers some clear advantages over the strict empirical approach. Irrespective of these other potential merits, the normative approach has been adopted herein as a practical necessity. Given present knowledge, it appears to provide a ready means for assessing the relevance of replacement cost measures.

[52] Robert R. Sterling, "On Theory Construction and Verification," *The Accounting Review*, 45 (July, 1970), 455n–56n.

[53] Piecemeal changes *within* the confines of the extant reporting model are frequently undertaken either independently or at the behest of external organizations such as the Securities and Exchange Commission.

CHAPTER THREE

The Nature of Replacement Cost Information

This chapter contains an introduction to the measurement of replacement cost income. Included is an illustration of the nature of replacement cost balance sheets and income statements. An example will be used to highlight the characteristics of replacement costing and to contrast these results with historical cost statements.

The feasibility of preparing replacement cost statements on a regular basis will also be examined in this chapter. This discussion will explore the objectivity of replacement costs, as well as the expense and effort required to produce such statements. These feasibility considerations are important; if a measurement method cannot be implemented, there is little need to analyze its theoretical merits.

One vitally important issue should be clarified at the outset. Replacement cost accounting is not a means of adjusting for economy-wide *price level* changes. Instead, it is a method that incorporates only those individual price changes that affect a specific firm. Individual price changes and economy-wide price level movements may be very different. To illustrate this difference, recall that the price level in the United States rose slowly but steadily throughout the 1960's. But despite this overall upward drift, the price of many individual commodities remained constant, or even declined over the same period (e.g., color television receivers). Using the same general price level index to adjust the statements of all firms assumes that the effects of price changes are uniform across firms. But in fact, this uniformity will seldom exist. Some firms may experience more than average price changes, others less than average changes. Indeed, some firms may experience price movements in the opposite direction from the economy as a whole. In order to avoid potentially erroneous adjustments, replacement costing focuses on the specific price changes that have affected a single firm.

REPLACEMENT COST INCOME

Reasons for
developing a replacement cost measure

A replacement cost income concept attempts to isolate two components of earned income that are not separated in the traditional historical cost income measure. Edwards and Bell identify these two components as the results of (1) operating activities, and (2) holding activities.[1] Figure 3–1 affords an easy means of explaining and visualizing the distinction between these two income components. In this highly simplified example of the product transformation process, assume that firms begin each period with an inherited stock of asset inputs. These initial inventories are necessary in order to provide firms with the capability to react to market and production uncertainties. A useful—albeit somewhat unrealistic—means of discussing the transformation process requires a distinction between (1) those periods in which production actually takes place and (2) those periods in which assets are merely held awaiting future transformation.[2] We shall refer to the former as production moments and to the latter as holding intervals. Figure 3–1 illustrates that increases in asset value over time can result from (1) value added by production of goods that are eventually sold (vertical movements), and (2) price changes during non-production intervals (horizontal move-

[1] Edwards and Bell, *Measurement of Business Income*. Although their book presented the most complete analysis of replacement cost income, Edwards and Bell were not the first to recommend separate disclosure of operating and holding activities. For example, this dichotomization of income was specifically suggested much earlier by C. Rufus Rorem, "Replacement Cost in Accounting Valuation," *The Accounting Review*, 4 (September, 1929), 171. (I am indebted to Mr. Jack Truitt of the University of Illinois for bringing this article to my attention.)

[2] Obviously, in many multi-product firms, production of all products is essentially continuous. This does not detract from the usefulness of our illustration, however. Because of the necessity for buffer stocks, invariably, not all assets will be in continuous use in production. Those that are not are thus considered to be "held" assets awaiting future deployment.

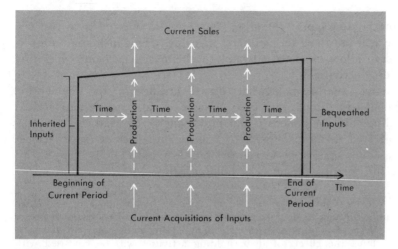

Current Sales

Inherited Inputs

Time — Production — Time — Production — Time — Production — Time

Bequeathed Inputs

Beginning of Current Period

End of Current Period

Time

Current Acquisitions of Inputs

FIGURE 3–1

Source: Edwards and Bell, *Measurement of Business Income,* p. 72. Originally published by the University of California Press; reprinted by permission of the Regents of the University of California.

ments). Edwards and Bell argue, as follows, for the separation of these events in accounting reports:

> The activities of the business firm in a particular time period resemble an escalator which has the ability to move to one side as well as upward. Any gains which accrue to the firm as a result of horizontal movements, or *holding activities,* are *capital gains.* Any gains made by the firm as a result of vertical movements, or *operating activities,* are *operating profits.*
>
> These two kinds of gains are often the result of quite different sets of decisions. The business firm usually has considerable freedom in deciding what quantity of assets to hold over time at any or all stages of the production process and what quantity of assets to commit to the production process itself. The opportunity to make profit through holding activities, that is, by holding assets while their prices rise, is probably not such an important alternative for most business firms as is the opportunity to make profits through operating activities, that is, by using asset services and other inputs in the production and sale of a product or service. The difference between the forces motivating the business firm to make profit by one means rather than by another and the difference between the events on which the two methods of making profit depend require that the two kinds of gain be carefully separated if the two types of decision[s] involved are to be meaningfully evaluated.[3]

Thus, in order to emphasize the different origin of each income segment, replacement cost income is fragmented into two components, operating

[3] Edwards and Bell, *Measurement of Business Income,* p. 73.

profit and holding gains. (Holding gains are also referred to as cost savings. We will use these terms interchangeably.) This dichotomization is intended to allow users to separately evaluate management's operating and holding activities.

There is another, somewhat related, justification for fragmenting replacement cost income into two components. In this alternative view, the holding gain component is not important *per se;* rather, it is separately reflected because we wish to remove the effect of price changes from those of operating performance.[4] Edwards and Bell also suggest this purpose for isolating the effect of holding gains:

> Even if the primary or sole objective of the business firm is to make a profit through its operating activities alone, it is still necessary to isolate the effects of holding activities, incidental though they may be. If this is not done, the effects of these holding activities will be confused with the effects of the firm's operating activities, making any meaningful evaluation of the firm's production decisions difficult if not impossible. Suppose, for example, that a firm expects to make $100 in the absence of price changes by pushing a group of inputs through the production process to final sale. If, during the period necessary for production to take place, the prices of the firm's inputs (already acquired) and outputs rise, the final profit reported according to present accounting procedures will be partly a result of holding activities and only partly a result of operating activity. The apparently favorable result of the production decision may lead the firm to make similar production decisions for the future. In this case, however, price changes may not occur, and gains from holding activities will not inflate reported operating profit.[5]

A brief example of the replacement cost computation will probably be helpful at this point. This example will illustrate the dichotomization of income into holding and operating components. Furthermore, it will also show the difference in the timing of income recognition between replacement costing and historical costing.

Assume that a firm buys an asset for $60 during 19x1. The asset is not sold during 19x1, but its replacement cost rises to $75 by the end of 19x1 and remains at that level throughout 19x2. The asset is then sold in 19x2 for $100. Historical costing recognizes the entire $40 of profit in 19x2, when the asset is actually sold ($100 selling price minus the historical cost of the asset sold, $60). Replacement costing, on the other hand, recognizes the $40 of total profit in two stages. First, 19x1

---

[4] This alternative justification for dichotomizing replacement cost income is introduced for an important reason. In Chapter 6 we will suggest that speculative decisions cannot be evaluated solely by reference to the holding gains component. If this position is correct, then this second justification for fragmenting the income components is the only supportable one.

[5] Edwards and Bell, *Measurement of Business Income*, pp. 73–74.

profit will reflect a portion of this total profit as a $15 holding gain (replacement cost of $75 minus historical cost of $60). Then, when the asset is finally sold in 19x2, additional profit of $25 will be recognized ($100 selling price minus the current replacement cost of the asset sold, $75). The two profit computations can be summarized as follows:

Portion of Total Profit Recognized in Each Year

	19x1	*19x2*	*Total Profit*
Historical cost	—	($100 — 60) $40	$40
Replacement cost	($75 — 60) $15	($100 — 75) $25	$40

Notice that historical costing recognizes the entire profit during 19x2. Replacement cost advocates suggest that this treatment is misleading since $15 of the total eventual profit arose during 19x1 as a consequence of holding activities. Thus, they would suggest that the *timing* of income recognition under replacement costing is more realistic. Furthermore, replacement cost advocates would suggest that the operating profit is only $25, not $40, as historical costing implies. That is, in the absence of future price changes, the firm could expect to realize a profit of just $25 from subsequent sales of similar assets. Therefore, they would also contend that the dichotomization of income facilitates a more realistic assessment of operating performance.

Although this simple example may be a useful means of introducing the issues discussed above, understanding the operation of a replacement cost system requires a more intricate illustration. We now turn to this type of example.

Replacement costing illustrated

In the example that follows, and throughout the remainder of the book, we will assume a stable *general* price level. The price changes that are introduced in this analysis will be limited to changes in the prices of specific assets. These specific price fluctuations are attributable to changes in supply and/or demand conditions for a single commodity rather than to economy-wide changes in the purchasing power of the dollar.[6] Adjustment procedures to reflect general purchasing power

---

[6] For a more detailed development of the difference between general and specific price changes, see Stephen A. Zeff, "Replacement Cost: Member of the Family, Welcome Guest, or Intruder?," *The Accounting Review,* 37 (October, 1962), 612–14.

changes could, if we wished, be coupled with replacement cost systems; however, doing so complicates the analysis without introducing any compensating substantive issues. Accordingly, we assume a stable general price level in order to simplify the analysis.[7]

To begin the example, consider the case of the *XYZ* Company, a retailer whose financial position appeared as follows on December 31, 19x0:

XYZ Company
Statement of Financial Position
December 31, 19x0

Assets		Equities	
Inventory (at historical cost, which equals market value)	$200	Owners' Equity	$700
Fixed Asset (purchased new on 12/31/x0, 5-year life, no salvage value)	500		
Total Assets	$700	Total Equities	$700

Operating events experienced by this firm during the year 19x1 were:

Sales	$1,100
Inventory purchases at historical cost	500
December 31, 19x1 ending inventory at historical cost	100
December 31, 19x1 ending inventory at market value	130
Cost of goods sold at replacement cost at the date of sale	675

Assume that the market price of the firm's fixed asset rose to $600 at the start of the 19x1 operating period. Given these events, the *XYZ* Company's traditional historical cost income for 19x1 would be $400, as shown in Table 3–1.

Observe carefully that the historical cost measurement process incorporates only those prices that were actually paid for the assets utilized in production. Operating profit is then simply the difference between the historical cost of the goods that were sold and the revenue received from such sales. No account recognition is given to any external changes in the price of the firm's assets that were not effected through actual transactions with outside entities.

In contrast, the *XYZ* Company's replacement cost income for 19x1 is shown in Table 3–2.

---

[7] Edwards and Bell present an illustration of how general price level changes can be incorporated into a more realistic replacement cost illustration (see pp. 233–69). Readers interested in a discussion of general price level adjustment procedures applied to a historical cost system should examine "Reporting the Financial Effects of Price-Level Changes," *Accounting Research Study No. 6*, (American Institute of Certified Public Accountants, 1963).

TABLE 3-1

XYZ Company
Income Statement (Historical Cost Basis)
For the Year Ended December 31, 19x1

Sales		$1,100
Cost of Goods Sold:		
Beginning inventory	$200	
Purchases	500	
Goods available for sale	$700	
Ending inventory (at historical cost)	100	
		600
Contribution Margin		500
Depreciation ($500 ÷ 5)		100
Operating Profit		$ 400

TABLE 3-2

XYZ Company
Income Statement (Replacement Cost Basis)
For the Year Ended December 31, 19x1

Sales			$1,100
Cost of Goods Sold (at replacement cost at the date of sale)			675
Contribution Margin			425
Depreciation (based on current market value, $600 ÷ 5)			120
Current Operating Profit			305
Realizable Cost Savings:			
Unrealized at the end of the year:			
On ending inventory	$30		
On fixed assets	80		
Unrealized Cost Savings		110	
Realized through use during the year:			
Inventory (as part of Cost of Goods Sold)	75		
Fixed Asset (through depreciation)	20		
Realized Cost Savings		95	
Total Realizable Cost Savings			205
Replacement Cost Income			$ 510

The cost savings (or holding gains) components in Table 3–2 can be explained as follows. Whenever the replacement cost of an asset rises after it has been purchased, a cost saving has occurred. This item represents the equity effect of the price change that occurred during the year.

For example, to reflect a price increase for some asset on the balance sheet, the following type of entry is necessary:

DR Asset account (dollar amount of debit equals
  price increase)   xxx
  CR Owners' equity or cost savings account   xxx

The theoretical justification for this treatment is that a firm has bene-fited from buying an asset *before* its price rises. The firm has "saved" to the extent that it bought the asset at a lower price than currently pre-vails. All savings of this nature that arise during the year are termed *realizable cost savings.* In Table 3–2, such savings for 19x1 totalled $205. Of this total, $95 relates to assets that were sold or used during the pe-riod; these are termed *realized cost savings.* The remainder, $110, relates to assets still on hand at the end of the period. This portion is called *unrealized cost savings.*

REALIZED COST SAVINGS

  Table 3–2 shows that realized cost savings for the *XYZ* Company during 19x1 were $95. That is, the product sold during the period phys-ically incorporated certain assets whose price had risen (i.e., inventory) and required the use of another asset whose price also rose (i.e., fixed assets). Of the total realized cost savings, $75 relates to the inventory that was sold during the year. That is, the replacement cost of the in-ventory actually sold during the year rose from its original cost of $600 to $675. (Notice that the replacement cost of goods sold reflects this in-crease. Current rather than historical costs are matched against revenue.)

  We will use accounting entries to illustrate some characteristics of cost savings. These entries would also be necessary in order to implement a replacement cost accounting system.

  For simplicity, assume that the entire $75 price rise in the inven-tory that was eventually sold took place instantaneously and before any sales were made. When the price of the inventory rose by $75, the firm would have made the following entry:

DR Inventory $75
  CR Realizable Cost Savings $75   (1)
  (To reflect a price rise in inventory on hand.)

Notice that the credit is initially made to realizable cost savings. After this entry is made, the inventory is carried on the books at its current market value. (If the firm wanted to keep track of the historical cost of its inventory, the debit would be made to a separate "Inventory-Price Change" account. Following this approach, the inventory account would contain only original cost and all price increases would be segregated in a separately designated asset account. For ease of exposition, we make no such distinction here.)

When the inventory on hand is finally sold, the asset account would be credited for the current market value of the goods sold:

DR Cost of Goods Sold	$675		
CR Inventory		$675	(2)

(To reflect the current cost of goods sold.)

Since the inventory has been sold, the cost saving of $75 has been realized. To reflect this, the following entry would also be made:

DR Realizable Cost Savings	$75		
CR Realized Cost Savings		$75	(3)

(To transfer the $75 cost saving to a realized savings account. Realized cost savings would then be transferred to retained earnings.)

Similar reasoning applies to the $20 of realized cost saving that relates to the fixed asset. The price of this asset rose by $100 at the start of 19x1. The following entry would be made to reflect this replacement cost increase:

DR Fixed Asset	$100		
CR Realizable Cost Savings		$100	(4)

(To reflect a price rise in the fixed asset.)

After making this entry, the carrying value of the fixed asset on the books of the company is $600, which is equal to its current replacement cost. Depreciation for the year is then based on this replacement cost. The entry would be:

DR Depreciation Expense	$120		
CR Accumulated Depreciation		$120	(5)

(To reflect one year's depreciation on a replacement cost basis. The asset has a 5-year life, no salvage value, a replacement cost of $600, and is depreciated on a straight-line basis.)

Notice that depreciation expense on a replacement cost basis is $20 higher than it would be on a historical cost basis. This difference represents one-fifth of the $100 price increase. That is, since one-fifth of the service potential of the asset has expired, one-fifth of the price increase has been realized through use. To reflect this, the following entry would also be made:

DR Realizable Cost Savings	$20		
CR Realized Cost Savings		$20	(6)

(To transfer $20 of cost saving to a realized savings account.)

UNREALIZED COST SAVINGS

Unrealized cost savings relate to assets still on hand at the end of the year. Such savings have yet to be realized through sale or use. Table 3–2 indicates that unrealized cost savings for 19x1 were $110. Of this amount, $30 pertains to the ending inventory. (That is, the historical cost of goods still on hand is $100; their replacement cost is $130.) The entry needed to reflect this cost increase is:

DR Inventory $30
   CR Realizable Cost Savings $30   (7)
    (To increase inventory on hand to its market value
    and to reflect the associated cost saving.)

The remaining $80 of unrealized cost savings relate to the unexpired portion of the fixed asset cost increase. Remember that the cost of the fixed asset rose by $100 during 19x1. One-fifth of this increase has already been realized through operations. That portion is a realized cost saving (see entry 6, above). The remainder, $80, will be realized in future periods and represents an unrealized cost saving.

In order to segregate unrealized cost savings in the accounts, the following entry would be made:

DR Realizable Cost Savings $110
   CR Unrealized Cost Savings $110   (8)
    (To transfer the unrealized cost savings on inven-
    tory, $30, and fixed assets, $80, to an unrealized
    cost savings account.)

After entries 1 through 8 are posted, the ledger accounts are no longer on a historical cost basis. Let us segregate the net effect of these replacement cost adjustments in the following five accounts:

Increases in Asset Carrying Value				*Increases in Replacement Cost Expenses Over Historical Cost Expenses*			
(1)	$ 75	(2)	$ 75	(2)	$75	To balance	$95
(4)	100	(5)	20	(5)	20		
(7)	30	To balance	110		95		95
	205		205				
Balance	$110			Balance	$95		

Unrealized Cost Savings				*Realized Cost Savings*			
To balance	$110	(8)	$110	To balance	$95	(3)	$75
	110		110			(6)	20
		Balance	$110		95		95
						Balance	$95

Realizable Cost Savings

(3)	$ 75	(1)	$ 75
(6)	20	(4)	100
(8)	110	(7)	30
	205		205

Notice carefully that unrealized and realized cost savings are each "associated" with a different type of financial statement change. Specifically, the total realized cost savings for the period ($95) exactly offset the increases in replacement cost expenses over historical cost expenses. (Historical cost expenses are $700; these same expenses on a replacement cost basis are $795.) Thus, one can view the recognition of realized cost savings as a reclassification within the profit account. Operating profits are reduced by $95 (the difference between historical and replacement cost expenses) and realized cost savings—another profit component—are increased by $95. Recognizing these cost savings leaves *total* profit unchanged. The only effect is to shift $95 from operating profit to cost savings.

Observe also that unrealized cost savings ($110) exactly equal the increase in asset carrying value on a replacement cost balance sheet. If these unrealized cost savings are also shown on the income statement (as many contend they should be), then total profit is increased. Notice that the amount of unrealized cost savings recognized during 19x1 is exactly equal to the difference between historical cost income ($400) and replacement cost income ($510). Thus, the recognition of unrealized cost savings is *not* equivalent to a reclassification between profit components. Instead, this cost saving does serve to change total profit. In this case, replacement cost income exceeds historical cost income by $110.

(One might ask whether it is essential to show unrealized cost savings on the income statement. The answer, of course, depends on whether these "savings" are viewed as income or as a capital adjustment. Both views are supportable. In this chapter we will include these items in the income statement. In Chapter 6, however, we will return to this issue and discuss the capital adjustment approach to unrealized cost savings. In that approach, unrealized cost savings are not shown on the income statement, but rather are carried directly to the balance sheet as an adjustment to owners' equity.)

BALANCE SHEETS

Comparative balance sheets prepared under both measurement bases as of the end of 19x1 appear in Table 3–3. These statements assume that all sales and purchases were made for cash.

TABLE 3–3

XYZ Company
Statement of Financial Position
(Historical Cost and Replacement Cost Basis)
December 31, 19x1

Assets	Historical Cost	Replacement Cost	Equities	Historical Cost	Replacement Cost
Cash	$ 600	$ 600	Beginning Own-		
Inventory	100	130	ers' Equity	$ 700	$ 700
Fixed Asset	$500	$600	Historical Cost		
Less: Accumu-			Income	400	
lated Depre-					
ciation	100	120	Replacement		
	400	480	Cost Income		510
Total Assets	$1,100	$1,210	Total Equities	$1,100	$1,210

Analysis of replacement costing

BALANCE SHEET CHARACTERISTICS

To some people, one of the more important characteristics of replacement costing is that it reestablishes the balance sheet as a major repository for useful financial information. After periods of pronounced price adjustments, the traditional balance sheet loses much of its economic significance. In such circumstances balance sheet carrying values bear little relationship to market values. Instead, historical cost balance sheet amounts represent past expenditures that are significant only because they await eventual write-off to the income statement.

In contrast, balance sheet carrying values in a replacement cost system are quite different. Replacement cost balance sheet values represent the amount that a firm would have to pay, as of the balance sheet date, in order to replace the assets shown in the statement or to satisfy reported liabilities. (Notice, however, that replacement costs will not necessarily reflect what those assets might bring if sold. Only a balance sheet prepared using net realizable values for all assets would reflect sales, or "exit," values. Under certain circumstances, however, replacement costs and "exit" values may tend to converge.[8])

---

[8] There are at least two different types of exit value. First, exit value can be defined as the proceeds that can be realized from selling assets in the ordinary course of operations. Second, exit value might also represent the proceeds that could be realized from an immediate liquidation at the best available price. Conceivably, these two exit values could differ. In Chapter 7 we will briefly explore the relationship between the exit value of current assets (on both bases) and the replacement cost of current assets.

Replacement costs have another balance sheet characteristic in addition to representing the current cost of duplicating assets (and perhaps occasionally approximating current liquidation prices). Specifically, if replacement of an asset is economically justified,[9] then the discounted present value of the asset's expected net inflows must equal or exceed its replacement cost. In other words, long-run enterprise viability requires replacement cost to at least represent the *minimum* value of an asset to a firm. Thus, the use of replacement costing results in balance sheet carrying values equal to the current minimum value *of those assets for which replacement is justified.*

It is conceivable, however, that firms will occasionally own assets that do not warrant replacement. That is, the cost of replacing some assets may exceed the expected discounted net inflows from using these assets. In these circumstances replacement cost will overstate the value of the asset to the firm. From a managerial perspective, the fact that eventual replacement is unwarranted does not necessarily mean that continued operation of an asset already owned is also unwarranted. On the contrary, as long as the asset's net present value exceeds its disposition price (or exit value), continued operation is justifiable. What, then, can be said about the utility of replacement cost measures when continued operation is warranted but eventual replacement is not?

In those instances where eventual replacement is not economically justified, there is still a reason for showing assets at their replacement costs for balance sheet purposes. Replacement usually becomes unjustified because the prices of assets used in operations have risen without any compensating adjustments in revenues. This makes it impossible to earn a normal profit at prevailing prices. Recording the replacement costs of assets in the balance sheet will, in the long run, tend to reflect this unprofitability. That is, current replacement costs will usually be higher than historical costs in such situations. When these higher replacement costs are matched against realized revenues, the resultant losses will tend to alert the statement reader that, in the long-run, it is uneconomical to replace these assets. (However, this situation may not be apparent to the reader unless external reports disclose performance on a process-by-process basis.)

This discussion naturally leads to an analysis of the income statement characteristics of replacement costing. Before concluding this

---

In general, the more perfect the market, the closer will be the correspondence between replacement costs and exit values. However, if the market for a given asset is highly fragmented or if costs of disposition, handling, etc., are quite high, replacement costs may greatly diverge from exit values.

[9] This would mean that the firm is recovering all costs of operation, in the long run, in addition to a normal profit.

analysis, we should indicate that a more exhaustive treatment of these balance sheet issues is contained in Chapter 6.

INCOME STATEMENT CHARACTERISTICS

In turning to an examination of the income statement characteristics of replacement cost accounting, it must be reiterated that one of the primary elements of this system is its separation of income into two components, current operating profit and cost savings. The former component is intended to be a measure of the efficiency of production and operations whereas the latter represents the gain or loss that arises as a consequence of holding activities.

Tables 3–1 and 3–2 indicate some advantages of isolating the current operating profit component of replacement cost income. In our earlier example, the replacement cost of the inventory used in generating sales rose during the period. Although the historical cost of the inventory sold was only $600, its cost in terms of current replacement prices increased to $675.[10] The historical cost contribution margin of $500 ignores this price increase. Strict reliance on this $500 figure suggests to owner-managers that operations have generated an increase in net assets (before depreciation considerations) equal to the contribution margin. However (depreciation considerations aside), were the firm to declare and pay a dividend of $500 in order to distribute the "profits" from operations, it would find that this dividend would contract the magnitude of its later operations. The reason, of course, is that $75 of the supposed $500 profit is not profit at all in a "real" sense.[11] If the

[10] For ease of exposition, we assume that all purchases were made at the beginning of 19x1, before prices rose. Furthermore, all sales were clustered toward the end of 19x1 after the new inventory price levels were reached.

[11] Notice carefully that the term "real" as employed herein differs from its traditional usage. Usually the terms "real profits" or "real costs" refer to the profit or cost after adjustment for general price level changes. Since we have assumed away such fluctuations in general purchasing power, our use of the term "real" is intended to reflect profits or costs after taking cognizance of specific price changes for individual assets.

To illustrate our use of the term "real," take the case of a retailer who buys refrigerators for $150 and sells them to customers for $200. (For simplicity we ignore direct costs of selling and overhead.) The retailer's profit on each refrigerator sold is obviously $50. This means that of the $200 proceeds from a single sale, the retailer will, after replenishing his stock, have $50 that can be withdrawn from the business without contracting his future level of operations. (That is, if he typically carries an inventory of one refrigerator, he can withdraw his $50 profit from the preceding sale, use the remaining $150 of sale proceeds to reestablish his inventory of one unit, and thus maintain his ability to generate future operating profits.)

Assume, however, that the wholesale price of the refrigerator suddenly increases to $175 between the time it is originally purchased and the time it is sold. Further

entire $500 were to be distributed to owners as a dividend, the firm would find itself unable to reestablish its previous physical inventory level at prevailing replacement prices.[12] The replacement cost statement clearly reflects this situation by denoting the contribution margin as $425 (Table 3–2). The replacement cost contribution margin of $425 also represents the amount that the firm may reasonably expect to generate from operations in the future, *barring subsequent changes in the level of operations and prices*.[13]

This point is further strengthened when one examines the margin that remains after deducting depreciation charges. If the process employed is a profitable one, it is likely to be continued in the future. Continuing a process necessitates eventual replacement of long-lived assets at the expiration of their useful economic lives. One means for assessing the current profitability of a process, and thus determining the desirability of its continuation in the future, is to charge all cost expirations to the income statement in terms of the current costs of the expired factors. Accordingly, the current operating profit of $305 on the replacement cost income statement indicates the contribution of the process after deducting *all* costs at prices that prevailed at the time of severance. This would appear to be a useful figure for determining the long-run profitability of the entity as a whole. (The impact of techno-

---

assume that the unit on hand is then sold for $200. Under these circumstances, the "real" operating profit on the unit just sold is not $50 (the difference between its historical cost and its actual selling price). To replace the unit sold, the retailer must now pay $175, not the $150 that the refrigerator just sold originally cost. Under this circumstance, if the retailer were to withdraw the $50 of historical cost "profit" from the enterprise, the remaining $150 of sales proceeds would buy only 86 percent of a new refrigerator. In effect, his distribution of "profit" has resulted in a 14 percent inventory contraction and a consequent reduction in potential operating activity. In real terms, the profit on the sale was only $25, since, in order to maintain inventory at a one-unit level, only $25 of the sale proceeds can be withdrawn from the business. Thus, for purposes of dividend determination, the reported current operating profit shows the maximum amount that can be distributed as a dividend in order to maintain future operating levels at their current level.

12 The importance of this decline in asset levels is that it may affect the ability of the firm to generate future operating inflows. Notice, however, that by maintaining physical asset levels, the firm does not necessarily maintain total operating flows at their previous level. Total operating flows will remain constant only if (1) operating levels are unchanged, and (2) input costs and output prices move in parallel fashion. Thus, by maintaining physical asset levels intact, the firm satisfies one condition necessary to maintain total operating flows. Whether total flows remain at the previous level is a function of the second condition as well.

13 If this assumption regarding stability of future costs and prices does not hold, the predictive ability of current operating profit could be diminished. In Chapter 6 we will see that under certain conditions current operating profit may be a reasonable predictor even if future costs and prices do change.

logical change on the assessment of current performance will be explored in Chapter 6.[14]) In this regard, Edwards and Bell state:

> Current operating profit . . . indicates whether or not the current proceeds from the sale of product are sufficient to cover the current cost of the factors of production used in producing that product. The factors of production are valued in this case not at prices which could be obtained by selling them outside the firm but at the prices which would currently have to be paid in order to bring the factors of production into the firm. The existence of a profit for a particular period indicates that the firm is making a positive long-run contribution to the economy; the production process in use by the firm is an effective means for converting resources having one value into an output having a larger value. If this profit exceeds interest on the current cost of the firm's assets at the beginning of the period, the production process of the firm is worth continuing. Current operating profit, therefore, is essentially the long-run profit associated with the existing process of production carried on under existing conditions. . . . Current operating profit is a measure of the amount of current output, in the sense of value added, which is profit.[15]

In addition to the current operating profit of $305, which indicates the profitability of the firm's *operations* in terms of prices prevailing at the time of sale, the firm was additionally able to increase the dollar value of its assets by virtue of its success in a somewhat unrelated sphere—its holding activities. Table 3–2 indicates that during the year the replacement cost of the firm's assets increased by $205. Gains of this type are denoted as realizable cost savings. They represent an increase that accrues to the firm by virtue of its good fortune in having purchased its assets when it did, at lower than current prices. Recording these increases in the cost savings account removes these price-induced gains from operating profit and allows the success of management's holding activities to be recognized. Simultaneously, the other portion of the entry either increases asset book values [16] or increases expense accounts to reflect current market prices.

---

[14] When technological change occurs, firms will not replace assets with identical assets at the end of their useful lives. Edwards and Bell suggest that replacement cost be defined by reference to the actual assets used in production rather than by reference to the current cost of obtaining the equivalent services from the technologically improved asset. In Chapter 6 we will see that when replacement cost is defined in this manner, a technological change does not necessarily diminish the usefulness of the resultant replacement cost financial statements.

[15] Edwards and Bell, *Measurement of Business Income*, pp. 98–99.

[16] In order to trace the functioning of the system through its complete cycle, consider the next period when the now higher priced asset is used in operations. At the time of expiration—if no further price changes take place—the book value of the asset will equal its then current market value. As the cost expiration is recognized, the resulting gross margin figure will represent the difference between the sales price and the current replacement cost of the expired factors of production. This replacement cost margin—or current operating profit—will differ from the profit that would

It will probably be helpful to illustrate the relationship between historical cost income and replacement cost income. This can be accomplished by preparing a reconciliation of the two profit figures, as in Table 3–4.

TABLE 3–4

XYZ Company
Reconciliation between Historical Cost and Replacement Cost Income
19x1

Replacement cost current operating profit	$305
Plus: Cost savings that were realized through sale or use during the year (realized cost savings)	95
Historical cost operating profit	400
Plus: Cost savings that were not realized through sale or use during the year (unrealized cost savings)	110
Total replacement cost income	$510

This reconciliation indicates that traditional historical cost operating profit ($400 in this example) is actually composed of two components:

1. the current operating profit segment of replacement cost income ($305), and
2. that portion of cost savings that relates to assets that have been consumed in whole or in part or sold during the current period ($95).

This second component of historical cost income is not really operating income. Instead, it is that portion of the spread between the historical cost of sales and sales revenues that must be retained within the enterprise so that operations may be continued at their pre-existing level. These realized savings arise because asset prices have changed between the time at which they were purchased and the time at which they were consumed in generating revenues. Because realized savings are not separately disclosed in the historical cost statement, these items are treated as if they were a component of operating profit. In fact, however, they are attributable to external price changes.

In addition to commingling a portion of holding gains with oper-

---

be recognized on a historical cost basis. In the situation just described, replacement cost income would be lower than accounting income since the expired cost has a higher carrying value in a replacement system.

ating profits (and thus making the separate assessment of operating activities difficult if not impossible), historical cost statements also do not necessarily recognize such gains in the periods in which they arise. In the example above, the $95 of realized gains during the operating period also happen to have arisen during the period. But this need not be the case in other situations, of course. When a holding gain occurs in one period but is recognized on a historical cost basis when it is realized in some other period, we not only obscure operating performance, but also make it difficult to determine the separate results of the current period's holding activities.

As Table 3–4 illustrates, the total profit obtained using replacement cost measurements will usually not equal the profit that is reflected using historical cost procedures. The amount of the divergence between the two income concepts equals $110 in the XYZ Company example. This difference is attributable to the unrealized cost savings on assets still held by the firm at the end of the period. Such market price changes are, of course, ignored in a historical cost system until they are validated by the firm's own external transactions. Replacement cost income, on the other hand, recognizes such changes as income in the period in which the gains arise, rather than waiting until the period in which they are realized through sale. This additional income component would appear to be an important and timely bit of information for use in evaluating the net impact of external price changes. When this $110 of unrealized cost savings is added to the $95 of cost savings that were realized during the period, the resultant $205 total cost savings figure reflects the total annual effect of price changes on assets held by the firm (see Table 3–2). Thus, a final characteristic of replacement cost income is that all holding gains—whether realized or unrealized—are included as a separately identifiable replacement cost profit component in the period in which they arise.

In summary, the replacement cost measurement framework incorporates three distinct characteristics of some special importance. First, assets are shown on the balance sheet at their current cost; thus, these valuations reflect the present outlay that would be required to replace owned assets. Second, the current operating profit component of total replacement cost income matches revenues with the current cost of generating those revenues. This procedure excludes from operating profit that portion that is eroded by price increases between the time of asset purchase and final sale. The resultant figure is a measure of the *current* profitability of operations.[17] Finally, the cost savings figure is a measure of the price changes that have affected the firm's assets during the current

---

[17] In Chapter 6 we will see that interdependencies between operating profit and cost savings will cause us to temper this statement under certain circumstances.

period. As such, this figure is an indicator of the net effect of a firm's holding activities.

FEASIBILITY OF REPLACEMENT COST MEASURES

To be useful, a theory must be capable of improving the practice of the discipline in which it originates. This criterion certainly applies to accounting theories. As one author suggests:

> But, if theorists . . . are unconcerned with immediate problems or practical problems, they forfeit the right to be considered as theorists—dreamers perhaps, but not theorists. The challenges lie out there in the real world in the first place, not in our heads.[18]

Replacement cost income, or any other proposed measurement method, must not only generate data that are theoretically more relevant to the user, but also the system must be capable of practical implementation. It therefore seems appropriate to consider the feasibility of the system just outlined. This brief examination should logically precede an analysis of the potential relevance of the output of a system. If a system cannot be implemented in practice, its utility is minimal despite other advantages it may possess.

Several researchers have examined the feasibility of actually implementing proposed alternative measurement systems. One of the earliest of these studies, by McDonald, suggests that accountants must establish some criteria by which feasibility can be evaluated.

> Feasibility criteria for accounting measures are standards by which we judge whether a particular method of measurement is practicable, given the goals for the accounting process.[19]

McDonald proposes several criteria such as dispersion, displacement, costliness, and timeliness. We will use these criteria here to evaluate the feasibility of implementing replacement cost measures.

The criterion of dispersion (objectivity)

Of the frequently cited criteria for evaluating the acceptability of a particular accounting measurement, perhaps the most popular is

---

18 R. J. Chambers, "Prospective Adventures in Accounting Ideas," *The Accounting Review*, 42 (April, 1967), 246.

19 Daniel L. McDonald, "Feasibility Criteria for Accounting Measures," *The Accounting Review*, 42 (October, 1967), 662.

objectivity. Increasingly, accountants have begun to reject the notion that objectivity resides exclusively in the object that is being measured. Instead, they suggest that objectivity is a function not only of the attribute of the object being measured, but also of the measurer, and the measurement system used. "Therefore, rather than basing the definition of objectivity on the existence of objective factors that are independent of persons who perceive them, it is far more realistic to define objectivity to mean simply the *consensus* among a given group of observers or measurers." [20] Since objectivity is considered to vary with the measurer, the measurement system employed, and the object being measured, it is important to realize that objectivity exists only as a matter of degree.

We will adopt this view and consider objectivity to be simply the degree of consensus among measurers. Thus, to measure, say, the objectivity of inventory valuation using replacement costing procedures, one would compute the dispersion among different measurers' inventory values. Using the variance as a measure of dispersion, one would define objectivity in the following manner:

$$V = \frac{1}{n} \sum_{i=1}^{n} (x_i - \overline{x})^2$$

where V is the degree of objectivity, n is the number of measurers, x_i, is the quantitative measure of an attribute developed by the ith measurer, and $\overline{x}$ is the mean value of all $x_i s$.[21] The measurement system used (e.g., replacement costing) and the object being measured (e.g., inventory) are constant for each calculation. Using this definition, the degree of objectivity will vary within a given measurement system depending on the object being measured; furthermore, for a given object (say inventory value), the degree of objectivity attaching to a measure of that object will vary from one measurement system to another.

EVALUATING THE OBJECTIVITY OF REPLACEMENT COSTING

One advantage in selecting a quantifiable definition of objectivity is that empirical testing is facilitated. Unfortunately, no tests of the relative objectivity of replacement costing have yet appeared in the accounting literature. Therefore, in order to evaluate the objectivity of replacement costing, we are currently forced to rely on logic and intuition rather than on empirical evidence. This means, of course, that

[20] Yuji Ijiri and Robert K. Jaedicke, "Reliability and Objectivity of Accounting Measurements," *The Accounting Review*, 41 (July, 1966), 476.
[21] *Ibid.*, 477.

the brief analysis that follows is tentative and must be tested at some later date.

This analysis of the relative objectivity of replacement costing versus historical costing will be limited to inventories and fixed assets. The reason for limiting the examination to these two categories is that financial assets (cash, receivables, payables) present few measurement problems and are not likely to diverge under the two measurement systems. Furthermore, inventory and fixed assets generally constitute the two most important nonfinancial asset categories.

Fixed asset accounting using replacement cost techniques (as defined by Edwards and Bell) [22] is quite similar to historical cost fixed asset accounting. The only difference between the two systems involves the carrying value on which depreciation charges are based. In a replacement cost system, depreciation charges are based on an allocation of current market price whereas a historical cost system uses actual past cost as the allocation base. However, the number of alternative depreciation patterns that can be used to make the allocation is the same for both systems. Since the procedures are alike in all respects except one, if a differential dispersion of measures exists, it must be attributable to the value used as a depreciation basis. Thus, to determine which of the two systems gives rise to more objective fixed asset measures, one need only determine which set of balance sheet carrying values is less dispersed. Although this is obviously an empirical issue, some very tentative *a priori* observations might be made.

One could contend that for fixed asset accounting, replacement cost results will usually be more diverse than historical cost measures. The reason why historical costing is likely to be relatively more objective is a function of the generally determinate initial asset carrying value employed in historical costing. All measurers using a historical cost system would arrive at a *basically* similar depreciation base for a given asset through reference to its original invoice cost. Close agreement on a depreciation base is not so likely among measurers using replacement costing. There are two reasons for this contention. First, reference to a *single* determinable invoice price to reflect current replacement cost is not feasible in many cases because there may be no active market for the asset. (If no market price exists for an asset, replacement cost must be estimated by indirect means such as specific price index adjustments, or appraisals. These estimation techniques necessarily require subjective judgment. That is, one must choose a price index or rely on an appraiser's expert opinion, and this would lead to a number of possible valuation bases. In such situations, replacement cost measures would

[22] Edwards and Bell, *Measurement of Business Income*, pp. 161–98.

be more diverse than those arrived at by historical cost procedures.) Second, even if an external market price exists for an asset at the close of the period, this price may vary slightly from one locale to another or from one supplier to another. Such differences, although likely to be small, will nevertheless precipitate different depreciation bases for different measurers. (In the ideal circumstance—that is, where no market price divergence exists—all measurers would agree on a market price. This would correspond to the historical cost case in which all measurers essentially agree on the amount of depreciable cost. Under these conditions, there would be little difference between the dispersion of historical cost and replacement cost fixed asset accounting. Realistically, however, a single market price would probably exist infrequently.)

Turning to inventory, the large number of inventory items and the divergent flow possibilities make it difficult, if not impossible in most situations, to determine the actual historical cost of goods on hand at the end of a period. That is, an arbitrary cost-flow assumption must be adopted in order to generate traditional financial reports. Furthermore, generally accepted accounting principles do not require correspondence between the cost-flow assumption used and the actual physical flow. As a consequence, the inventory valuation and cost of goods sold calculations under historical costing may vary widely. (The situation is aggravated by the fact that the financial statement impact of inventory costing is cumulative. That is, reported cost of goods sold for 19x1 could diverge not only because LIFO was chosen by one measurer and FIFO by another in 19x1 but also because LIFO or FIFO was also used in each of the preceding years, thus causing differences in the beginning inventory figures for 19x1 under each basis.)

In contrast, replacement cost inventory procedures are much less diverse. Latitude in the selection of a cost-flow assumption does not exist. Inventories are valued using their current market price as of the balance sheet date, and cost expirations are recorded at the price that prevailed at the time of severance.[23] Although the market price may vary between suppliers and thus increase the valuation possibilities, competitive circumstances should tend to minimize such differences. In summary, it appears defensible to suggest that inventory measures using replacement costs would tend to be less dispersed than their counterpart measures utilizing historical costs. We base this statement on the belief that differences in ending replacement market values would, on the average, tend to be smaller than corresponding differences between ending historical cost inventory values computed using, say, LIFO

---

[23] Certain approximations are usually made in order to avoid overly burdensome clerical costs, but the differential effects of these alternative assumptions are probably small.

versus FIFO. Obviously, this is an empirically testable proposition that must be subjected to closer scrutiny before a final assessment is possible.

In summary, although historical costing might tend to generate more objective (i.e., less divergent) measures in the area of fixed asset accounting, replacement costing appears to be more objective for inventory accounting. If empirical evidence confirms these expectations, it would follow that in capital intensive firms, historical cost measurements would tend to be more objective overall. Similarly, for those firms in which inventories assume greater importance vis-à-vis fixed assets, replacement costing would tend to be more objective, on balance. Of course, each of these statements must be tempered by the realization that individual price structures, the rapidity of price changes, and the availability of current market data in each situation could invalidate these expectations.

No empirical studies have been performed to compare the dispersion of replacement cost versus historical cost measures. However, such studies do exist in the area of net realizable value (or current cash equivalent) fixed asset accounting. McDonald found that net realizable value depreciation charges were less dispersed than those computed using historical cost depreciation methods.[24] McKeown reported similar results.[25] In his sample firm McKeown found that approximately 75 percent of the fixed asset items had a lower depreciation dispersion using the net realizable value method than they had using generally accepted accounting principles.[26] Although neither of these dispersion studies is directly relevant to our particular problem, they are cited as evidence of the fact that the mere abandonment of generally accepted accounting principles need not necessarily lead to a reduction in the objectivity of the resultant measures.[27] (In another sense, these findings are consistent

[24] Daniel L. McDonald, "A Test Application of the Feasibility of Market Based Measures in Accounting," *Journal of Accounting Research,* 6 (Spring, 1968) 38–49. In this study, McDonald used a questionnaire approach and asked respondents to select a depreciation pattern for an automobile fleet. One must be cautious in generalizing the results of this study to other types of fixed assets since exit values are perhaps more readily available in the automotive market.

[25] James C. McKeown, "An Empirical Test of a Model Proposed by Chambers," *The Accounting Review,* 46 (January, 1971), 12–29.

[26] *Ibid.,* 20–21.

[27] Another study in this same area came to different conclusions. (See Robert R. Sterling and Raymond Radosevich, "A Valuation Experiment," *Journal of Accounting Research,* 7 (Spring, 1969), 90–95.) These authors found the variance of market based values to exceed that of cost based measures. Perhaps this finding is attributable to the instructions given to the respondents. They were invited to "take a guess at the fair market value as of today" (91). It is questionable whether the respondents would use this valuation procedure in preparing *actual* financial statements. On the other hand, the studies cited above may be biased in the other direction because they were undertaken in markets for which current prices are available. Sterling and Radosevich con-

with our hypothesis regarding the relative objectivity advantage of replacement cost inventory measures. The logic is as follows: The computation of net realizable value depreciation corresponds closely to the determination of cost of goods sold and cost savings on a replacement cost basis. That is, end of period market values are subtracted from the total of beginning market value plus asset additions to determine the periodic depreciation charge. Since this process generates relatively less dispersion among financial statement figures, and since this process roughly corresponds to replacement cost inventory accounting, these findings suggest that replacement cost inventory measures might similarly tend to be less dispersed.)

AVAILABILITY OF MARKET PRICE DATA

Before concluding this examination of the dispersion criterion, we should return for a moment to the question of the availability of current market price data. As already pointed out, this issue has important implications for the dispersion of replacement cost measures. *Ceteris paribus,* the greater is the availability of actual market price data, the less need there is for subjective, alternative valuation procedures, and thus the less would be the dispersion of the resultant measure.

The limited empirical evidence that relates to the availability of market price data is inconclusive. For example, Dickerson, in a case study of the feasibility of implementing Edwards and Bell's income framework, found that fixed asset market prices for his sample firm were generally unavailable. He was therefore forced to rely heavily on index-based valuations. However, Dickerson suggests that there would be little difficulty in obtaining market prices for the various inventory components.[28] Dockweiler, in a similar feasibility study, was able to determine market prices for only 3 percent of fixed assets and for only 50 percent of in-process and finished goods inventories.[29] Dockweiler's results must be interpreted cautiously, however. The statements to which he was applying replacement cost procedures were for periods several years prior to the time of actual research (1968). Thus, he was forced to seek somewhat distant market prices. One would not expect similar difficulties

---

clude, "in general, we would expect current values to be more objective for types of assets which have well established market price indicators, such as automobiles. For a class of other assets, with markets that are not so well defined, the current values would be less objective" (95).

[28] Peter J. Dickerson, *Business Income—A Critical Analysis* (Berkeley, California: Institute of Business and Economic Research, University of California, 1965).

[29] Raymond C. Dockweiler, "The Practicability of Developing Multiple Financial Statements: A Case Study," *The Accounting Review,* 44 (October, 1969), 736–38. The percentages quoted are based on the historical cost of the fixed assets and inventory.

to arise if the price inquiries were made at or near the statement date.[30] Inventories did not constitute an important facet of McKeown's study, but market values for these items were readily obtainable. Furthermore, in contrast to Dickerson's results, McKeown was able to use direct means to value 90 percent of the fixed assets (by value) for his case company.[31]

The apparent conclusions of these studies are somewhat conflicting. In part, this may be explained by differences in the characteristics of the companies surveyed. It is reasonable to expect that the availability of market price data will vary across industries and types of companies. Many additional studies will be needed to identify the factors that tend to facilitate accurate determination of market prices. However, we can tentatively summarize the findings of existing studies as follows. First, adequate market price data are seemingly available to account for the materials component of inventories. Dockweiler's somewhat contrary results are probably influenced by the lag between the time of the study and the dates for which market prices were requested. If the price inquiries were undertaken closer to the balance sheet date, one would expect Dockweiler's results to improve considerably. Second, with regard to fixed asset market prices, no clear statement regarding the availability of market measures is possible. Further research is needed to clarify this issue. Certainly the studies that have been undertaken provide no compelling evidence to indicate insurmountable valuation problems.[32]

The criterion of displacement

Displacement, like dispersion, refers to the magnitude of the distribution of a set of measures around some central point. Dispersion is an index of the distribution of all measures around the mean of these measures (and thus represents the degree of consensus among measurers). In contrast, displacement represents the departure of each individual's

[30] As Dockweiler himself states (*ibid.,* 736): "Part of the reason greater use could not be made of market prices is the fact that it was necessary to seek prices which existed up to three and one-half years prior to the period when the research was conducted. In most cases, neither . . . [the case company] . . . nor its suppliers had old price lists or catalogs on hand."

[31] McKeown, "Test of a Model," 20.

[32] On this same point, Dickerson (*Business Income,* pp. 34–35) concludes: ". . . it seems clear that Professors Edwards and Bell have succeeded in devising a reasonably efficient method of restating inventories, tangible fixed assets, and regularly-marketed money claims in terms of current costs by means of year-end adjustments. They have not been successful in the areas of intangible fixed assets and money claims for which there is no regular market."

We should mention that intangibles also present rather difficult problems under a historical cost system, whereas the money claims issue is a relatively minor one for many enterprises.

measure of some object from the "ideal" measure of that same object. To illustrate: [33]

$$D = \frac{1}{n} \sum_{i=1}^{n} (x_i - x^*)^2$$

where D is by definition the measure of displacement, n is the number of measurers, x_i is the quantitative measure of an object developed by the ith measurer using a given measurement system, and x^* is the ideal measure of the object.

The notion of an "ideal measure" is obviously a difficult one, especially in accounting. However, many accounting theorists believe that the discounted present value of the expected net cash flows of an asset constitutes the conceptually "best" measure of asset worth for many purposes.[34] One of the strongest arguments in support of replacement cost measurement is based on the theoretical relationship between the replacement cost of an asset and its discounted present value. In brief, proponents of this position would contend that at any point in time the replacement cost of an asset is the most objective possible approximation of its discounted present value—the theoretically best measure of asset worth. In other words, proponents of replacement costing would suggest that the displacement of replacement cost measures is less than that of other possible measures of asset worth such as historical costs and net realizable values. This argument will be explored in some depth in Chapter 4.

The criterion of timeliness

If information is to be useful in decision making, it must be available at the time the decision is made. Because of the complexity of a particular measurement process, or time-lags in the retrieval of necessary inputs, one can conceive of situations in which data will not be available until after the time for the required decision has passed. It seems relevant to ask whether the additional computational procedures required by replacement cost reporting would delay the distribution of financial statements enough to make them out-dated at the time of receipt.

As an illustration of the potential problem, McDonald indicates that traditional depreciation expense can be computed for present and future periods immediately after determining the purchase cost and depreciable life of the asset. In contrast, market-based depreciation cannot

[33] Ijiri and Jaedicke, "Reliability and Objectivity," 480–82.

[34] For example, Committee on Accounting Standards, *Accounting and Reporting Standards for Corporate Financial Statements and Preceding Statements and Supplements* (Madison, Wis.: American Accounting Association, 1957), p. 4.

be calculated until the end-of-period price is known.[35] The question, then, is whether this time differential is likely to be significant. From the sparse evidence available and the known characteristics of the reporting process, the answer is "probably not." For instance, current practice presently requires much end-of-period information before statements can be prepared (e.g., receivables, and inventory balances). The resulting time-lag between the end of the period and the actual date on which statements are distributed is probably long enough to absorb the rather minor (and overlapping) delays that could arise in a market-based measurement system. Furthermore, one could reasonably expect such insignificant delays to further diminish once market-based reporting is adopted:

> . . . it is likely that if the practice of seeking year-end purchase prices became regular and widespread, such information would become more readily available than it is presently. Vendors would grow tired of answering letters and telephone calls and would prepare and mail out to their customers each year end the latest price lists for their products.[36]

Two available studies indicate the actual time needed to prepare market-based statements from traditional accounting records. In both studies the total conversion time was quite short.[37] Furthermore, since these were first-time conversions, the total time included certain start-up costs that would be unnecessary if market value statements were to be prepared on a continuing basis in succeeding years. In this regard, Dickerson suggests that "it is possible that preparation of the data in subsequent years might take as little as one-third of first-year time. . . ."[38] Although conversion time will vary with the size of the firm, Dickerson further suggested that "with the additional mechanical aids to computation available to the larger firm, this increase is unlikely to be in direct proportion to asset-volume increase."[39]

The criterion of costliness

From these time estimates another criterion, that of costliness, could be computed. For example, McKeown estimates the recurring costs of his application to be small.[40] Whether even small additional costs are

---

35 McDonald, "Market Based Measures," 43.

36 Dockweiler, "Multiple Financial Statements," 741.

37 Dickerson, *Business Income*, p. 34; and James Charles McKeown, "An Application of a Current Market Value Accounting Model," (unpublished Ph.D. dissertation, Michigan State University, 1969), p. 112.

38 Dickerson, *Business Income*, p. 34.

39 *Ibid.*

40 McKeown, "Market Value Accounting Model," 113.

warranted would require a comparison between these costs and the expected benefits from providing the market value reports. Because of the difficulty in estimating these benefits, the decision must be an intuitive one based largely on the absolute levels of the costs themselves.

SUMMARY

We illustrated the computation of replacement cost income at the start of the chapter. Although the assumed economic events were highly simplified, it was observed that replacement cost statements incorporate three characteristics. First, balance sheet values are presented in terms of current market prices; the resultant book values thus represent the cash outflow that would be required to duplicate existing facilities and satisfy existing debt obligations. Second, the replacement cost current operating profit figure is the result of matching realized revenues with the expired *current* costs of generating those revenues. Thus, operating profit excludes a basically artificial element that arises under historical costing whenever specific price changes occur. Third, the effects of asset price changes are recognized in the period in which they occur and are segregated in cost savings components of income. This separation is reputed to facilitate the evaluation of holding activities and, by isolating the effect of price changes, maintain the integrity of operating results.

The feasibility of implementing such a replacement cost system was also scrutinized. Of primary concern in the existing institutional environment is the dispersion, or the degree of objectivity, of the resultant replacement cost measures. *A priori* analysis suggested that, relative to replacement costing, historical cost fixed asset accounting appears to possess more objectivity, where objectivity is defined as the dispersion among different measurers' calculations. On the other hand, it appeared that replacement costing might generate more objective measures than historical techniques in the area of inventory accounting. These observations, as well as the overall relative objectivity of each system, require empirical testing. Although no such evidence is currently available, several piecemeal studies were cited to indicate that departure from established measurement techniques does not necessarily lead to diminished objectivity.

Another feasibility criterion examined was that of displacement, that is, the degree of correspondence between a series of measures and the normatively ideal representation of that attribute of an object. It was indicated that one of the more compelling theoretical advantages of replacement costing is attributable to the supposed relation between such measures and the net present value of assets, an oft advanced "ideal" representation of asset worth. This argument will be examined in some detail in Chapter 4.

The final feasibility criteria were timeliness and costliness. There is no evidence to indicate that the greater computational complexity of replacement costing would so delay the availability of replacement cost reports as to diminish their usefulness. Furthermore, available studies indicate that the preparation time for developing such reports is relatively short; therefore, the incremental costs of this system are likely to be small in relation to the potential benefits.

CHAPTER FOUR

Information for
Predictions—
The Lead-Indicator
Method

In Chapter 2 we identified two methods by which an income concept could conceivably generate information for predictions (1) the extrapolation method, and (2) the lead-indicator method. As we will see in Chapter 5, the extrapolation method centers on the predictive ability of the current operating profit component. The lead-indicator concept, on the other hand, involves not just the current operating profit component but rather *total* replacement cost income.

In this chapter we develop and explore the theoretical foundation which suggests that total replacement cost income generates information which is a lead indicator for the future distributable operating flows of an enterprise. This contention is quite important since, in contrast to simple extrapolation, an effective lead indicator allows users to anticipate turning points. The ability to anticipate turning points would greatly improve users' predictions of future distributable operating flows in a dynamic environment. Since future distributable operating flows are thought to be a prime determinant of future dividends, this improved ability to predict distributable operating flows would simultaneously enhance users' predictions of future dividends.

The theoretical foundation for the lead-indicator method is somewhat complex. Accordingly, this entire chapter will be devoted to a critical analysis of the relationships necessary if total replacement cost income is to generate information which is useful as a lead indicator. In order to provide a background for this analysis, a digression into the possible reasons for treating realizable cost savings as income is necessary.

RATIONALE FOR TREATING REALIZABLE COST SAVINGS AS INCOME

Edwards and Bell define total replacement cost income as the sum of two components (1) current operating profit, and (2) realizable cost savings. (Reali*zed* cost savings are not income of the period unless these savings coincidentally became reali*zable* during the the same period.[1]) Notice that realizable cost savings are not considered to be a direct capital adjustment. For example, the credit that arises from recognizing cost increases is not immediately entered in a balance sheet equity account. Rather, this cost change is first credited to an income account, realizable cost savings, and thus affects reported replacement cost income.

It is important to understand why realizable cost savings are considered to be income of the period in which they arise. To develop this understanding, we will now explore three potential reasons for treating realizable cost savings as income rather than as a capital adjustment.

Realizable cost savings as "subjunctive income"

Edwards and Bell, in their development of the replacement cost concept, suggest the following reason for including realizable cost savings in income:

> The difference . . . [between an asset's historical cost and its market value at the balance sheet date] . . . represents a cost saving, a saving at-

---

[1] To clarify this point, refer to the brief example on pp. 60–61. In that example, an asset was purchased for $60 during 19x1 and its replacement cost rose to $75 by the end of 19x1. There were no further changes in replacement cost, and the asset was sold for $100 in 19x2. Replacement cost income recognizes the $40 total profit in two components, (1) $15 of cost saving during 19x1, and (2) $25 of operating profit during 19x2. Notice that the cost saving became realizable during 19x1 and was recognized as part of total replacement cost income during 19x1. But when this cost saving is actually realized through sale in 19x2, replacement cost income is not affected. Only the $25 of operating profit that arose during 19x2 influences 19x2's replacement cost income. Thus, realizable cost savings affect replacement cost income of the period in which they arise, but realized cost savings have no income statement effect. (Of course, if the cost saving arises in the same period in which it is realized, then replacement cost income does include the cost saving. The reason is not because the saving was realized during the period, but rather because it became reali*zable* during the period.)

tributable to the fact that the input used was acquired in advance of use. This saving is attributable to holding activities. . . .[2]

Notice that this is a highly operational rationale for the treatment accorded realizable cost savings. But Edwards and Bell offer no other, less mechanistic, explanation. Considering the importance of this income component to their theory, it is surprising that until recently no one had explored the theoretical dimension of realizable cost savings. Such an analysis of the nature of the concept and what it is intended to measure is absolutely essential to an understanding of the characteristics of total replacement cost income. Therefore, the analysis now turns to the simple issue of *why* realizable cost savings are included in income.

As an initial approach to the issue, we can explore the implications of the rationale suggested by Edwards and Bell themselves. One might immediately ask whether a firm actually benefits from purchasing an asset whose price subsequently rises. (Treating the realizable cost saving as income certainly implies that the firm has benefited.) From one perspective it might actually appear that the firm's position has *worsened* after the price rise. That is, all subsequent replacements of the asset after the price rise will necessitate a greater outflow than similar replacements before the price rise. Following this logic, the resultant price increase might conceivably be treated as an enterprise *loss* rather than as a gain.

Edwards and Bell never directly address themselves to this question. However, it is possible to construct an answer to this issue based on other parts of their theory. Generating this hypothetical response is instructive since it reveals the rationale that apparently underlies their realizable cost savings notion. They would probably suggest that, irrespective of anticipated movements in eventual selling prices, a firm benefits from increases in the prices of owned assets and these increases should accordingly be included in income. Were the firm not to have purchased an asset before its price increased, subsequent replacement would necessitate a greater cash outflow because of the higher price. The cash saving generated by the fortuitous (or planned) timing of asset purchases is thus a real benefit to the firm, they would contend.

It is apparent that the nature of the realizable cost savings income component that follows from this reasoning is essentially an opportunity cost measurement. The cost saving is included in income because it represents the opportunity "gain" accruing to the firm because it purchased its asset when it did rather than at a later date.[3] One author describes such concepts using the term "subjunctive gains and losses":

2 Edwards and Bell, *Measurement of Business Income*, p. 93.

3 See Lawrence Revsine, "Replacement Cost Reports to Investors: A Relevance Analysis" (unpublished Ph.D. dissertation, Northwestern University, 1968), pp. 42–43.

> . . . a company is considered to have sustained a "loss" from a business interruption when its financial position after the interruption is less than it might have been at that time if the business had not been interrupted (even though its financial position may, in fact, be greater after the interruption than before it, if, say, operations in only one of its many factories were interrupted). This type of loss differs from an intertemporal loss in two respects: (1) it is a comparison between two amounts at the same point of time [rather than at two different times, as in the case of an intertemporal loss] . . ., and (2) one of the terms of the comparison is the amount that a measurable property of an object *might have been* if prior events had been different from what they were (if the interruption had not occurred in the example).[4]

Thus, a subjunctive gain necessitates a comparison between events that actually occurred and events that might have occurred if conditions were different. Incorporating such opportunity costs into an accounting measurement system introduces many troublesome issues. Theoretically, there are an unlimited number of possible courses of action available to a firm. Selecting one such conceivable event for juxtaposition with actual events is difficult to defend.[5]

Viewed from a slightly different perspective, there is another reason why this opportunity cost explanation for treating realizable cost savings as income presents theoretical difficulties. Simply stated, this income component does not relate exclusively to the performance of a single entity. Instead, realizable cost savings require an implicit comparison among the activities of several firms. To see why this implicit comparison must be made, consider the following, alternative explanation for Edwards and Bell's treatment of realizable cost savings:

> A realizable cost saving is a legitimate income item because it measures a firm's cash position advantage relative to other firms in the industry which were not in the fortunate position of holding an asset over a period of rising prices. When these other firms (which may have had temporarily depleted inventories or may have been late entrants into the industry) replenish their asset supplies, they must do so at prevailing (higher) prices. As a consequence, their cash outflow necessary to purchase equivalent assets will exceed the cash outflow of firms which experienced the holding gain.

[4] Paul Rosenfield, "Reporting Subjective Gains and Losses," *The Accounting Review*, 44 (October, 1969), 788. The term "subjunctive" was chosen because "describing gains or losses of this type requires the subjunctive mood of the verb because the description requires an *if*-clause in which the condition is contrary to fact." (788–89)

[5] It is possible to compare observed results with some *ex post* optimum strategy in order to generate a meaningful figure that reflects the deviation between what the enterprise did and what it *should have done* given perfect foreknowledge. For a discussion of such a system, see Joel S. Demski, "An Accounting System Structured on a Linear Programming Model," *The Accounting Review*, 42 (October, 1967), 701–12. Rosenfield ("Subjective Gains and Losses," 796) introduces this notion of an optimum opportunity cost and contends that there is no reason to believe that the opportunity notion imbedded in realizable cost savings approaches this ideal.

Thus, to explain the treatment of realizable cost savings as income, a hypothetical cash flow comparison must be made *among firms*. More traditional income concepts relate to the performance of a single entity and do not require such comparisons in the interpretive process.[6]

Both the opportunity cost and interfirm comparison explanations for the treatment of realizable cost savings are merely variants of the same basic rationale. Whichever explanation is selected, however, will either (1) introduce interfirm comparisons directly into the measurement process or, (2) present almost insurmountable measurement difficulties. For these reasons, both variants of this rationalization must be rejected as an appropriate theoretical explanation for the inclusion of cost savings in income. Accordingly, we will now examine another potential explanation for treating realizable cost savings as income.

Realizable cost savings as wealth enhancement

Rejecting the implicit Edwards and Bell explanation for the income treatment of realizable cost savings necessitates the substitution of some alternative rationale. One such alternative might be called the "wealth enhancement" approach. It is generally related to the now familiar Hicksian income definition:

> . . . we ought to define a man's income as the maximum value which he can consume during a week, and still expect to be as well off at the end of the week as he was at the beginning.[7]

A holding gain would thus qualify as income because it would represent an enhancement in the value of assets under the control of the firm. This enhancement could be converted into a realized gain by liquidating the appreciated asset. That portion of sale proceeds in excess of original cost constitutes income [8] that could be distributed as a dividend while maintaining original dollar capital intact.

A holding gains rationalizaton of this type has had only moderate appeal to accountants [9] since it emphasizes possible liquidation as an

[6] Revsine, "General Purpose Reports," 39–40.

[7] J. R. Hicks, *Value and Capital* (2nd ed.) (Oxford: Clarendon Press, 1946), p. 172.

[8] We reiterate that a stable *general* price level is assumed throughout this study.

[9] For two significant exceptions, see Chambers, *Accounting, Evaluation and Economic Behavior;* and Robert R. Sterling, *Theory of the Measurement of Enterprise Income* (Lawrence: The University Press of Kansas, 1970).

underlying motive for recognition.[10] In general, *any* accounting income component that emphasizes liquidation, or "escape values," is destined to receive a somewhat mixed reception from accounting theorists; such concepts are at variance with prevailing assumptions of enterprise continuity—the going-concern concept of accounting. Liquidation-oriented income components also seem inconsistent with the information needs of investors. This user group is presumably concerned with dividend flows from investment opportunities. Since in the long run dividends are generated by operating assets rather than by liquidating them, an income concept that is based on a liquidation assumption seems ill-suited to such information needs.[11]

There is another reason for rejecting liquidation-oriented explanations for the treatment of realizable cost savings. Beyond the fact that this approach is seemingly not useful in forecasting future events, its appearance as a rationale for a replacement cost concept is *particularly* inappropriate. A replacement cost concept is not intended to depict movements in exit values (selling prices). The fact that a firm experiences cost savings on held assets does not necessarily mean that the liquidation value of these assets has also risen.[12] Thus, if holding gains were really intended to reflect wealth enhancement, representation of such effects would necessitate the use of exit values instead of replacement costs in the income model.

In summary, the wealth enhancement explanation for including realizable cost savings in income is seemingly of doubtful relevance to investors. There are two reasons for this contention. First, the relationship between proceeds from liquidation of appreciated assets and long--

---

[10] One might argue that the wealth enhancement position does not require liquidation. The contention would be that cost savings are recognized only to maintain real capital intact. However, this counter-argument is unsatisfactory since it does not explain why something that merely maintains capital intact is treated as income. To support this capital maintenance argument, the cost saving should be carried directly to the balance sheet and never enter into the computation of income.

[11] A similar position is taken by Eldon S. Hendriksen, *Accounting Theory* (rev. ed.) (Homewood, Ill.: Richard D. Irwin, Inc., 1970), p. 265.

[12] The issue here is *not* whether entry values will tend to approximate exit values. In general, they will not. Edwards and Bell discuss, at some length, the prerequisite conditions that are necessary in the various markets in order that the two values will tend to coincide. (*Measurement of Business Income,* pp. 75–76). The real question is whether *movements* in replacement costs will tend to approximate *movements* in exit values. In this regard Rosenfield ("Subjunctive Gains and Losses," 792) says:

. . . the purchase price and the selling price do not necessarily move in the same amount, or even in the same direction, over time. Forces which tend to cause the purchase prices of commodities of an enterprise to rise or fall may also tend to cause the selling prices . . . to rise or fall, but whether or not this relationship exists can only be determined by examining the [particular] circumstances.

term future flows to investors is uncertain. Second, changes in replacement costs are probably not a reliable indicator of changes in asset liquidation values—the essence of wealth enhancement.

Realizable cost savings as an indicator of change in operating flow potential

Rosenfield examined and rejected both of the preceding theoretical justifications for Edwards and Bell's treatment of realizable cost savings. As a consequence of his findings, he concluded that the inclusion of this component in total replacement cost income made the resultant profit figure "unintelligible," "uncorroborable," and "irrelevant." [13] Yet there is one additional theoretical justification for the treatment accorded realizable cost savings that is potentially the most significant of all. Thus, any dismissal of the concept at this stage is premature.

This final justification for the income treatment accorded realizable cost savings relies on the theoretical, but plausible, assumption that asset market values are determined by discounting, at some appropriate rate, future operating flows expected to be generated from using the asset.[14] Hypothetically, then, it would seem to follow that *changes* in market values should reflect *changes* in the stream of future operating flows expected to be generated by assets. Hence, a holding gain would qualify as a legitimate income inclusion because the price change on which the holding gain is based is a reflection of enhanced future earning power. It is apparent that if this explanation is indeed correct, then an income concept that includes these realizable cost savings would be highly relevant to the needs of readers concerned with levels of future operating flows.

The belief that realizable cost savings may be related to *changes* in future operating flows is important. This relationship, if true, could lend support to the contention that total replacement cost income generates data which are a lead indicator for future distributable operating flows. Since future distributable operating flows are a prime determinant of future dividends, the ability of replacement costing to act as a lead indicator for operating flows would make this concept highly relevant to the information needs of long-term investors.

The validity of this lead-indicator relationship will be scrutinized in the remainder of this chapter.

13 *Ibid.*, 795–97.

14 Committee on Accounting Standards, *Accounting and Reporting Standards for Corporate Financial Statements*, p. 4.

REPLACEMENT COST INCOME
AND THE LEAD-INDICATOR NOTION [15]

The accounting literature contains little research that explores the relevance of replacement cost income to a given, defined use. Nevertheless, it is possible to reconstruct from the literature a justification for the dissemination of replacement cost reports to investors. This justification is based on the assumption that replacement cost income is a surrogate for economic income.[16] Since economic income [17] embodies changes in the service potential of assets, economic income is quite obviously a lead indicator for future operating flows. The ability of replacement cost income to approximate economic income would then explain its presumed relevance to investors. That is, insofar as replacement cost is a surrogate for economic income, then replacement cost income would also be a lead indicator for future operating flows.

Beaver, Kennelly, and Voss maintain that before we empirically test the predictive ability of a concept, the theory supporting such contentions must be developed.[18] However, the notion that replacement cost

---

[15] The material in the remainder of this chapter is adapted from Revsine, "Replacement Cost Income." It is reproduced with permission of the Editor of *The Accounting Review.*

[16] Proponents of this surrogation argument implicitly suggest that historical cost income is not as accurate an approximation of economic income as is replacement cost income. Since this issue has been treated elsewhere in the literature [see Sidney S. Alexander (revised by David Solomons), "Income Measurement in a Dynamic Economy," *Studies in Accounting Theory,* ed. W. T. Baxter and S. Davidson (Richard D. Irwin, Inc., 1962), pp. 174–88], we need not dwell on it here.

[17] Although economic income, as the term is used in this study, will be more rigorously defined below, a brief explanation is given now for those readers unfamiliar with the concept. Economic income is a comparative statics income concept. It is computed by comparing the change in the value of an enterprise between two points in time. Value at any moment in time, according to this concept, consists of two components. The first is measured as the discounted present value of the expected future net cash flows of the firm. The second is the value of the net liquid assets on hand. The sum of these two components is called total economic value. The change in total economic value over time thus reflects *both* changes in *realized* liquid assets and changes in the cash generating *potential* of the firm.

[18] Beaver, Kennelly, Voss, "Predictive Ability," 677:

The use of the predictive ability criterion presupposes that the alternatives under consideration have met the tests of logic and that each has a theory supporting it. . . . Theory provides an explanation why a given alternative is expected to be related to the dependent variable and permits the investigator to generalize from the findings of sample data to a new set of observations. Consequently, a complete evaluation involves both *a priori* and empirical considerations.

93

income is a surrogate for economic income (and thus is a lead indicator for future operating flows) has never been rigorously examined by its proponents. Therefore, in the following sections we will develop an *a priori* model to assess the theoretical validity of this relationship between replacement cost income and economic income. (In the remainder of this chapter, we will refer to this relationship as simply the "lead-indicator notion" for ease of exposition. We must remember that this abbreviated reference really reflects a two-stage process. First, it incorporates the surrogate relationship between replacement cost income and economic income, and second, because of this surrogate relationship, it also denotes ability to predict future operating flows using replacement cost information.)

References in the literature

A brief examination of prior references to the lead-indicator notion in the accounting literature accomplishes two objectives. First, it indicates that some accounting theorists have—at least implicitly—used the supposed relationship between replacement cost income and economic income as a rationale for replacement cost reporting. Second, these passing references should indicate that the basic nature of the assumed relationship between the two concepts remains to be explored.

Illustrative of the support given to the lead-indicator notion in the literature is the statement by Zeff:

> But it can be argued that [Edwards and Bell's] "business profit" is not too bad an approximation of the current increment in the present value of future net receipts [economic income].[19]

Corbin advances a similar view:

> Given a satisfactory degree of competition, the prices of assets in the market place would then be based on estimates of their future income streams made by many independent individuals; market prices would serve as objective, indirect estimates of value. One could go to the stock exchanges to get present value estimates for stocks and bonds, to the commodities markets or dealers' catalogues for inventories and equipment, to the real estate markets for land and buildings, etc. In this manner the values of all assets and liabilities, *except Goodwill,* could be determined indirectly each period, in order to calculate net income as the increase in an enterprise's net [present] value during the period.[20]

---

[19] Zeff, "Replacement Cost," 623. However, in a later article [Stephen A. Zeff and W. David Maxwell, "Holding Gains on Fixed Assets—A Demurrer," *The Accounting Review*, 40 (January, 1965), 70], Professors Zeff and Maxwell seem to recant this earlier position.

[20] Donald A. Corbin, "The Revolution in Accounting," *The Accounting Review*, 37 (October, 1962), 630.

Other authors have made similar explicit contentions that replacement cost income is a surrogate for economic income.[21] In addition, this lead-indicator notion is implicit in certain other replacement cost income studies.[22]

However, none of these references contain a detailed examination of the conceptual foundation for the lead-indicator relationship. Nor is such an examination found in other studies that are highly critical of the lead-indicator notion.[23] Therefore, the basic nature of the relationship between replacement cost income and economic income must be explored.

Theoretical foundation

In this section, a model that provides the heretofore absent theoretical foundation for the lead-indicator notion will be developed. We shall see that in a perfectly competitive economy, the correspondence between replacement cost income and economic income is precise. Later, we will utilize the developed model to assess the validity of the lead-indicator notion in an imperfect, but more realistic, competitive environment.

Before this lead-indicator foundation is developed, we should isolate several characteristics of perfectly competitive economies that merit special emphasis. First, perfect competition implies the existence of perfect resource mobility. All firms are assumed able to adjust capital levels instantaneously in response to changed market conditions. Second, as a consequence of this resource mobility and other characteristics of a perfectly competitive economy,[24] the price of every asset at the be-

---

21 See, for example, Henry W. Sweeney, "Income," *The Accounting Review*, 8 (December, 1933), 325, and his earlier article, "Capital," *The Accounting Review*, 8 (September, 1933), 189–91; and Joel Dean, "Measurement of Real Economic Earnings of a Machinery Manufacturer," *The Accounting Review*, 29 (April, 1954), 257.

22 See, for example, Edwards and Bell, *Measurement of Business Income*, p. 25; Bedford, *Income Determination Theory*, p. 91; and Staubus, "Current Cash Equivalent," 650–61. Professor Staubus explicitly refers to the asset valuation case. His comments extend to the income determination case by implication only.

23 Robert L. Dickens and John O. Blackburn, "Holding Gains on Fixed Assets: An Element of Business Income?," *The Accounting Review*, 39 (April, 1964), 312–29; and Howard J. Snavely, "Current Cost for Long-Lived Assets: A Critical View," *The Accounting Review*, 44 (April, 1969), 344–53.

24 These other characteristics of a perfectly competitive economy are: (1) each buyer and seller is so small in relation to the market in which he operates that he cannot influence the price of what is sold therein, and (2) there are no artificial constraints placed on prices, supply, or demand. See, for example, Kalman J. Cohen and Richard M. Cyert, *Theory of the Firm: Resource Allocation in a Market Economy* (Englewood Cliffs, N. J.: Prentice-Hall, Inc., 1965), pp. 49–51.

ginning of the ith period (P_i) is equal to the discounted present value at the beginning of the ith period of the net cash flows expected to be generated by asset operations (V_i); i.e.,

$$P_i = V_i \tag{1}$$

Finally, at any moment in time, all firms in a perfectly competitive economy have identical expectations regarding cash flows to be generated by owned assets.[25]

Economic income (as the term is used in this study) is measured as the change, over some period of time, in the value of a firm's assets. The total value of a firm's assets at any point in time can be determined by discounting, at the prevailing market rate of return, the expected net cash flows from asset utilization and adding to this the value of net liquid assets on hand. The total economic income figure that results from a comparison of beginning and ending period asset values can be fragmented into two components: (1) distributable operating flow (more frequently termed "expected income"), and (2) unexpected income.[26]

[25] This is a derivative of the familiar perfect knowledge assumption. Since this general characteristic of perfect competition is frequently misunderstood, amplification is warranted. In this regard Cohen and Cyert state (*ibid.*, p. 50):

> This [perfect knowledge] assumption should be interpreted as meaning that all buyers and sellers in the market are aware of all current opportunities. . . . We do not assume perfect ability to forecast the future, but only perfect knowledge of current opportunities.

[26] Hicks, *Value and Capital*, pp. 171–88; Alexander (revised by Solomons), "Income Measurement," pp. 174–88; and Bedford, *Income Determination Theory*, pp. 25–27. If for simplicity we assume that all cash flows occur on the last day of each period, these two components of economic income can be isolated symbolically in the following manner:

$$(Ye)_i = V_{i+1} - V_i$$

where $(Ye)_i$ represents the economic income for the ith period, V_i is the envisioned value of the firm's assets at the beginning of the ith period, and V_{i+1} is the envisioned value of the assets at the beginning of period $i+1$. Thus:

$$V_i = \sum_{j=i}^{n} \frac{F_j(i)}{(1+r)^{j+1-i}} + L_i \tag{a}$$

where $F_j(i)$ represents the expected net cash flow in the jth period as envisioned at the beginning of the ith period, r equals the market rate of return, n represents the terminal date of the planning horizon, and L_i is the value of the net liquid assets at the beginning of the ith period. Similarly:

$$V_{i+1} = \sum_{j=i+1}^{n} \frac{F_j(i) + \Delta F_j(i+1)}{(1+r)^{j-i}} + L_i(1+r) + R_i \tag{b}$$

where ΔF_j $(i+1)$ represents the change in the originally envisioned i^{th} period cash

Distributable operating flow represents the maximum amount of resources generated by operations that can be distributed to owners without lowering the level of future physical operations.[27] The distributable operating flow (D_f) component of total economic income is the product of the market rate of return (r) and the beginning of the period net present value of assets (V_i). Thus:

$$D_f = rV_i \qquad (2)[28]$$

The unexpected income component of economic income is equal to the sporadic increase in asset net present value that develops as a result of

---

flow now viewed from the beginning of period $i+1$, and R_i is the actually realized cash inflow of the ith period. Subtracting [a] from [b] and rearranging yields:

$$(Ye)_i = \sum_{j=i+1}^{n} \frac{F_j(i)}{(1+r)^{j-i}} - \sum_{j=i}^{n} \frac{F_j(i)}{(1+r)^{j+1-i}} + L_i r + R_i + \sum_{j=i+1}^{n} \frac{\Delta F_j(i+1)}{(1+r)^{j-i}} \qquad (c)$$

$$\underbrace{\text{distributable operating flow}} \qquad \underbrace{\text{unexpected income}}$$

This particular dichotomization of the income components is appropriate only if it is assumed that R_i, the actually realized inflow of the ith period, equals $F_i(i)$, the expected ith period inflow as envisioned at the beginning of the ith period. However, if R_i diverges from $F_i(i)$ then equation (c) must be altered slightly.

[27] This assumes that all expectations are realized and that no changes in future prices occur. Footnote 31, *infra.*, shows numerically how a dividend equal to distributable operating flow provides for constant future physical operating levels and constant future dividends.

[28] From footnote 26 we have, for distributable operating flow:

$$D_f = \sum_{j=i+1}^{n} \frac{F_j(i)}{(1+r)^{j-i}} - \sum_{j=i}^{n} \frac{F_j(i)}{(1+r)^{j+1-i}} + L_i r + R_i \qquad (c')$$

which, after performing the indicated subtraction, yields:

$$D_f = \sum_{j=i+1}^{n} \frac{(1+r)F_j(i) - F_j(i)}{(1+r)^{j+1-i}} - \frac{F_i(i)}{(1+r)} + L_i r + R_i \qquad (d')$$

Since $F_i(i)$ equals R_i in this *ex ante* income conceptualization, we can substitute $F_i(i)$ for R_i in equation (d') and simplify:

$$D_f = \sum_{j=i+1}^{n} \frac{rF_j(i)}{(1+r)^{j+1-i}} - \frac{F_i(i)}{(1+r)} + L_i r + F_i(i)$$

$$D_f = \sum_{j=i}^{n} \frac{rF_j(i)}{(1+r)^{j+1-i}} + L_i r$$

$$D_f = r[\sum_{j=i}^{n} \frac{F_j(i)}{(1+r)^{j+1-i}} + L_i]$$

$$D_f = rV_i$$

changes in expectations regarding the level of future operating flows from assets.

We will now demonstrate that, theoretically, replacement cost income is virtually identical to economic income in a perfectly competitive economy. Replacement cost income contains two general components: (1) an operating profit segment, and (2) a price change segment. In the terminology of Edwards and Bell these components are called current operating profit and realizable cost savings, respectively. Current operating profit is generally measured as the difference between revenues for the period and the replacement cost of those assets consumed in generating revenues. If an economic depreciation concept is used to measure the expiration of long-lived assets (i.e., a concept that measures the periodic decline in the discounted earning power of an asset [29]) the resulting actual rate of return from operations for a single-asset firm is given by:

$$r_a = \frac{C_i}{P_i} \qquad (3)$$

In (3), r_a represents the actual operating rate of return, C_i is the current operating profit, and P_i, as before, denotes the market price of assets. Given a perfectly competitive environment, the following relationship should hold in equilibrium:

$$r_a = r \qquad (4)$$

Substituting V_i for P_i and r for r_a in equation (3) and rearranging gives:

$$C_i = rV_i \qquad (5)$$

[29] Another way of viewing economic depreciation is that it is an allocation of book value to time periods that permits the rate of return on assets to remain constant, if no changes occur in anticipated or realized cash flows. See, for example, Lerner and Carleton, *Financial Analysis*, pp. 50–51. The computation can be illustrated in the following fashion. Assume that a fixed asset has a 3-year life and no salvage value. Its cost is $299.55 and it is expected to generate annual net inflows of $110. The internal rate of return promised by this asset is approximately 5 percent. Economic depreciation for this asset would be:

	Year			
	1	*2*	*3*	*Total*
Book value of asset at beginning of the period	$299.55	$204.53	$104.76	—
Cash inflow	$110.00	$110.00	$110.00	$330.00
Income (5% of beginning of period book value)	14.98	10.23	5.24	30.45
Economic depreciation	$ 95.02	$ 99.77	$104.76	$299.55

It will be seen that the depreciation figure is a residual one which permits recognition of a 5 percent return on book value in each year.

A comparison of equations (5) and (2) indicates that:

$$C_i = D_f \qquad (6)$$

Thus, in a perfectly competitive economy, the current operating profit component of replacement cost income is equal to the distributable operating flow component of economic income.[30] This equivalence means that current operating profit would thus reflect the maximum amount of resources generated by operations that could be distributed in the current period without reducing the level of future physical operations (and thus, if costs and prices are constant, future dividends).[31]

[30] Notice that the conditions under which this relationship holds are rather limited. First, this relationship is valid only for economies in which all characteristics of perfect competition are satisfied and, because of equation (4), only in equilibrium. Second, equation (6) is valid only if the specific depreciation concept used in the replacement cost model is that of economic depreciation. However, Edwards and Bell (pp. 178–80) exclude economic depreciation from their model on both theoretical and practical grounds. Therefore, current operating profit as computed by Edwards and Bell need not necessarily equal distributable operating flow. Finally, a change in the composition or level of ending inventory of processed goods can destroy the equation (6) relationship. (See Edwards and Bell, pp. 105–8.) This is the case since the entry value replacement cost concept promulgated by Edwards and Bell specifically excludes value added by production.

[31] This can easily be demonstrated by means of a simple example. Using the basic data from footnote 29, let us assume that the firm pays a dividend equal to the distributable operating flow of each period. If we further assume that the firm reinvests undistributed cash flows at 5 percent, the future flow pattern would appear as follows:

	Year			
	1	2	3	Total
Book value and market value of asset at beginning of period, V_{i1}. (Book value and market value are presumed equal since economic depreciation is used.)	$299.55	$204.53	$104.76	—
Undistributed cash flow, V_{i2}:				—
From year 1		95.02		
From years 1 & 2 ($95.02 + 99.77)			194.79	—
Total Assets	$299.55	$299.55	$299.55	
Net cash inflow:				
From asset operation	$110.00	$110.00	$110.00	$330.00
From reinvestment of undistributed cash flows of previous periods	0.00	4.75	9.74	14.49
Total cash inflow	110.00	114.75	119.74	344.49
Distributable operating flow:				
From asset operation (rV_{i1})	14.98	10.23	5.24	30.45
From reinvestment of undistributed cash flows (rV_{i2})	0.00	4.75	9.74	14.49
Total distributable operating flow (equals dividend paid)	14.98	14.98	14.98	44.94
Undistributed cash flow (equals economic depreciation)	$ 95.02	$ 99.77	$104.76	$299.55

In similar fashion the second component of replacement cost income—realizable cost savings—is a direct counterpart of the second component of economic income—unexpected income. Realizable cost savings are equal to the change in the market price of assets held during the period. Unexpected income consists of the discounted value of the changes in the amount of future flows expected from operating owned assets. In a perfectly competitive economy, such changes in cash flow expectations are directly translated into changes in asset market value [equation (1)]; therefore, the realizable cost savings component of replacement cost income is equal to the unexpected income component of economic income.[32]

Since each component of replacement cost income is equal to its counterpart component of economic income, then total replacement cost income must also equal total economic income. Thus, replacement cost income would be a lead indicator for *future* distributable operating flows.[33] To estimate future distributable operating flow, the following approach would be used. Since replacement cost income is equal to economic income in a perfectly competitive environment, the equity value shown on a replacement cost balance sheet would be equal to the net present value of the firm [equation (1)]. Multiplying this net present value by the market rate of return on assets would provide an estimate of the succeeding year's distributable operating flow [equation (2)].

We see that if the firm distributes the total amount of distributable operating flow as a dividend at the end of each period, the following consequences result. First, the accumulated undistributed cash flow at the end of the third year ($299.55) is precisely the amount needed to buy a replacement asset *and thus maintain future physical operations at their existing level.* Second, when the dividend distribution is equal to the amount of distributable operating flow, then future distributable operating flow (and thus future dividends) remains constant. This demonstrates that when prices are stable, distributable operating flow represents the maximum amount that the firm can distribute as a dividend and still maintain physical operations and future dividends at their existing levels.

[32] This correspondence between realizable cost savings and unexpected income is precise only if replacement cost depreciation is measured as the periodic decline in the earning power of an asset (economic depreciation). Only then will the difference between the book values of assets and ending market values correspond to the unexpected income component of economic income. If replacement cost depreciation is computed on a basis other than economic depreciation, realizable cost savings will vary from unexpected income by the amount of the divergence between economic depreciation and replacement cost depreciation as actually computed.

[33] We should point out, however, that total replacement cost income is not equal to future distributable operating flow for any *single* future year. The reason is that realizable cost savings reflect the discounted present value of the entire stream of operating flow changes in the single year in which these changes first become apparent. That is, replacement cost income absorbs the entire impact of the flow change in the year of the associated asset price change. Since this flow change will usually be spread over several future periods, the realizable cost savings would have to be allocated to each of these future periods in order to predict individual year's future distributable operating flows.

ILLUSTRATIVE CORRESPONDENCE

A brief, numerical example illustrating the correspondence between replacement cost income and economic income in a perfectly competitive economy follows. The data for this example are identical to those used to illustrate economic depreciation in footnote 29. That is, a firm owns a single asset that costs $299.55. The asset is new, has a 3-year life and is expected to generate annual net cash inflows of $110. Given these assumptions, the asset's time-adjusted rate of return is expected to be 5 percent, which also equals the prevailing market rate of return.

Assume that in the first year of operations the expected net inflows of $110 are actually realized. The computation for replacement cost income in this first year would show:

Replacement Cost Income
For the Year Ended December 31, 19x1

Current Operating Profit:	
Net cash inflow	$110.00
Depreciation:	
(see computation in footnote 29)	95.02
Current Operating Profit	$ 14.98
Realizable Cost Savings	0.00
Total Replacement Cost Income	$ 14.98

Economic income would be:

Economic Income
For the Year Ended December 31, 19x1

Distributable Operating Flow:	
rV_i (0.05 × $299.55)	$14.98
Unexpected Income	0.00
Total Economic Income	$14.98

A summary of the two computations for 19x1 would show:

Replacement Cost Income
Current Operating Profit + Realizable Cost Savings
$14.98   +   0

Economic Income
Distributable Operating Flow + Unexpected Income
$14.98   +   0

Now assume that on January 1, 19x2 it is suddenly perceived that net cash inflows for the year 19x3 will be $95. In a perfectly competitive, frictionless economy, the equilibrium price of the asset will immediately fall from $204.53 ($299.55 original cost minus $95.02 depreciation) to $190.93. This latter figure is derived by discounting the new, lower 19x3 flow at the prevailing 5 percent rate.

19x2	$110 × 0.9524 =	$104.76
19x3	95 × 0.9070 =	86.17
New Price for 1-Year-Old Asset		$190.93

If 19x2 inflow expectations are indeed realized, replacement cost income for 19x2 would be: [34]

Replacement Cost Income
For the Year Ended December 31, 19x2

Current Operating Profit:		
Net cash inflow		$110.00
Depreciation:		
Value of the asset at 1/1/x2	$190.93	
Value of the asset at 12/31/x2:		
19x3 flows ($95 × 0.9524)	90.48	$100.45
Current Operating Profit		$ 9.55
Realizable Cost Savings:		
Value of the asset after adjustment	$190.93	
Value of the asset at 12/31/x1	204.53	
Realizable cost savings		(13.60)
Total Replacement Cost Income		$ (4.05)

Economic income for 19x2 would be:

Economic Income
For the Year Ended December 31, 19x2

Distributable Operating Flow:	
rV_i (0.05 × $190.93)	$ 9.55
Unexpected Income:	
Decrease in 19x3 expected flows	
($15 × 0.9070)	(13.60)
Total Economic Income	$ (4.05)

The summarized 19x2 results for the two income concepts are:

Replacement Cost Income
Current Operating Profit + Realizable Cost Savings
$9.55   + $(13.60)

---

[34] For ease of exposition, we have ignored reinvestment of periodic inflows.

Economic Income

Distributable Operating Flow + Unexpected Income
$9.55   + $(13.60)

If no further changes in expectations occur, and if operating results for 19x3 are as anticipated, replacement cost income for 19x3
would be:

Replacement Cost Income
For the Year Ended December 31, 19x3

Current Operating Profit:		
Net cash inflow		$ 95.00
Depreciation:		
Value of the asset at 12/31/x2	$90.48	
Value of the asset at 12/31/x3	0.00	
		90.48
Current Operating Profit		$ 4.52
Realizable Cost Savings		0.00
Total Replacement Cost Income		$ 4.52

Economic income for 19x3 would be:

Economic Income
For the Year Ended December 31, 19x3

Distributable Operating Flow:	
rV_i (0.05 × $90.48)	$ 4.52
Unexpected Income	0.00
Total Economic Income	$ 4.52

The 19x3 summarized results are:

Replacement Cost Income

Current Operating Profit + Realizable Cost Savings
$4.52   +   0

Economic Income

Distributable Operating Flow + Unexpected Income
$4.52   +   0

Thus, the calculations in this section illustrate that under certain
circumstances total replacement cost income equals total economic income. Furthermore, the corresponding subcomponents of each concept
are also equal. Although our analysis assumed a perfectly competitive
environment in which all firms have homogenous expectations, this cor-

respondence between the two income concepts can also be demonstrated to exist in total when there is divergence among firms' expectations.[35]

The lead-indicator notion in imperfectly competitive economies

OPERATING PROFIT CORRESPONDENCES

Removing the conditions of perfect competition introduces imperfect resource mobility and other market imperfections into the economy. These imperfections change the equalities in (1) and (4) to mere approximations. Then, performing substitutions similar to those in the perfect competition illustration, (5) becomes:

$$C_i \cong rV_i \qquad (5')$$

Thus, under conditions of imperfect competition, current operating profit is merely an approximation for distributable operating flow. It should prove useful to illustrate more explicitly some precise circumstances that transform the equalities in (1) and (4) to mere approximations and thus make the relationship between current operating profit and distributable operating flow an approximate one.

1. Cost differences among firms. Even in a simple imperfect competition case where there is a primary capital good used exclusively by one industry, costs of production are liable to differ dramatically among firms. Certain firms in the industry may employ older, less efficient support facilities for the asset in question; or, one firm might be situated in a higher-cost labor market than are its competitors. Both of these possibilities would raise the costs of using the capital good and thus lower the expected net cash flows accruing to these higher-cost firms. Assume that an industry-wide *minimum* acceptable rate of return exists. Theoretically, high-cost firms would not be induced to purchase a capital asset unless its price were low enough to yield a prospective return at least as great as the minimum rate. That capital price (market value) that yields exactly the minimum rate of return to the marginal firm, however, would afford a larger return to the lower-cost, efficient firms in the industry. Thus, even if one assumes identical target rates of re-

[35] It can be shown that under conditions of divergent expectations, total replacement cost income and total economic income are equal for firms whose expectations prove, *ex post,* to be correct; furthermore, each of the sub-components of each concept is equal to its counterpart component in the other concept. For firms whose expectations are not borne out by subsequent events, there will be divergence between the two sub-components of each concept; however, even for these firms, *total* replacement cost income will equal *total* economic income. These continued correspondences presume that economic depreciation is used to determine total replacement cost income.

turn throughout an industry, the market value of a capital asset need not equal the discounted present value of future cash flows for all firms using the asset. "Except for marginal purchasers, the buyer's discounted expectations must be greater than his cost." [36]

If a capital good is simultaneously employed by several different industries, the disparity between market prices and discounted cash flows could be even more pronounced. In this instance, it is not solely differing efficiency or resource market placement that causes this disparity between prices and net present values. Rather, the production characteristics of the industry itself might contribute to the differential. One industry may be inherently more profitable than another because the nature of the final product produced involves lower production costs.

The inter-industry cost differentials could conceivably be more dramatic than efficiency-induced differentials within a single industry. Thus, the disparity between market prices and discounted cash flows could be very large even if one assumes an identical minimum target rate of return for all industries using the capital asset.

2. Revenue differences among firms. A disparity, similar to that encountered with regard to production costs, could also exist in imperfect competition with respect to the revenues generated by capital asset use. There is no reason to assume that all firms that employ a given capital good within a single industry would enjoy identical gross cash inflows from sales of final goods. Various market imperfections could exist that would result in differences in the unit price or physical volume of sales. Those firms favorably situated with regard to final markets could enjoy a level of gross cash flow per asset in excess of that garnered by less fortunate competitors. However, the prevailing market price for the capital asset might also be influenced by the expectations of the less favorably placed competitors. The equilibrium market price might be low enough to afford these firms a "normal" rate of return, despite their expected lower gross inflows. For these less profitable firms, the asset market value would indeed be equal to the discounted expected future flows from the asset. It follows, however, that the asset owned by a favorably placed firm would again have a net present value in excess of its market price. [37]

This differential could become more pronounced if many industries use a similar type of capital asset. The final product produced by certain of these industries could enjoy greater demand than the output of other

---

[36] Carl T. Devine, "Asset Cost and Expiration," *Modern Accounting Theory*, ed. Morton Backer (Englewood Cliffs, N. J.: Prentice-Hall, Inc., 1966), p. 143.

[37] Again, it is assumed that all firms in the industry have identical discount rates. This somewhat unrealistic assumption is relaxed in the next section.

industries.[38] These industry differences might also contribute to a disparity between asset market price and the present value of future operating flows.

3. Discount rate differences among firms. To this point, the discussion has assumed that the cost of capital for all firms in an industry and all industries in the economy is similar. The sole cause for divergence between asset market price and discounted future flows was the assumption of the existence of various market imperfections in the industry under examination. But these same market imperfections, constraints on the free movement of capital, and differences in risk can cause disparities in the actual cost of capital. Since the discount rate is a function of extant conditions confronting firms in an imperfectly competitive economy [39] and also of existing risk differences,[40] then the notion of a uniform cost of capital is no longer appropriate.

To illustrate the difficulty introduced by diverse discount rates, assume that some industries have a different capital cost than other industries. Because of operating characteristics and market imperfections, this differential is expected to persist. Capital asset selling prices will be determined by discounting assets' expected net cash flows using, in some ill-defined fashion, that discount rate appropriate to the marginal purchasers of the asset. The price that results will not necessarily equal the discounted present value of the asset to other firms in the economy. Thus, if several industries employ the same capital asset in the production process, divergent discount rates among industries could alone cause a disparity between market prices and present values.

The impact of these three illustrations on the correspondence between current operating profit and distributable operating flow can be summarized as follows: Each general situation described above tends to

---

38 These gross cash flow differentials are briefly discussed in Bedford, *Income Determination Theory*, p. 28; and Ronald S. Edwards, "The Nature and Measurement of Income," *Studies in Accounting Theory*, p. 112.

39 D. R. Scott, "The Capitalization Process," *Journal of Political Economy*, 18 (March, 1910), 219. Scott says:

> Each of the competing entrepreneurs whose bids make up the demand makes his own estimate of the incomes that will come to him from the use of the instrument in question, and he also computes the present worth of those incomes by the use of a time-discount rate peculiar to himself. . . . Each sort of goods must go through a market to have a market value put upon it. Even though a good is unique and has never been sold, its value comes to be estimated according to the offers the owner must refuse in order to keep it.

40 For an illustration of this point, see David F. Drake, "The Pattern of Depreciation," (unpublished Ph.D. dissertation, University of Chicago, 1963), pp. 87–99. Risk-aversion premiums are also discussed, for example, in Lerner and Carleton, *Financial Analysis*, pp. 113–15.

transform the equality between asset prices and values described in (1) into an approximation. Thus:

$$P_i \simeq V_i \tag{1'}$$

This means that V_i cannot legitimately be substituted for P_i in (3), and thus (5) and (6) also become only approximations. That is, in a realistic economic environment, current operating profit will merely be an approximation of distributable operating flow. How good this approximate relationship will be and how stable it is over time are empirical issues which have yet to be investigated.

HOLDING GAINS CORRESPONDENCES

An approximate correspondence can similarly be attributed to the cost savings and unexpected income components. Even in imperfectly competitive economies, an asset's price will approximate its average net present value. Theoretically, changes in an asset's operating flow potential precipitate appropriate changes in its price. Proponents of the lead-indicator notion apparently would contend that just as market price is related to asset net present value, so too the *change* in asset market price is related to the *change* in asset net present value. Therefore, realizable cost savings, measured as the change in the market price of owned assets, would approximate unexpected income for a period, measured as the change in the net present value of asset operating flow potential.

The basis for the lead-indicator contention in "realistic" economies should now be evident. There are two distinct sub-correspondences underlying this supposed relationship between total replacement cost income and total economic income: (1) that the current operating profit component of replacement cost income is an indirect measure of the distributable operating flow component of economic income, and (2) that the realizable cost savings component of replacement cost income is an indirect measure of the unexpected income component of economic income.

However, there are *a priori* grounds for questioning the validity of the relationship between changes in asset prices and changes in service potential in realistic economies. Therefore, below, we will examine the reasonableness of this assumption of positive covariance between asset prices and operating flows. Furthermore, we will explore the impact of this covariance assumption (and its possible invalidity) on the relationship between total replacement cost income and total economic income.[41]

41 Heretofore, we have concentrated on the underlying correspondences between the sub-components of each income concept in order to develop the theoretical foundation for the lead-indicator notion in a comprehensible manner and to explain why this

Market prices and cash flow potential

The hypothesized relationship between replacement cost income and economic income rests, in part, on the assumption that changes in asset prices are in direct response to changes in the level of operating flows expected to be generated by assets. In an aggregate sense, this relationship between realizable cost savings and unexpected income is probably valid. Barring changes in the discount rate, and the like, such a relationship between asset prices and asset operating flows must exist in the long run for the economy as a whole. However, for any individual firm in the economy there is no necessary relationship between movements in asset prices and movements in operating flows. Actually, there are three possibilities regarding asset market price changes and changes in the revenue generating potential of assets to a firm. As an asset price changes:

A. Future flows resulting from asset operation could change in the same direction as the price change.
B. Future operating flows could remain constant.
C. Future operating flows could change in the opposite direction.

These three possibilities will be referred to as Type A, Type B, and Type C asset price changes, respectively.[42]

If replacement cost income and economic income are indirectly related, there ought to be rather close correspondence between movements in each. This suggests that Type A price changes should predominate in order to validate the lead indicator notion.[43] However, if Type B and Type C price changes can be expected to occur with some frequency, and if such price changes precipitate divergence between the direction of movement in total replacement cost income and total economic income, then replacement cost income will not always be a surrogate for economic income.

This type of condition is illustrated in the following section.

---

surrogate relationship has been extended to realistic economies by its proponents. When firms' expectations differ, however, we can demonstrate that these two underlying correspondences are not necessarily independent. Since divergence of expectations is the norm in realistic economies, and since our concern centers on the total relationship between the two income concepts, in the remainder of the chapter we shift our focus from the sub-components to concentrate instead on the relationship between total replacement cost income and total economic income.

[42] It should be reiterated that for ease of exposition the general purchasing power of the monetary unit is assumed herein to be stable. Therefore, the influence on market prices of general inflation or deflation can be ignored.

[43] More specifically, not only must asset prices and operating flows move in the same direction, but also the magnitude of the price change must correspond to the magnitude of the change in the present value of expected operating flows.

An illustrative Type C price change. Assume that the gamma industry manufactures a particular consumer good called a gamma. The industry is characterized by perfect competition but it has earned an above-normal rate of return during 19x0. Furthermore, assume that these abnormal returns induce capital movement into the gamma industry during 19x1 as new firms attempt to take advantage of the inordinately high returns available. This movement will initially tend to raise asset prices for all firms in the gamma industry, including the established firms. Asset prices will rise because of the demand for fixed assets by entering firms; this demand is added to the replacement demand for productive equipment on the part of firms already producing gammas in the gamma industry. Unless perfect elasticity of supply in the capital goods industry is assumed, this increase in demand for gamma-producing equipment will serve to raise the price of such equipment. However, the output of final goods, gamma, will not immediately increase since it is assumed that a certain lead-time is necessary before the new firms entering the industry are able to utilize the new capacity for gamma production. Thus, in this initial stage, no change in the magnitude of established gamma firms' operating flows occurs, but asset prices are bid upward.

After the necessary lead-time passes, however, the gamma industry's new firms begin production in 19x2. Utilization of this new capacity increases the supply of final output available. With demand constant (and not perfectly elastic), this increase in supply will tend to reduce the price obtained for each gamma unit sold; furthermore, the volume attained by new firms is assumed to be garnered at the expense of established firms. Each established firm, if we assume a constant demand for final output of the industry, will experience both a shrinking market and a decline in per unit gamma selling price. Furthermore, in an increasing-cost industry, the increased output will trigger increases in the price of variable inputs used in production. The forces originally set into motion by the disparity of rates of return between the gamma industry and the remainder of the economy will eventually eliminate the disparity by (1) raising the costs of factors of production, including fixed inputs, (2) lowering the average selling price of output, and (3) fragmenting the market into smaller individual shares.

The net effect of these results on the established firms in the industry will be: (1) a rise in the market price of capital assets used in production, and (2) a fall in expected future flows associated with operating the gamma-producing equipment. Hence, a Type C price change (opposite movements in asset prices and future flows) is the likely result of this sequence of events. Thus, although it is apparently true that at the aggregate level changes in operating flow expectations translate directly into changes in asset prices, the possible existence of Type B and Type

C price changes would indicate that this correspondence need not exist at the micro level.[44]

Given the magnitude of fixed asset dollar values relative to income, it is conceivable that a proportionally small change in replacement costs could exert a proportionally large impact on reported income.[45] If the price changes experienced by a firm are predominately of Type B and/or Type C, serious divergence between reported replacement cost income and economic income could result. This divergence means that replacement cost income could be moving in one direction while the expected future operating flows of the firm are moving in the opposite direction.

We will now illustrate numerically this possibility for divergence between the direction of movement of the two income concepts. The situation described in the gamma industry example will form the basis for the illustration. Numbers will be inserted for conceptual clarity.

Impact of Type C changes on conventional replacement cost income. Earlier in the chapter we developed the theoretical basis underlying the correspondence between replacement cost income and economic income. To effect this correspondence, economic depreciation was used to compute replacement cost income. As was indicated at that time, Edwards and Bell reject the use of economic depreciation. Thus, the standard computation of depreciation in a replacement cost framework uses a more traditional allocation scheme, e.g., straight-line depreciation applied to market values. Since our objective in this section is to illustrate possible divergence between *conventional* replacement cost income and economic income, we now will use a conventional computation procedure to determine replacement cost income. That is, in order to illustrate the divergence between conventional replacement cost income and economic income, conventional depreciation procedures must be employed.

To begin the illustration, assume that the gamma industry (which was described above) is in temporary disequilibrium in 19x0. Gamma-producing equipment, which has a 3-year life and no salvage value, is

---

44 One might argue that the example is incomplete since it begins at a point of disequilibrium and ends when equilibrium has been restored. Although this format was chosen for ease of exposition, there are two additional answers to such objections. First, a firm may enter the process at any point in the cycle. Accordingly, the relevant cycle for analysis is that time span over which the *individual* firm experiences a price change. To contend otherwise is to again confuse individual-firm and economy-wide phenomena. Second, even in this form, the example illustrates the potentially serious year-to-year divergence that can occur between replacement cost income and economic income. Insofar as reported year-to-year income changes have information content, the predictive ability of statement users could be seriously impaired by these divergences.

45 This point is raised by Dickens and Blackburn, "Holding Gains on Fixed Assets," 318.

expected to generate annual cash inflows of $110. Given an economy-wide normal rate of return of 5 percent, the equilibrium value of the asset would be:

Year	Net Inflow	Discount Factor (at 5%)	Present Value
19x0	$110	0.9524	$104.76
19x1	$110	0.9070	99.77
19x2	$110	0.8638	95.02
		Equilibrium Market Price	$299.55

The actual market price of the asset, given the temporary disequilibrium, is $250.

If first-year expectations are realized, economic income for 19x0 is:

Original Firm
Economic Income
For the Year Ended December 31, 19x0

Distributable Operating Flow:	
rV_i (0.05 × $299.55)	$14.98
Unexpected Income:	
From changes in expected future flows	0.00
On acquisition	49.55
Total Economic Income	$64.53

Notice that there is now a divergence between the price of the asset ($250) and its value to the firm ($299.55). Economic income treats this divergence as income in the period of acquisition. Conventional replacement cost computations take no cognizance of such divergences. To do so would necessitate recognition of acquisition income in the accounts. This would inject subjective values into the computational processes and would in essence be an abandonment of the market price basis for asset valuation. Since our objective is to illustrate divergence between conventional replacement cost income and economic income, we choose to use conventional computation procedures to determine replacement cost income. Accordingly, acquisition income will not be recognized. Thus, the standard computation for replacement cost income for 19x0 would be $26.67, as shown at the top of p. 112.

Since the inordinately high economic rents in this industry have persisted, new entrants are attracted during 19x1. It becomes apparent that, as a consequence of their entry, net cash flows generated each year by the gamma-producing equipment will fall to $95 starting in 19x2. (For simplicity, we assume that 19x1 flows are unaffected and that this change in expectations is perceived instantaneously on January 1, 19x1.)

Original Firm
Replacement Cost Income
For the Year Ended December 31, 19x0

Current Operating Profit:	
Net cash inflow	$110.00
Depreciation:	
$250 cost of asset ÷ 3-year life	83.33
Current operating profit	$ 26.67
Realizable Cost Savings	0.00
Total Replacement Cost Income	$ 26.67

If it is assumed that the market reestablishes an equilibrium price for gamma-producing equipment, the price of the 1-year-old asset of the type owned by the Original Firm will become $190.93. The computation is:

Year	Net Inflow	Discount Factor (at 5%)	Present Value
19x1	$110	0.9524	$104.76
19x2	95	0.9070	86.17
Equilibrium Market Price			$190.93

Replacement cost income for the Original Firm for 19x1 and 19x2 would be computed as follows:

Original Firm
Replacement Cost Income
For the Year Ended December 31, 19x1

Current Operating Profit:			
Net cash inflow			$110.00
Depreciation:			
$190.93 market value of asset ÷			
2-year remaining life			95.46
Current Operating Profit			$ 14.54
Realizable Cost Savings:			
Book Value of asset at 12/31/x0:			
Original cost	$250.00		
19x0 depreciation	83.33		
		$166.67	
Market value at 1/1/x1		190.93	
Realizable Cost Savings			24.26
Total Replacement Cost Income			$ 38.80

Original Firm
Replacement Cost Income
For the Year Ended December 31, 19x2

Current Operating Profit	
Net cash inflow	$95.00
Depreciation	95.47
	(0.47)
Realizable Cost Savings	0.00
Total Replacement Cost Loss	$ (0.47)

Economic income for 19x1 and 19x2 would be:

Original Firm
Economic Income
For the Year Ended December 31, 19x1

Distributable Operating Flow:	
rV_i (0.05 × $190.93)	$ 9.55
Unexpected income:	
Decline in expected 19x2 cash inflows	
($15 × 0.9070)	(13.60)
Total Economic Income	$ (4.05)

Original Firm
Economic Income
For the Year Ended December 31, 19x2

Distributable Operating Flow:	
rV_i (0.05 × $90.48)	$ 4.53
Unexpected Income	0.00
Total Economic Income	$ 4.53

Table 4–1 summarizes reported profit on each basis over the 3-year period.

TABLE 4–1

Summary of Reported Profit

Measurement Basis	19x0	19x1	19x2	Total
Replacement Cost Income	$26.67	$38.80	$(0.47)	$65.00
Economic Income	64.53	(4.05)	4.53	65.00

The comparative results for 19x1 are especially interesting. Reported replacement cost income is not only positive for this period, but has actually increased by almost 50 percent when compared to 19x0 replacement cost income. Examination of the replacement cost income statement for 19x1 indicates that this increase is attributable to the holding gain that was reported during 19x1. Since the expected future operating flows of the Original Firm actually decreased during 19x1, the price change that gave rise to the holding gain is of Type C; that is, the market price of the asset rose while its operating flow potential to the firm actually fell. By incorporating such Type C holding gains, replacement cost income could present a misleading picture of enterprise potential. That is, replacement cost income—the reputed lead indicator of future operating flows—could *increase* during the very period that the operating flow potential of the firm has *decreased*.

It is not difficult to develop other examples of Type B or Type C price movements. The conditions that give rise to these types of price changes (e.g., demand shifts in other industries, shifts in relative input prices, and technological changes) [46] appear to be representative of reasonable, real-world phenomena. If Type B and Type C price changes are numerous, it is possible that total replacement cost income may sometimes be a misleading indicator of changes in expected future operating flows.

In summary, we have seen that, theoretically, replacement cost income may indeed be a lead indicator for future operating flows. But we have also seen that this lead-indicator notion requires covariance between changes in asset prices and changes in operating flow potential. When such covariance exists, the price change is of Type A. However, to the extent that Type B and C price changes predominate in a given situation, replacement cost income could conceivably give a misleading indication of future operating flow potential. Thus, in order to determine whether replacement cost income is an effective lead indicator, we need to determine empirically the extent and frequency of Type B and Type C price changes.

Consequences of an invalid lead-indicator relationship

One rationalization for the dissemination of replacement cost reports to investors relies on the validity of the lead-indicator argument. Investors are not primarily interested in the historical financial data provided to them in published financial statements, this argument goes. No

---

[46] For a development of such examples, see Revsine, "Replacement Cost Reports," pp. 76–93.

rational investor purchases stock in a company because of its past profit performance; rather, it is the prospect of future profitability that induces investment.[47] Given this investor emphasis on the potentialities confronting the firm, lead-indicator proponents have advocated the relevance of a replacement cost report to investors. They contend that since replacement cost income is supposedly a surrogate for economic income, and since economic income incorporates the very potentialities of concern to investors, it follows that replacement cost reports should provide an indirect means for communicating potentialities to the market. This is the foundation for considering replacement cost to be a lead indicator for expected future operating flows.

However, a replacement cost report that contains Type B and/or Type C price changes could result in an investor making seriously misleading inferences regarding a company's prospects. This result is particularly likely if alternative information regarding future events is not superior to accounting data and readers are forced to base forecasts on some variant of reported income. For example, if future dividend flows are indeed of paramount importance to the investor, then the income concept reported to investors ideally should vary in the same direction and by the same magnitude that discounted operating flow expectations vary. Thus, reported income should increase whenever the operating flow potential of the firm increases and should decrease whenever the operating flow potential decreases.[48] However, replacement cost income might not achieve this result whenever a Type B or Type C asset price change occurs. For example, in a Type C price change situation, replacement cost income theory necessitates the recognition of a realizable cost saving in response to a rise in asset price. This realizable cost saving will be recognized in the year of the price rise despite the fact that future flows accruing to the firm already owning an asset whose price has risen are expected to fall. Such a firm is clearly in a deteriorated long-run operating flow position relative to its position before the price rise. Yet it must show "income" as a consequence of the price change. Clearly, following the lead-indicator notion, the term "income" should be reserved for those instances in which an augmentation of operating flow potential has occurred. This is not necessarily the case using the replacement cost income framework, however.

[47] See, for example, Sprouse, "The Measurement of Financial Position and Income," 106; Staubus, *Accounting to Investors*, p. 50; *A Statement of Basic Accounting Theory*, p. 23; and Vatter, *The Fund Theory of Accounting*, p. 72.

[48] Cf. Committee on Accounting Procedure, *Accounting Research and Terminology Bulletins* (final ed.) (New York: American Institute of Certified Public Accountants, 1961), pp. 87–88; and Harold Bierman, Jr., and Sidney Davidson, "The Income Concept —Value Increment or Earnings Predictor," *The Accounting Review*, 44 (April, 1969), 241.

The importance of this possible divergence is this: if replacement cost income always equals economic income, then the owners' equity on a replacement cost basis would exactly equal the net present value of the firm in perfect competition. This net present value could be used in conjunction with the prevailing normal rate of return on assets in order to estimate future distributable operating flows (see equation 2, p. 97). However, if replacement cost income diverges from economic income, then the replacement cost owners' equity figure will similarly diverge from the net present value of the firm. Thus, users' estimates of future distributable operating flows would be adversely affected.

As noted earlier, in imperfect competition replacement cost income merely approximates economic income. Thus, the relationship is not precise, as it can be in perfect competition. As a result, replacement cost owners' equity could also differ from the net present value of the firm in imperfect competition because of the existence of goodwill, i.e., the ability to earn extraordinary returns. But as we will see in Chapter 7, goodwill is more easily measured in a replacement cost system since replacement costing facilitates valid interfirm comparisons. (That is, replacement costing obviates the need for certain arbitrary allocations and reduces the distortion caused by differences in the timing of asset purchases.) Thus, extraordinary returns would be reflected in r_a, the firm's replacement cost operating return. By observing the amount of the extraordinary return, a user has a basis for estimating the magnitude of goodwill. This goodwill figure, when added to the replacement cost equity value, should approximate the present value of the firm. This present value estimate could then be used, in conjunction with the prevailing normal rate of return for a given risk level, to generate an estimate of future distributable operating flow. In this manner, the lead-indicator method could be employed in imperfectly competitive environments, despite the possible existence of goodwill.

However, this goodwill estimate presumes that the extraordinary returns will persist in future periods, i.e., that r_a will be somewhat stable. In order for r_a to be stable, Chapter 6 suggests that there must be covariance between changes in asset prices and individual firms' operating flows. This reinforces our observation that distributable operating flow forecasts in a replacement cost system will theoretically be accurate only if Type A changes predominate. And this need for covariance exists in both competitive and imperfectly competitive environments.

SUMMARY

Little research attention has been given in the accounting literature to the lead-indicator method of indirect prediction. Since the rationale for attributing predictive ability to *total* replacement cost income relies on the lead-indicator method, an analysis of this approach was presented in this chapter. The theoretical basis for lead-indicator assertions was developed first. It was shown that under certain rather rigid conditions replacement cost income and economic income are identical. Furthermore, initial *a priori* analysis suggested that replacement cost income might also approximate the results of economic income measurements under more realistic circumstances. Since economic measurements explicitly incorporate operating flow potential, the ability of replacement cost income to approximate economic income would explain its predictive significance to investors.

While our analysis emphasized income relationships, this was done only for ease of exposition. The potential lead-indicator advantage of replacement cost income can also be explained from a balance sheet perspective. That is, if replacement cost income is in fact a surrogate for economic income, then balance sheets prepared under each concept would also be similar. An investor—knowing the equity value on a replacement cost balance sheet—could then treat this value as an approximation of the net present value of the firm. Multiplying this figure by the appropriate normal market rate of return on assets would thus provide an estimate of future distributable operating flows.

However, closer examination of the realizable cost savings component of total replacement cost income introduces the possibility of divergence between asset price changes and the direction of change in operating flow potential. This possible divergence suggests that changes in replacement cost income could be moving in a direction *opposite* to changes in operating potential. The occurrence of such price movements could destroy the indirect relationship between replacement cost income and economic income. This would suggest that replacement cost income might not be a dependable lead indicator for operating flow potential. Unfortunately, our analysis could not be extended beyond the stage of *a priori* reasoning. Empirical evidence in this area is absent.

Thus, in summary, this chapter explored one aspect of the reputed predictive ability of replacement cost income. No conclusions are yet possible because of the paucity of evidence in the prediction area. Nevertheless, it is hoped that by isolating and analyzing issues, this chapter has contributed to a better understanding of the theoretical problems involved. A corollary benefit exists to the extent that our review highlights areas in which further empirical research is needed.

CHAPTER FIVE

Information for Predictions— The Extrapolation Method

Information for predictions is intended to provide the decision maker with a basis for generating his own predictions of future events. The normative investor decision model developed in Chapter 2 requires information about future dividend payments. We suggested that the best starting point for developing this information is to estimate future distributable operating flows because future distributable operating flows are generally the prime determinant of future dividend paying ability for most firms. Furthermore, operating flows are often sufficiently stable so that reasonable forecasts are possible. Accordingly, in this chapter we analyze the ability of replacement costing to provide information for predicting future distributable operating flows.

We have already identified two methods by which replacement costing might generate information for predictions: (1) the extrapolation method, and (2) the lead-indicator method. In this chapter we will explore the utility of replacement cost data as a basis for generating *extrapolations* of future operating flows. Chapter 4 examined the ability of replacement costing to serve as a *lead indicator* of future operating flows.

Together, Chapters 4 and 5 provide a detailed analysis of the theoretical relevance of replacement cost information for predictions.[1]

CURRENT OPERATING PROFIT AS A PREDICTOR—
A PRIORI CONSIDERATIONS

One of the reputed predictive advantages of replacement cost data relates to the current operating profit component. Some authors have contended that this current operating profit component of total replacement cost income can provide a basis for predicting future flows.

The contention that current operating profit can be extrapolated in order to generate useful predictions originates with Edwards and Bell. They state:

> The significance of current operating profit may extend to periods other than the current period if certain assumptions are valid. Current operating profit can be used for predictive purposes if the existing production process and the existing conditions under which that process is carried out are expected to continue into the future; current operating profit then indicates the amount that the firm can expect to make in each period over the long run.[2]

If Edwards and Bell's qualifying assumption—stability of all production conditions—is temporarily accepted, the rationale for this predictive ability contention is apparent. The dollar magnitude of current operating profit represents the profit contribution at the current level of input and output prices. If the production process, technology, volume, and prices

---

[1] The normative issue of who should generate these predictions depends on which view of market behavior is accepted. If one adopts the traditional view, then individual investors would generate their own predictions based on a careful analysis of accounting reports. Their objective is to maximize expected returns at a given risk level. Alternatively, if one adopts the efficient markets approach, such individual efforts to earn extraordinary returns using publicly available data are deemed to be fruitless because all publicly available data is presumed to be instantaneously impounded in security prices. Following the efficient markets approach, information for prediction is instead needed to allow the market to continuously determine appropriate security prices. Accounting information would provide one basis for instantaneously incorporating available evidence regarding future operating flows—the prime determinant of security worth. The greater the accuracy of the predictive basis provided by accounting information, the less the need for subsequent price adjustments because of predictive errors. Minimizing predictive errors would thus tend to promote more efficient capital resource allocation. Following this efficient markets approach, the rationale for examining the predictive ability of replacement costing is to assess the utility of this data *for the market as a whole*. But irrespective of which approach we adopt (i.e., the traditional approach or efficient markets approach), the ability to predict future operating flows is of crucial importance.

[2] Edwards and Bell, *Measurement of Business Income*, p. 99.

are stable, succeeding years' current operating profits will equal those of the current period. Obviously, these stability assumptions are rather unrealistic and are likely to occur only infrequently. Notice, however, that even if one makes these same stability assumptions, no similar predictive ability can be attributed to historical cost operating profit. That is, extrapolating the current period's historical cost margin, even under *ceteris paribus* conditions, will often be an unreliable indicator of succeeding periods' "real" operating margins.[3] This will be true if input prices have changed while old costs constitute a significant portion of currently reported expenses. Replacement costing advocates would contend that the inability of historical cost operating profit to generate reliable estimates of future flows even under the most favorable condition of stable prices disqualifies the concept as a useful basis for predictions. In contrast, current operating profit at least has the potential for generating reasonable estimates under certain, albeit unrealistic, circumstances.

The more pressing issue, however, is whether current operating profit has the theoretical potential to generate reasonable forecasts in a more realistic economic environment. In analyzing this issue, empirical evidence is needed. A limited amount of empirical evidence is actually available in this area. But before we examine this evidence, some nonempirical observations will be made regarding the predictive ability of current operating profit.

On an intuitive level, it would appear that whenever there is a fairly stable upward trend of input prices beyond the present period, current operating profit would tend to outpredict historical operating profit. Both would tend to overstate future operating flows in this situation, but historical cost measures would be farther from the actual figure—especially when the FIFO inventory flow assumption is used. Furthermore, the slower the inventory turnover, the greater the relative predictive advantage of current operating profit.

When price trends are downward, the use of the lower of cost or market inventory figure would tend to equalize the two methods. Even in this situation, however, if fixed asset prices are also declining, the current operating profit estimate would tend to be superior since generally accepted accounting principles often do not require adjustments to the depreciable base of fixed assets. While current operating profit would thus appear to have a *relative* theoretical advantage over historical operating margin, it is unclear whether this measure can generate reasonably accurate forecasts of expected operating flows in an absolute sense.

---

[3] In Chapter 3, we defined "real profits" to mean profits after adjusting for specific price changes. Such profits represent that amount that can be withdrawn from a business without contracting its level of operating activity.

To illustrate a potential deficiency of current operating profit forecasts in an absolute sense, consider a situation in which there is a cyclical or otherwise fluctuating operating flow pattern. In such situations, no *single year's* operating margin figure—irrespective of how it is measured—can forecast such a fluctuating stream. Forecasts based on existing levels of operating profit are, in essence, simple trend analyses. One of the primary deficiencies of trend analyses is that such extrapolations can never anticipate turning points. Such changes can be incorporated into later forecasts only after they occur. Furthermore, whenever there is a lag between the period of asset purchase and the periods in which an asset generates increased flows, the early period operating profits do not necessarily provide an appropriate basis for estimating future operating flows.

A POTENTIAL INCONSISTENCY

We should point out that the reputed ability of current operating profit to predict *future* distributable operating flows is potentially inconsistent with the lead-indicator approach discussed in Chapter 4. In Chapter 4 we showed that the most defensible explanation for treating cost savings as income was based on an assumed covariance between asset price changes and expected changes in assets' operating flows. If the expected operating flow changes do occur, then future distributable operating flows may be different from current distributable operating flows. But notice that simple extrapolations of current operating profit take no cognizance of such expectations. Thus, using only current operating profit as a basis for extrapolating future distributable operating flows seemingly ignores the potentially relevant cost savings data.

However, this inconsistency can be explained. We will see that the extrapolation approach implicitly assumes that Type A changes predominate. That is, to support the predictive ability of current operating profit, as an asset's price changes, a similar change must occur in its ability to generate operating flows. Furthermore, operating flows must adjust so quickly that the Type A change is totally reflected in the current period's current operating profit. This covariance between prices and flows would change expenses and revenues similarly (leaving current operating profit approximately the same) and thus seemingly provide a valid extrapolation base.[4]

4 An alternative rationalization for the apparent inconsistency exists. In this view, proponents of the extrapolation approach would implicitly contend that all three types of price changes occur (that is, Types A, B, and C) and that no one type predominates. For a firm with many assets, these price changes would cancel out; on the average, cost savings would not reflect changes in operating flow potential. Accordingly, cost savings could be ignored in generating estimates of future distributable operating flows.

On the basis of this discussion, it should be apparent that the lead-indicator and extrapolation approaches are somewhat interdependent. Nevertheless, subtle differences between the two methods exist. Both have been advanced in support of replacement costing and each has its separate advocates. While we have pointed out the interdependence between the two approaches, we will, for expository ease, treat the lead-indicator approach and the extrapolation approach as two independent hypotheses in the remainder of the study.

CURRENT OPERATING PROFIT AS A PREDICTOR— EMPIRICAL EVIDENCE

It is possible to approach the issue of predictive ability of current operating profit on a conceptual level, as we did above. However, predictive ability is essentially an empirical question and can be resolved only by examining actual evidence. Several empirical studies regarding the predictive ability of current operating profit have appeared in the accounting literature. Unfortunately, none have investigated the ability of current operating profit to predict distributable operating flows. Instead, the researchers selected income and cash flow as the objects of prediction. Thus, these studies do not provide direct evidence about the relevance of current operating profit predictions for the normative investor model introduced in Chapter 2. Nevertheless, we must review these studies for two reasons. First, they are relevant to the general issue of current operating profit predictions. Second, these studies introduce issues that must be considered in the design of subsequent, relevant predictive ability tests.

Operating profit as a predictor of income [5]

Although predictive ability claims were often advanced in support of replacement costing, the appropriate *object of prediction* was never clearly specified. Recently, two studies appeared that tested the relative ability of current operating profit to predict future *income*.[6] These studies selected future income as the object of prediction because some earlier

---

[5] Much of the material in this section is adapted from Lawrence Revsine, "Predictive Ability, Market Prices, and Operating Flows," *The Accounting Review,* 46 (July, 1971), 480–89. It is reproduced with permission of the Editor of *The Accounting Review.*

[6] Frank, "Predictive Significance of Two Income Measures," 123–36; and John K. Simmons and Jack Gray, "An Investigation of the Effect of Differing Accounting Frameworks on the Prediction of Net Income," *The Accounting Review,* 44 (October, 1969), 757–76.

studies suggested that the superiority of current operating profit rested on the ability of this concept to predict future income. For example:

> Income from ordinary operations . . . facilitates prediction of future income from ordinary operations, assuming that costs other than depreciation are also stated in current terms.[7]

Also:

> Since income from operations and holding gains or losses result from different causes, they can be expected to have different patterns of recurrence. Effective prediction of future income is facilitated by reporting them separately.[8]

However, the theoretical basis that explains why *income* forecasts are useful is unspecified. Income is an artifact. One can nominally define income by mere resolution and the resultant definition has no necessary external validity.[9] This does not automatically mean that predictions of income are useless. What it does mean is that because income is an artifact, one must explain *why* income predictions are useful. That is, some transformation must be developed between future artifact values and users' decision models. Since those who explored the ability of replacement costing to predict future income did not specify this transformation, the logic that supports *income* predictions merits closer scrutiny. Accordingly, we will now analyze the apparent reasons for desiring to predict future income in order to determine whether the results of these income prediction studies are relevant to our inquiry.

REVIEW OF PRIOR INCOME PREDICTION STUDIES

Frank, in the first of two recent studies in the income prediction area, used actual firm data as the basis for testing the predictive ability of current operating profit.[10] Two types of tests were performed. In one, Frank determined the error magnitude that resulted from using one year's current operating profit to predict succeeding years' current operating profit. This error rate was then compared with that which resulted from using one year's historical operating income as a basis for predict-

---

[7] Committee on Concepts and Standards—Long-Lived Assets, "Accounting for Land, Buildings, and Equipment," *The Accounting Review*, 39 (July, 1964), 696.

[8] 1964 Concepts and Standards Research Study Committee—The Realization Concept, "The Realization Concept," *The Accounting Review*, 40 (April, 1965), 320.

[9] For a discussion of nominal, denotative, and real definitions see Cohen and Nagel, *Logic and Scientific Method*, pp. 227–31.

[10] Frank, "Predictive Significance of Two Income Measures."

ing succeeding years' historical operating income.[11] The income concept that best predicted *its own* future values was deemed to be the better predictor. Frank rationalized this test in the following manner:

> If the predictability of an income concept is of primary concern, the errors which result from attempting to forecast future values of income from past values of that same income series would be of interest.[12]

Frank found that for his sample data, the error rate for current operating profit forecasts exceeded those of historical operating income forecasts.

In his second test Frank chose historical operating income as the object of prediction. He compared the results of current operating profit forecasts and historical operating income forecasts to determine which of the two concepts generated the better predictions of later years' historical operating income. His justification for this second test was that

> . . . another approach [beyond that of the first test] is needed if current-cost income is to be regarded only as possible supplementary information, included to enhance the accuracy of predictions of the primary accounting income figure. The relative accuracy of forecasts of accounting income based on past values of accounting income should then be compared with forecasts of those same values but based on past values of current-cost income.[13]

The results of this test again indicated that current operating profit forecasts were generally not superior to those of historical operating income. That is, Frank found that historical operating income—not current operating profit—tended to yield the most accurate forecasts of succeeding years' historical operating income.

A second study, by Simmons and Gray (hereafter, S & G), also examined the predictive ability of various income measures.[14] Once again, the predictive ability criterion related to the efficiency of the various concepts in predicting future income levels, this time in a simulated environment. The S & G simulation indicated that, in general, total historical cost income and/or total price adjusted cost yielded better linear projections of their own future values than did current operating profit for its future values.

On the basis of the foregoing studies, one might conclude that the

---

[11] Frank defines historical operating income as ". . . net sales less cost of sales, selling, general and administrative, and other normal operating expenses" (p. 126).

[12] *Ibid.*, 131.

[13] *Ibid.*, 125.

[14] Simmons and Gray, "Differing Accounting Frameworks."

reputed predictive ability of current operating profit has been severely challenged. However, such an inference would be premature. Both studies accepted future income as the variable to be predicted on the basis of very casual references in the literature. Since the selected object of prediction is crucial to the evaluation of predictive ability, it would seem that closer scrutiny of the theoretical foundation underlying income predictions is warranted before available evidence can be evaluated.

WHY FORECAST AN ARTIFACT?

Most of the *a priori* observations in the literature suggest rather ambiguously and without elaboration that knowledge of current operating profit facilitates estimates of future income.[15] This imprecision generates two questions. First, since there are many conceivable methods for measuring income, it is not clear which definition is being used by proponents of the predictive ability notion. Second, since income in any case is an artificial construct, one must explain why income predictions are useful. That is, the transformation between future income and users' decisions must be specified. The subsequent discussion will concentrate on this second point—the theoretical justification for income predictions. Once this intended purpose for income estimation is identified, the issue of which (if any) income concept ought to be predicted will become clearer.

Income as a surrogate. The claim that income prediction is useful implicitly rests on one of several possible presumptions. Probably the most pervasive is the belief that income is a surrogate for some class of events of interest to users. In the simplest form of this rationale, future income would itself be a proxy for whatever future events are deemed important. One could test the validity of such claims by examining the covariance between predicted future income values and the events which these values supposedly approximate.[16]

In this section, we will illustrate this surrogation rationale for predicting income. To do this, agreement regarding which particular events

15 See, for example, sources cited in footnotes 7 and 8, *supra*. Edwards and Bell are even more vague (p. 99):

> Current operating profit can be used for predictive purposes if the existing production process and the existing conditions under which that process is carried out are expected to continue into the future; current operating profit then indicates the amount [of what?] that the firm can expect to make in each period over the long run.

16 In the less testable form, income prediction is considered relevant because users are presumed to know the transformation between earnings and whatever object is relevant to their model. Without knowledge of the object, the transformation, and its stability, this second form is untestable. Accordingly, it is difficult to use this rationale to support income prediction.

are presumably of ultimate concern to users is not necessary. What is important is an understanding that income prediction is relevant not for its own sake but rather because of the correspondence between future income and some other events that constitute the real object of prediction. In accordance with the normative investor model developed in Chapter 2, we will use distributable operating flow as the object of prediction. But it must be emphasized that the resultant analysis, although phrased in terms of distributable operating flows, is general in nature and would apply equally well to some alternative object of prediction.

Once the object of prediction is selected, a rationale for income predictions immediately follows. In this case, one would predict income because future income is thought to be a surrogate for future distributable operating flows.[17] Since distributable operating flows are a prime determinant of future dividends, such forecasts would be useful to investors. It is then apparent that income projections are not themselves of primary interest to the user; rather, it is the relationship between projected income and future distributable operating flows that is important.

Indeed, one can suggest that this relationship between current operating profit and distributable operating flow was also implicit to the predictive ability assertions of replacement costing proponents. *These*

---

[17] Operating flows represent the amount of cash and other liquid resources generated by operating activities. Distributable operating flow is used in the Hicksian sense as that amount of resources that can be distributed to owners without constricting the level of future physical operations. In Chapter 4 (footnote 28) distributable operating flow was defined as the product of (1) the company's prevailing rate of return, and (2) the initial discounted asset value.

To illustrate the computation of distributable operating flows, consider the following situation. A company pays $299.55 for a fixed asset that has a 3-year life and no salvage value. The asset is expected to generate net inflows of $110 in each of the three years. (The expected internal rate of return and reinvestment return is 5 percent.) The book value shown for each year is the sum of the then current present value of the asset's flows and the accumulated value (at 5 percent) of the undistributed operating flows.

	Year			
	1	*2*	*3*	*Total*
Book value of asset plus undistributed cash flows	$299.55	$299.55	$299.55	
Operating inflow	$110.00	$110.00	$110.00	$330.00
Return on previous periods' undistributed cash flows	0.00	4.75	9.74	14.49
Economic depreciation	(95.02)	(99.77)	(104.76)	(299.55)
Distributable operating flow (5% of book value)	$ 14.98	$ 14.98	$ 14.98	$ 44.94

If distributable operating flows are paid as a dividend in each period, the firm will retain precisely the amount of funds needed to replace the asset at the end of year 3.

Other authors have called this *ex ante* computation, the "expected economic income" of the period. See, for example, Bedford, *Income Determination Theory*, pp. 25–27.

proponents were really suggesting that future current operating profit is the theoretically correct object for prediction since this measure constitutes the best possible estimate of future distributable operating flows.

The reasoning that supports this amended predictive ability assertion relies on two distinct, and testable, sub-assertions:

1. In the absence of contrary evidence, the actual current operating profit figure for any given year constitutes the best estimate of the current operating profit that will be realized in the succeeding year.
2. The estimate of the succeeding year's current operating profit is the best *ex ante* measure of the succeeding year's distributable operating flow.

Let us briefly explore the logic that supports these two sub-assertions.

1. Estimating the succeeding year's current operating profit. In an environment in which relative prices, risk, and technological processes are constantly changing, one can seldom make very accurate estimates of future current operating profits. Furthermore, when changes in operating variables have no discernible pattern, detailed trend analyses are of limited benefit. For lack of a better method in such situations, a reasonable basis for estimating future flows is to extrapolate the most recent period's results under the assumption that no further changes will occur. If, indeed, no further price changes occur (and if volume is constant), then the following period's current operating profit will be equal to the present period's current operating profit.[18] Furthermore, even with the existence

---

[18] In Chapter 6 we will see that this assertion must be amended slightly.

As we suggested earlier in this chapter, when the historical cost operating margin includes old prices that have since changed, the current period's historical cost margin will not necessarily be a good predictor of the following period's "real" operating margin.

On the other hand, by ignoring all price fluctuations unless validated by a firm's transactions, historical cost systems may have an advantage under certain conditions when price changes are largely the result of technological advances. This is particularly true when a company continues to utilize what has suddenly become a technologically more primitive asset. If no active market exists for the primitive asset, its carrying value in a replacement cost system must be derived from index number adjustments. Such indices usually cannot isolate the price impact attributable to technological change; i.e., the associated revenue increases or cost decreases. Thus, the recognized holding gain will include the price impact of technological change even though the primitive asset has obviously not experienced a technological gain. Rather than a holding gain, one could contend that the owner of the primitive asset might better reflect the loss occasioned by the partial obsolescence of the existing asset. (See, for example, David Green, Jr., and George H. Sorter, "Accounting for Obsolescence—A Proposal," *The Accounting Review*, 34 (July, 1959), 433–41.)

This problem, although potentially important, is not insurmountable. Recent efforts at developing indices that isolate the price effect of technological change have met with some success (e.g., John C. Musgrave, "The Measurement of Price Changes in Construction," *Journal of the American Statistical Association*, 64 (September, 1969), 771–86.) Furthermore, in some cases a market for the older type assets may also exist. Specific appraisals can also be used to separate the price effect from the influence of technological change.

of future price changes, the superiority of current operating profit forecasts can still be argued to hold. That is, unless there is strong evidence to suggest a shift in the direction of price and output levels, it can be contended that the best estimate of the following period's current operating profit will usually be generated by simple extrapolations of the present period's current operating profit.

2. Future current operating profit as a measure of future distributable operating flows. The assertion that forecasts of future current operating profit constitute a reasonable approximation of future distributable operating flows rests on some rather involved relationships that were explored in the last chapter. Briefly, to effect this correspondence, some connection between asset prices and the present value of an asset's cash flows is required. It can be shown that in a perfectly competitive economy in which all firms have similar expectations, asset prices and values are identical and the correspondence between current operating profit and distributable operating flow is exact. In more realistic environments, a reasonable extension suggests that current operating profit will approximate distributable operating flow. For this relationship to hold, asset values to an individual firm must continuously approximate the prices of these assets. This again requires the existence of covariance at the individual firm level. That is, movements in asset prices must correspond to movements in asset values. (Some implications of this relationship will be explored further in Chapter 6.)

Figure 5-1 summarizes the reasoning that supports operating profit forecasts. If the argument outlined above is correct, then current operating profit of one year provides the best basis for predicting current

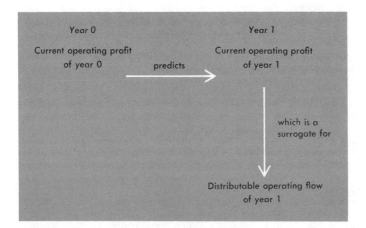

FIGURE 5–1

operating profit of the following year,[19] which in turn is a surrogate for that year's distributable operating flow. Thus, forecasts of current operating profit would provide a means for estimating future distributable operating flows—a primary determinant of future dividend flows.

Income and the efficient markets hypothesis. There is another justification for the relevance of earnings predictions that has only recently been advanced in the accounting literature. This explanation relies on the findings of a large body of empirical evidence that supports what is popularly described as the "efficient markets model." This research suggests that the capital markets apparently behave in an "efficient" fashion.[20] More specifically, these studies indicate that securities' prices fully reflect publicly available information, including, of course, reported earnings,[21] and that such prices react quickly and in an unbiased fashion to new information.

If securities' prices are indeed influenced by accounting earnings, then a seemingly powerful and rational motive for predicting future income is introduced. By predicting future earnings, the market is better able to predict future stock prices since these prices will be a function of whatever future earnings materialize. Despite the fact, then, that earnings are a nominally defined artifact, since the market apparently takes cognizance of measures of this artifact, a better prediction basis would enhance market price determination.

THE OBJECT OF PREDICTION

Both Frank and S & G attempted to test prior claims regarding the predictive ability of current operating profit. Since the theoretical basis for these claims had never been developed in the literature, both studies were forced to interpret predictive ability assertions literally. As a consequence, their experiments treated income prediction as relevant *per se.*

19 The results of one recent simulation study support this *a priori* contention regarding the superiority of future operating flow estimates based on current operating profit measures. See Melvin N. Greenball, "Evaluation of the Usefulness to Investors of Different Accounting Estimators of Earnings: A Simulation Approach," *Empirical Research in Accounting: Selected Studies,* 1968, Supplement to Volume 6, *Journal of Accounting Research,* 27–49, and the discussion comments on this paper by Andrew C. Stedry, *ibid.,* 58.

20 See Fama, "Efficient Capital Markets," 383–417.

21 Tests of the efficient markets model with regard to accounting information can be found in Ray Ball and Philip Brown, "An Empirical Evaluation of Accounting Income Numbers," *Journal of Accounting Research,* 6 (Autumn, 1968), 159–68; and William H. Beaver, "The Information Content of Annual Earnings Announcements," *Empirical Research in Accounting: Selected Studies,* 1968, Supplement to Volume 6, *Journal of Accounting Research,* 67–92.

In contrast, our analysis suggests that income is a valid object for prediction only under two possible circumstances (1) that the particular income concept to be predicted is a good reflection of some other object that is of ultimate concern to users (the "ultimate object" justification), or (2) that market prices of securities react to whatever concept is selected as a reporting basis (the "efficient markets" justification). But, we will now show that these two justifications are interdependent and, indeed, the second eventually reduces to the first.

To illustrate, we must briefly reconsider the efficient markets hypothesis. This hypothesis does not suggest that the market's reaction to financial data is necessarily accurate. On the contrary, the hypothesis states that if the financial events "promised" by current information (to which the market has reacted) fail to materialize, subsequent price corrections will ensue. Thus, in the longer run, insofar as share prices are affected by internal events, it is these events and not reported income that determine investment worth.

It follows that if the income concept included in external reports is not a reasonable precursor of distributable operating flow (or whatever other object of prediction is selected), eventually an efficient market will "discount" similar information in later periods. That is, if the market is frequently misled by a deficiency in the income model employed, then eventually the market will compensate for such inaccurate data and alter its short-term response to reported accounting information. To contend otherwise is to deny the possibility of learning on the part of persons in the market.[22]

---

[22] This learning phenomenon has implications for the future relevance of external accounting information. Empirical studies indicate that in the recent past, accounting data have been an important element in the market's decision-making processes (see references in footnote 21, *supra*). This indicates that, at a minimum, accounting data have been perceived to be relevant to security worth. However, all the empirical work regarding the reaction of an efficient market to accounting information has used pre-1966 data. The fact that accounting reports have been perceived to be relevant in the past is no guarantee that they will continue to be so perceived in the future. Recently, the accountant's income determination process has been the subject of many critical and (to some non-accountants) highly illuminating articles in the financial literature. To the extent that these articles have alerted investors to certain deficiencies of the traditional model as a forecast basis and to the manipulative potential occasioned by alternative accounting principles, one could assume that the market would react more warily to future accounting data. (It would be interesting to replicate some of the recent studies in the area using data for periods in which various accounting lawsuits and the purchase-pooling controversy received attention in the financial press. The purpose, of course, would be to observe whether the market's reaction to accountants' reports diminished as a consequence of the information content of the adverse publicity.)

From the perspective of the accounting profession, a decline in the perceived relevance of external accounting measures would have serious repercussions. Since there are many competing sources for financial information in an efficient market, if users perceive deficiencies in traditional measures, then the market is also searching for

Thus, the efficient markets justification for income prediction eventually reduces to the ultimate object justification. More generally, the market can be assumed to react to reported income in the long run only insofar as the income concept used is a good indicator of the ultimate object of prediction. Therefore, the crucial issue in predictive ability is not the relative ability of an income concept to predict itself, but rather the relative ability of a concept to predict whatever object is thought to be of concern to users. Similarly, the ability of an income concept to predict some other income concept is irrelevant unless the other (predicted) income concept is itself related to some ultimate object of prediction.

Assertions regarding the relative predictive ability of current operating profit were probably based on the belief that this concept is a better indicator of some future events, such as distributable operating flows. To test the validity of these assertions, as Frank and S & G attempted to do, the relative ability of the two income concepts in predicting those future events must be determined.[23] Income prediction tests are thus irrelevant unless a transformation is specified between income and some ultimate object of prediction. Since Frank and S & G proposed no such transformation, their findings are not directly relevant for assessing the predictive ability of current operating profit.[24]

CRITERION FOR ASSESSING PREDICTIVE ABILITY

The area of income prediction generates disagreement not only with the object of prediction often selected, but also with the *criterion*

---

alternative information sources. If such alternatives materialize, growth of the accounting profession would be impeded; the primary impetus for external reporting would then be occasioned by legal or quasi-legal requirements and growth would depend on the imposition of *new* legal requirements, rather than from continuing user demand for more information.

[23] In the illustrative situation in which distributable operating flows are assumed to be the appropriate object of prediction, a relevant test of these predictability assertions would require a determination of the relative ability of the two income concepts in predicting future distributable operating flows. Alternatively, if one accepts the theoretical relationship between current operating profit and distributable operating flows (see Chapter 4, pp. 95–99), then a variant of Frank's second experiment would constitute an appropriate test. Here, the relative ability of historical cost operating margin and current operating profit in predicting future current operating profit would be tested. (Remember that in Frank's somewhat similar test, the object of prediction was future historical cost operating margin.) Whichever concept proves to be the better predictor of future current operating profit would automatically be considered the better surrogate for predicting future distributable operating flows.

[24] It should be apparent that these comments are not intended to be critical of either Frank or S & G. They cannot be faulted for testing the apparent rationale for assertions that previously appeared in the literature. Any criticisms must be directed toward proponents of replacement costing who did not develop the theoretical basis on which their assertions rested.

sometimes employed to assess predictive ability. For instance, since some analysts recommend straight-line extrapolation as a prediction basis, S & G tested the ability of several income concepts to generate a straight-line pattern.[25] Although S & G do not necessarily espouse this as a valid criterion for assessing the predictive ability of a given concept,[26] others may. The result is essentially a stability criterion; it suggests that the smoother the pattern of year-to-year income movements for a particular concept, the better the predictions generated by that concept. However, since the income of a firm over its lifetime will be known only on dissolution, but in total will be the same irrespective of the measurement basis used,[27] the process of assigning income to periods is essentially an allocation.[28] The stability criterion suggests that those measurement bases that more equally allocate total income are the most useful. But this criterion seems to lose sight of the inherent nature of the object that is being forecasted. If the object to be forecasted is itself volatile (e.g., operating flows in periods of market adjustment) then a measurement method would be desirable insofar as it is similarly volatile. To illustrate this phenomenon, consider the life cycle of a firm depicted in Figure 5–2.

The horizontal axis of this illustration measures time and the vertical axis represents the distributable operating flow over a given period of time. The solid line W-Z represents the level and pattern of actual, *ex post* operating flows. Obviously, the total configuration of these realized flows cannot be known until t_n, the terminal date of the enterprise. But in order to make a wide range of decisions, an *ex ante* estimate of the operating flow stream must be made initially and revised periodically in an uncertain environment. In Figure 5–2, the dashed line A-C represents one such *ex ante* estimate, this one made at t_0. Visual inspection indicates that *ex post*, total flows were larger than originally anticipated at t_0; furthermore, the pattern of yearly flows departed from expectations. The realized pattern encompassed three distinct stages— one of slow, steady growth in operating inflows, one of more rapid

---

[25] S & G described their test in the following fashion (761):

Since straight-line extrapolation is the prediction method assumed, the income pattern which most closely adheres to a straight-line will have the best predictive value.

[26] *Ibid.*, 758.

[27] Income in this context is defined simply as the difference between the initial and ending capital of the firm adjusted, of course, for additional investment and dividends. For a somewhat different definition and view of lifetime income see Keith Shwayder, "The Capital Maintenance Rule and the Net Asset Valuation Rule," *The Accounting Review*, 44 (April, 1969), 304–16.

[28] For an exhaustive development of this issue, see Arthur L. Thomas, *The Allocation Problem in Financial Accounting Theory*, Studies in Accounting Research No. 3 (Menasha, Wis.: American Accounting Association, 1969).

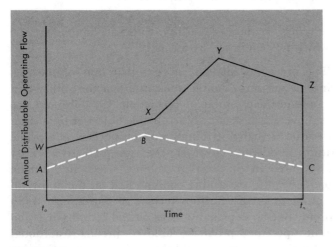

FIGURE 5–2

growth, and finally, one of decline in net flows. The "kinks" in the operating flow pattern, which (perhaps unexpectedly) transport the firm from one stage to another, are what make the selection of a predictive basis (or income measure) so difficult. If the pattern were stable, one would select an income concept that is itself stable as a basis for predicting future operating flows. (In essence, S & G, and perhaps to a lesser extent, Frank, were searching for such stable concepts.) But since the real pattern is subject to certain "jolts," the problem is more difficult. Simple linear extrapolation can never presage turning points. Ideally, one would want to select as a forecasting basis whatever income concept minimizes the deviation between anticipated and realized flows. To accomplish this, the measure must possess at least two attributes. First, *within each stage* it must be sufficiently stable to allow reasonable forecasts of future flows until the termination of that stage. Second, it must provide evidence of movement from one stage to another at the earliest possible moment. If possible, the selected forecast basis should be sufficiently sensitive to incorporate those variables that portend the jolt before they actually exert their influence.[29]

Realistically, it may be expecting too much of an income concept that incorporates past and/or present events [30] to give *forewarning* of change. But this sensitivity to impending changes is the standard against which alternative concepts must be measured. Sensitivity implies—indeed,

[29] Once again, this is the "lead-indicator" reporting concept that was discussed in Chapter 4.

[30] Remember that potential data inputs to an income concept are limited to past and present events; forecast data are generally deemed to be outside the legitimate purview of existing professional practice. (See Chapter 2, pp. 37–40.)

at the appropriate times, requires—volatility. Such a standard is the antithesis of that which was employed by S & G.[31]

Summary. The preceding analysis suggests that tests of the predictive ability of income measures should concentrate on the ability of a concept to reflect some ultimate object of prediction. We advanced distributable operating flow as a theoretically acceptable object of prediction for investors. Our reason is that distributable operating flow is a prime determinant of future dividends. However, the two predictive ability studies that were reviewed in this section did not select an ultimate object of prediction. Instead, these studies concentrated on the ability of current operating profit to predict various income measures, e.g., traditional operating profit. But no explanation was offered for why it is important that current operating profit be able to predict traditional operating profit. That is, these tests established no transformation between the selected income concepts and some ultimate object of prediction. For this reason we conclude that the evidence generated by these studies is not relevant to our inquiry. Such evidence does not indicate whether current operating profit can predict those real events of ultimate interest to investors.

Operating profit
as a predictor of future cash flows

There are currently no studies that test the ability of current operating profit to predict distributable operating flows. However, studies that test the ability of current operating profit to predict other ultimate objects have been performed. The object of prediction in these studies is future cash flows.[32] Two of the most exhaustive studies of this nature were prepared by Greenball. Simulation was used as the methodology in each. In the first study, Greenball developed a firm model that contained several variable parameters.[33] Variable values were randomly generated for each iteration of the simulation and income was computed for each

---

[31] By reacting quickly to many variables, it might be suggested that a volatile reporting measure could precipitate sufficient price instability to lead to a disorderly market. Thus, a more stable measure might be preferred not for its predictive potential but as a practical concession to an orderly market. However, one could reply that a stable measure—by suppressing knowledge of impending changes until actual occurrence—might lead to less frequent, but even more violent, price fluctuation as users are periodically "surprised." Empirical evidence regarding user reaction to various types of messages is needed to resolve the issue.

[32] The traditional cash flow definition is used, that is, accounting earnings plus non-cash expenses, plus (or minus) changes in receivable-payable and inventory balances.

[33] Melvin N. Greenball, "The Accuracy of Different Methods of Accounting for Earnings—A Simulation Approach," *Journal of Accounting Research*, 6 (Spring, 1968), 114–29.

run using several measurement bases. The standard against which each measurement method was compared in order to determine its predictive ability was called the *permanent earnings* of the firm. Basically, this "ideal" was defined as the average net cash flow of the period.[34]

The results of the study indicated that current operating profit computed on both an absorption and direct costing basis performed slightly better with respect to estimating the *current* period's average net cash flow than did historical cost income computed on both bases. However, there was a consistent, slight downward bias using current operating profit.[35] This study did not explicitly attempt to use different accounting methods to estimate future values of permanent earnings. Technically, then, it does not support the proposition that current operating profit is a better predictor of *future* cash flows. Because it is a better estimator of the current period's flows over the long run, one might infer that predictive ability would also be enhanced. But it is unnecessary to infer beyond the limits of this study, since a subsequent study by Greenball addresses the prediction problem more directly.

In this second simulation study,[36] Greenball attempted to determine which accounting earning measure led to the best investor performance. Since investor performance was essentially a function of realized cash inflows over the life of the firm, it would follow that earnings measures that facilitated better performance would have tended to generate better estimates of future cash flows. Greenball found that in his simulated environment, investors using current operating profit significantly outperformed those using historical cost methods.[37] Given the assessment criterion, this result would indicate that current operating profit was a better estimator of *future* cash flows than was historical costing.[38]

In interpreting the results of any simulation, great care must be taken to avoid unwarranted generalizations. One never can be sure whether the observed findings are representative of real-world phenomena or attributable to the unique environment of the simulation itself. This observation is particularly relevant in this instance since the systematic rate of growth in one of Greenball's studies was zero. Whether the ob-

---

[34] *Ibid.*, 115–19.

[35] *Ibid.*, 127. In other words, the absolute value of the divergence between current operating profit and permanent earnings was slightly less than the divergence between historical cost and permanent earnings. But, taking cognizance of the sign of the divergence, current operating profit tended to understate permanent earnings by more than did historical costing.

[36] Greenball, "Usefulness of Different Accounting Estimators," 27–49.

[37] *Ibid.*, 43–47.

[38] It is interesting, however, that the historical cost measure did tend to outperform *total* replacement cost income.

served results would be duplicated in a more realistic environment that incorporated growth is unclear. Furthermore, although simulation affords a means for gathering evidence of a preliminary nature, the results of an experiment using actual data are often more compelling because results observed in a real-world situation, even though they may be identical to those generated in the simulated environment, dispel lingering doubts regarding the realism of the simulated environment. Unfortunately, in the area of current operating profit, the empirical work available is often not directly relevant to the issue currently under examination. Nevertheless, it may prove instructive to review one of these efforts.

Staubus performed an experiment that is tangentially relevant to our inquiry.[39] The purpose of his study was to test the usefulness of accounting for inventories as opposed to immediately charging such outlays to expense. He used the degree of correlation between each alternative (i.e., accounting for inventories versus immediate charge-off) and future cash flows accruing to the investor as the criterion for determining which accounting treatment was superior. Whichever method had the higher r value was deemed to be the better predictor. Staubus' research technique was an interesting one. Rather than attempting to estimate the expected value of an equity share in order to discern the predictive ability of inventory measures, he used actual, observed data on a retrospective basis. His methodology consisted of running a series of regressions between actual, past accounting flows and actual share prices and dividend data for other, more recent past periods. Some of the accounting flows employed inventory accounting, others did not. Those accounting methods that correlated most closely with actually observed equity values over past periods were deemed to be the better predictors.

In this study Staubus did not specifically examine the predictive ability of current operating profit. Indeed, operating profit in general was not tested in the study since depreciation effects were excluded. But, since inventory accounting is one important element of total operating profit, his conclusions are of interest. In one aspect of his study, Staubus attempted to determine whether LIFO or FIFO flow measures correlated more closely with discounted stock values. Although LIFO is not, strictly speaking, a replacement cost method, if inventory turnover is relatively high, the income statement results of LIFO measures would tend to approximate the cost of goods sold component included in the current operating profit calculation. Thus, the outcome of this aspect of Staubus' experiment might be interpreted as evidence regarding the predictive ability of current operating profit. Having made this statement, two

[39] George J. Staubus, "Testing Inventory Accounting," *The Accounting Review,* 43 (July, 1968), 413–24.

crucial caveats must be reiterated. First, LIFO cost of goods sold is not identical to replacement cost of goods sold, although the results of the two methods may converge under certain circumstances. Second, inventory accounting is only one aspect of determining total current operating profit.

In analyzing the results of these LIFO-FIFO correlations, Staubus found a slight tendency in favor of LIFO. That is, LIFO inventory accounting procedures tended to improve the correlation between accounting flows and equity values by a greater amount than did FIFO measures. This result was not observed for every period examined nor was the LIFO superiority very pronounced in certain test runs.[40] On the basis of these somewhat conflicting and inconclusive results, Staubus declined to attribute greater predictive ability to the LIFO measures. Because of the divergence between Staubus' test measures and current operating profit as traditionally defined, the implications of these results cannot necessarily be generalized.

SUMMARY

This is the second of two chapters that explore the nature of replacement cost information for predictions. In this chapter, we examined the ability of current operating profit to provide a basis for extrapolations.

A priori arguments suggest that current operating profit has the *theoretical* potential to improve estimates of future distributable operating flows. The reasoning is that current operating profit of one year is—in the absence of price and volume changes—an indicator of the succeeding period's current operating profit. In turn, by equation (2) of Chapter 4, this succeeding year's current operating profit is a surrogate for that year's distributable operating flow. While it is quite possible that these relationships may continue to hold in an environment that includes price and volume changes, no conclusions can be forthcoming until empirical evidence is available. Experimental research in the area has been sparse to date.

In the first part of the chapter we analyzed two recent empirical studies that utilized the extrapolation method for generating predictions. These studies interpreted predictive ability to mean the ability of a concept to provide a basis for future income estimates. However, we argued that since income is an artificial construct, forecasts of future income levels are not relevant *per se*. Rather, two possible reasons exist for

40 *Ibid.,* 421–24.

desiring to predict income. First, income may be thought to be related to some real events that constitute the ultimate object of prediction. Second, stock market prices may be thought to react to whatever income concept is externally reported. It was suggested that in a rational market, this second justification for income predictions must eventually reduce to the first. Thus, only one justification for income prediction survives; that is, such forecasts are useful only insofar as the income concept being predicted is a reasonable indicator of some real event(s) of concern to users. Therefore, tests of the relative predictive ability of alternative income constructs must specify the ultimate object of prediction and determine the correspondence between income forecasts and future values of that selected object. Since the studies that have heretofore appeared in the literature treated future *income* as the desired object of prediction, we lack relevant evidence to evaluate the relative predictive ability of various income concepts.

A caveat regarding the criterion used to assess predictive ability was also introduced. To be a useful predictor, an income concept need not be relatively stable from period to period. If the object of prediction is volatile, then the best possible predictor would be similarly volatile with a reasonable lead. This suggests that the criterion for assessing predictive efficiency must be related to the object for which a prediction is desired.

If progress is to be made in the prediction area, future researchers must empirically test the ability of different measurement constructs to generate reasonable estimates of defensible objects of prediction.

Greenball designed two simulations that meet this criterion. Greenball's simulations generated results that seemingly supported the superiority of current operating profit forecasts of future cash flows. Unfortunately, there is no empirical evidence in the literature that reinforces these findings. Only Staubus' study is at all relevant, and his results show only a weak superiority for LIFO-based flow measures. Further studies that examine the relationship between current operating profit of one year and various objects of prediction could provide the needed evidence.

In summary, the paucity of relevant evidence in the prediction area makes it impossible to evaluate conclusively the extrapolation basis provided by current operating profit. Nevertheless, this chapter has outlined a theoretical foundation that is needed to guide later empirical tests. Hopefully, this background will hasten the accumulation of evidence regarding extrapolation bases.

CHAPTER SIX

Additional Issues

Some additional problems relating to the measurement and interpretation of replacement cost income will be discussed in this chapter. One of these issues—the ability of total replacement cost income to reflect changes in operating flow potential—is carried over from Chapter 4. Three other problems not previously introduced will be treated briefly as well.

IS REPLACEMENT COST INCOME A LEAD INDICATOR?

In Chapter 4 we built a structural correspondence between replacement cost income and economic income in order to determine whether replacement costing is a surrogate for economic income. The existence of such a relationship between the two concepts is important because economic income incorporates expectations about future operating flows. *If* replacement costing is a surrogate for economic income, then it too would be related to future operating flows. This would mean that movements in replacement cost income could conceivably be lead indicators for movements in future distributable operating flows.

The relationship between replacement cost income and economic income was developed in terms of two sub-correspondences between components of each total income concept. The relevant relations can be depicted in the following fashion:

Replacement Cost Income $\overset{?}{\underset{=}{\sim}}$ Economic Income
$=$ $\qquad\qquad$ $=$
Current Operating Profit $\overset{?}{\underset{=}{\sim}}$ Distributable Operating Flow
$+$ $\qquad\qquad$ $+$
Realizable Cost Savings $\overset{?}{\underset{=}{\sim}}$ Unexpected Income

Our overriding concern centers on the relationship between *total* replacement cost income and total economic income. Concentration on the sub-correspondences is justified only for ease of exposition.[1]

The primary question is whether replacement cost income does indeed approximate economic income and thus serves as a lead indicator for *future* distributable operating flows. This, of course, is to date an unexplored empirical issue.

Evidence regarding price changes

There is no empirical evidence regarding the covariance between movements in replacement cost income and economic income. *A priori* analysis in Chapter 4 suggested that individual price changes may be important to the correspondence between these two income concepts. That is, if price changes and changes in a firm's expected future operating flows do not move in harmony, the total correspondence between replacement cost income and economic income would be weakened.

Thus, evidence regarding the actual existence of Type B and C price changes would seem to be crucial. Here too, however, the needed

---

[1] Unfortunately, an analysis of the correspondence between the sub-components is clouded by the fact that the two concepts can agree in total even though their sub-components may diverge because the sub-components are interdependent under certain circumstances. Accordingly, divergence in one sub-correspondence may exactly offset divergence in the other, thus maintaining the total equality. Despite this possibility, our emphasis on the sub-correspondences appears useful for the following reason. Potentially, the most serious cause for divergence between *total* replacement cost income and *total* economic income is the existence of Type B or Type C price changes. This type of effect is most easily seen by concentrating only on one component of each income concept. Furthermore, the impact of such price changes do not "wash out" between income components; that is, total replacement cost income and total economic income will diverge as a consequence of such price changes. Therefore, it does not seem necessary to complicate our analysis by considering both sub-correspondences simultaneously.

empirical evidence is lacking. Studies which examine the relation between changes in asset prices and changes in an *individual* firm's operating flows are unavailable. Until such studies are undertaken, we must continue to utilize *a priori* analysis in considering the issue of the predictive ability of total replacement cost income.

The theoretical utility of replacement cost income as a lead indicator seems to rest largely on the predominance of Type A price changes. Realistically, one could ask whether Type A changes would, in fact, constitute the bulk of all price changes experienced. That is, can anything be said concerning the relative frequency and materiality of Type B or Type C price changes?

In answer, it would seem that the factors that are needed to give rise to Type B and C price changes (e.g., imperfections in factor markets, demand shifts in other industries, technological changes, etc.) are both plausible and likely real-world phenomena.[2] As one author states:

> A change in an asset's replacement cost can be caused by many things—a war in South Africa, a strike in Chile, an increase in freight rates, an increase in wages, the production of a new and cheaper substitute product, etc., and only a few of those changes would have any bearing at all on the future cash receipts or disbursements *of any particular firm*. And even if an increase in cost did indicate an increase in future net cash receipts, the cost increase certainly would not be a reliable measure of the increase in the asset's real value.[3]

An empirical test for the existence of Type B and C price changes appears possible. If asset prices and operating flows generally do move in concert, one would expect firms' real rates of return [4] (using replacement cost income) to remain fairly constant over some period of time. Equation (3) in Chapter 4 represents one possible approximation of firms' real rates of return.[5] If this ratio of current operating profit to the

[2] Revsine, "Replacement Cost Reports," 76–90.

[3] Snavely, "Current Cost for Long-Lived Assets," 347.

[4] As in previous chapters, "real rate of return" means that return which exists after adjusting for specific price changes.

[5] Equation (3) states operating return to be:

$$r_a = \frac{C_i}{P_i}$$

where C_i represents current operating profit of the ith year, and P_i denotes the market price of the firm's assets in the ith year. Obviously, no single year's rate would provide a totally accurate test of this hypothesis. To illustrate, consider the following. Even in the absence of asset price changes, year-to-year changes in the time pattern of operating flows could occur. Thus, any *single* year's operating profit figure may not be representative of expected future events; the use of a single year's operating profit figure could precipitate changes in the estimated real rate of return that would not reflect actual

market value of productive assets changes dramatically, it can be deduced that such rate of return fluctuations would imply less than perfect correspondence between changes in prices and changes in flows. Thus, one test for the existence of Type B and Type C price changes involves monitoring movements in replacement cost rate of return ratios for individual firms over some period of time. Relatively large fluctuations in the rate of return over time would tend to suggest the absence of *aggregate* correspondence between changes in asset prices and changes in cash flows.[6] Pending development of such evidence, however, we will have to limit our analysis of the existence of such price changes to the *a priori* arguments presented previously.

Adjustments required for Type B and Type C price changes

As the analysis in Chapter 4 illustrated, the entire notion of replacement cost as a lead indicator depends heavily on the predominance of

---

changes in the long-run rate of return. Thus, the suggested test must span a several year period.

A more general difficulty also exists with regard to the proposed test. Changes in the rate of return will reflect *ex post*, realized events. The correspondence between replacement cost income and economic income relies on covariance between price changes and *ex ante* flow expectations. Thus, the suggested test makes the rather heroic assumption that actual, realized events are a valid proxy for original expectations.

[6] Studies of this nature have been performed on an industry-wide basis using accounting and tax return data (for example, see George J. Stigler, *Capital and Rates of Return in Manufacturing Industries*, Princeton, N.J.: Princeton University Press, 1963). While this study found a large amount of short-term stability in rates of return for all industries, and longer-term stability in concentrated industries, these findings are not clearly relevant to our situation. There are two reasons for this. First, the assumption of covariance between prices and flows relates to *individual firms*, whereas the available evidence is on an industry-wide basis. Second, while Stigler adjusted for price changes, his adjustment technique used highly aggregated economy and industry-wide data. Thus, the resultant data probably do not approximate the replacement cost data needed to test our hypothesis.

There is an indirect method for testing the covariance between changes in asset prices and changes in future operating flows. To the extent that market frictions are small, there would seem to be fewer opportunities for divergent movements between asset prices and operating flow potential. Thus, one could test to determine the degree of friction in various sectors of the economy. Results which indicate a general absence of frictions would provide evidence of the existence of conditions which tend to support the covariance assumption.

The extent of friction might be examined by testing the amount of dispersion among various firms' replacement cost operating rates of return. In Chapter 7 we will suggest that the use of replacement costs facilitates inter-firm comparisons by reducing the number of artificial, accounting-induced differences between firms' results. Thus, differences among firms' replacement cost rates of return would provide evidence of market imperfections and frictions which tend to destroy the correspondence between prices and values. To support the posited surrogate relationships, the rate of return dispersion among groups of firms that employ common resource inputs must be small.

Type A price changes.[7] Since the possible existence of other types of price changes cannot be dismissed, it seems fair to examine the adjustments that would be necessitated by Type B and Type C changes. That is, we will now analyze whether the supposed lead indicator advantages of replacement cost income can be maintained in an environment that is assumed to include Type B and Type C price changes. The fixed asset and inventory cases will be treated separately.

FIXED ASSET PRICE CHANGES

If Type B and Type C price changes do indeed occur in the real world, then caution must be exercised in preparing replacement cost reports. For example, if a Type C price change occurs, the holding gain or loss recognized under a replacement cost system may lead to some anomalous interpretations of periodic performance. That is, the expected future operating flows of a firm may have fallen because of external events, yet the reliance of replacement costing on market-wide price changes may dictate the recognition of a holding gain. Lacking sufficient information, the market as a whole may be ignorant regarding the impact of market-wide price changes on the unique operating flow position of the individual firm. Thus, the information conveyed by an increase in reported total replacement cost income under such circumstances may be misleading.[8]

What accounting options are available to help prevent such misevaluations? One of the more obvious possibilities is to merely deny income statement recognition to unrealized holding gains and losses. Following this approach, as an asset's market price changed, a balance sheet debit would continue to be made in order to reflect the current replacement cost of owned assets. However, the credit portion of the entry could be closed directly to some balance sheet capital account and would never

[7] For perfect correspondence to exist, not only must the direction of the change in prices and flows agree, but also the magnitude of the price change must exactly equal the discounted value of the expected increase in flows.

[8] Notice that this possible misevaluation does not necessarily imply market inefficiency because information that is not available to the market cannot be impounded in securities' prices. One example of information that is not readily available to the market is information regarding the covariance between market-wide price changes and individual firm operating flows. However, replacement cost income purports to incorporate such changes in expected flows via the price mechanism. But if Type B and Type C price changes predominate, replacement cost income may be an inadequate indicator of future operating flows. Since the market may have no better indicator of expected changes in operating flows, it may rely on changes in reported replacement cost to provide such evidence. Thus, when the relationship between replacement cost income and economic income is faulty, the market could be led to an erroneous interpretation of changes in reported replacement cost income. That is, it could interpret an increase in reported replacement cost income as evidence of an increase in expected future flows when, in fact, no such increase is expected.

appear as a component of reported income. The advantages of this approach are two-fold. First, cost expirations in the current operating profit section of the income statement would continue to reflect the pro rata portion of current market costs that have been utilized in generating revenues. Thus, operating profit would reflect the difference between current market revenues and current market costs. The second advantage of treating the credit as a capital adjustment is that the potentially misleading Type B and Type C price changes are denied income statement impact.

Unfortunately, this approach would not avoid the difficulties introduced by Type B and Type C price changes. That is, reflecting all holding gains directly in capital would still cause the Type B and C price changes to affect owners' equity and thus distort estimates of future distributable operating flows generated from this figure.[9] Furthermore, this approach would also exclude from total replacement cost income the legitimately includable Type A changes.

A preferable approach would necessitate a selective elimination from income of those price changes that do not reflect expected changes in operating flows while including those that do correspond to expected flow changes. One means of accomplishing this result in a world of uncertainty is to employ the concept of economic depreciation in measuring the expiration of the service potential of fixed assets. This measurement device allows subjective expectations to be incorporated at the firm level. Unfortunately, the use of economic depreciation also has a disadvantage because it constitutes an abandonment of replacement costing for fixed assets. An example employing economic depreciation will serve to illustrate both the advantages and deficiencies of this alternative approach to the holding gains problem.[10]

The data employed to illustrate the advantages of using economic depreciation are based on our Chapter 4 illustration of a Type C price change (pp. 110–114). For convenience, all relevant statements will be reproduced here.

Recall that gamma-producing equipment had a market value of $250 on January 1, 19x0. This equipment has a 3-year life and is expected to generate annual net cash inflows of $110. Given a desired rate of

---

[9] Specifically, if one adopted a balance sheet approach and attempted to predict future distributable operating flows based on the replacement cost equity balance, then price changes would have to be differentiated by type. That is, unless Type B and C price changes are isolated on the balance sheet, the owners' equity figure cannot be treated as an approximation of the present value of the firm. As a consequence, the appropriate normal rate of return cannot be multiplied by owners' equity in order to estimate distributable operating flow.

[10] This illustration is adapted from Revsine, "Replacement Cost Income," 522–23.

return of 5 percent, the subjective value of the gamma-producing equipment is approximately $300, computed as follows:

Year	Net Inflow	Discount Factor (at 5%)	Present Value
1st	$110	0.9524	$104.76
2nd	110	0.9070	99.77
3rd	110	0.8638	95.02
Subjective value			$299.55

It was assumed in Chapter 4 that the Original Firm, a member of the gamma industry, purchased the asset on January 1, 19x0. If all expectations of operating performance during 19x0 were realized, then economic income for the original firm for 19x0 would be:

Original Form
Economic Income
For the Year Ended December 31, 19x0

Distributable Operating Flows:		
rV_i (5% × $299.55)		$14.98
Unexpected Income:		
From changes in future flows	$ 0.00	
On acquisition (difference between subjective value, $299.55, and cost, $250.00)	49.55	
Total Unexpected Income		49.55
Total Economic Income		$64.53

If economic depreciation is inserted into the basic replacement cost framework (in contrast to our approach in Chapter 4), then depreciation charges must be based on the subjective value of the asset rather than on its current market value. In order to bring the carrying value of the asset up to this subjective value, an acquisition income component must be recognized. This acquisition income component would be measured as the difference between the subjective value of the asset ($299.55) and its cost ($250.00).[11] Once economic depreciation is used in the replacement cost computation, total replacement cost income equals total economic income for 19x0. This is illustrated at the top of page 146.

Although it is encouraging that total replacement cost income and total economic income are equal for 19x0, an even more dramatic correspondence occurs in 19x1 during a period in which a Type C price change occurs. To review the facts of the illustrative situation, recall that

[11] For an illustration and discussion of this approach, see Bedford, *Income Determination Theory*, p. 176.

Original Form
Replacement Cost Income
(Computed Using Economic Depreciation)
For the Year Ended December 31, 19x0

Current Operating Profit:			
Net cash inflow			$110.00
Economic depreciation:			
Value of the asset at $1/1/x0$		$299.55	
Value at $12/31/x0$:			
19x1 flows ($110 × 0.9524)	$104.76		
19x2 flows ($110 × 0.9070)	99.77		
		204.53	
Total Depreciation			95.02
Total Current Operating Profit			14.98
Realizable Cost Savings:			
Acquisition income:			
Value to the firm		299.55	
Cost		250.00	
			49.55
Total Replacement Cost Income			$ 64.53

the prospect of abnormal returns in the gamma industry induced new entrants. As a result of this entry, 19x2 net inflows were expected to fall to $95. (For simplicity, we assume that 19x1 flows were unaffected and that the consequences of increased entry were perceived instantaneously on January 1, 19x1.) If the market reestablishes an equilibrium price for a 1-year-old gamma-producing asset, its market value will rise to $190.93.[12] As shown in Chapter 4, economic income for 19x1 is:

Original Form
Economic Income
For the Year Ended December 31, 19x1

Distributable Operating Flow:	
rV_i (5% × $190.93)	$ 9.55
Unexpected income:	
Decline in expected 19x2 cash inflows	
($15 × 0.9070)	(13.60)
Total Economic Income	$(4.05)

[12] This price is computed as follows:

Year	Net Inflow	Discount Factor (at 5%)	Present Value
19x1	$110	0.9524	$104.76
19x2	95	0.9070	86.17
Equilibrium Market Price			$190.93

If economic depreciation is again employed in a replacement cost framework, reported income for 19x1 on this basis would be:

Original Form
Replacement Cost Income
(Computed Using Economic Depreciation)
For the Year Ended December 31, 19x1

Current Operating Profit:		
Net cash inflow		$110.00
Economic depreciation:		
Value of the asset at 12/31/x0	$204.53	
Value at 12/31/x1		
19x2 flows ($95 × 0.9524)	90.48	
		114.05
Total Current Operating Profit		(4.05)
Realizable Cost Savings		0.00
Total Replacement Cost Income		$(4.05)

Notice that the use of economic depreciation serves to maintain the correspondence between replacement cost income and economic income even in the face of a Type C price change. Indeed, the reason is that price changes involving fixed assets are ignored using an economic depreciation concept. If a price change does reflect an expected operating flow effect, then this change is incorporated in the depreciation calculation itself. For example, notice that the replacement cost computation does not explicitly incorporate the new price of $190.93 for a 1-year-old asset when economic depreciation is used. Even at the time of purchase in 19x0, the asset's carrying value on the amended replacement cost basis is $299.55, not its original cost—and market value—of $250.00. In the interests of completeness, the correspondence between the two income concepts during 19x2 is illustrated in footnote 13, below and on p. 148.

13

Original Form
Economic Income
For the Year Ended December 31, 19x2

Distributable Operating Flow:	
rV_i (5% × $90.48)	$ 4.52
Unexpected Income	0.00
Total Economic Income	$ 4.52

Aside from the fact that it is an abandonment of the market price method for valuing fixed assets, one of the primary objections that can be raised against the use of economic depreciation is its subjectivity. For example, the carrying value of a firm's assets might be influenced by overly optimistic forecasts of future flows. Although this argument is undeniably true, it is also ironic. It would appear that from the standpoint of objectivity, the least defensible aspect of *current* reporting practice is that of depreciation. Selecting a particular useful life and allocation pattern for a long-lived asset is obviously a subjective judgment made by management. In a relative sense, traditional allocation patterns might be preferred to that of economic depreciation because they are systematic and—once selected—less subject to management manipulation. But traditional patterns are still essentially arbitrary.

It is not our purpose in this section to argue for the adoption of economic depreciation procedures. Before economic depreciation becomes a feasible accounting alternative, many of the audit controls discussed in Chapter 2 in connection with direct predictive information would have to be developed. Nevertheless, if the substitution of one subjective depreciation construct (economic depreciation) for another (traditional depreciation) promises to improve the correspondence between replacement cost income and economic income, such subjective procedures merit closer scrutiny. The reason, of course, is apparent. If one can improve the correspondence between replacement cost income and economic income, then the replacement cost equity value will approximate the present value of the firm. Multiplying this equity balance by the prevailing rate of return will then allow one to generate an estimate of future distributable operating flow.

Original Firm
Replacement Cost Income
(Computed Using Economic Depreciation)
For the Year Ended December 31, 19x2

Current Operating Profit:		
Net cash inflow		$95.00
Economic depreciation:		
Value of the asset at 12/31/x1	$90.48	
Value at 12/31/x2	0.00	
		90.48
Total Current Operating Profit		4.52
Realizable Cost Savings		0.00
Total Replacement Cost Income		$ 4.52

INVENTORY PRICE CHANGES

Fortunately, the adverse effects of Type B and Type C price changes are mitigated somewhat in the case of inventories because of the rapid turnover of inventories relative to fixed assets. The more rapid the turnover of a given asset, the less of that asset must be held, on average, to facilitate a given volume of sales. The lower the amount held, the smaller the potentially misleading Type B or Type C gain. Furthermore, the higher the turnover, the greater the proportion of the holding gain that is both realizable and realized in the same period; this means that the total profit impact from recognizing a Type B or Type C price change will tend to "wash-out" in the period of the price change.

To illustrate more concretely, consider the following situation. A firm has an inventory turnover of 5. It owns a fixed asset that has a market value of $100,000 and a 10-year remaining life on June 30, 19x1. The carrying value of average inventory is $5,000. On July 1, 19x1, a 10 percent increase occurs in the market price of both the fixed asset and the inventory. (The general price level is assumed constant.) Realizable cost savings of $500 will be recognized on the inventory and $10,000 on the fixed asset.

The inventory turnover of 5 means that typical items complete a cycle from acquisition to sale in 2.4 months. Thus, on the average, by the end of 19x1 all of the material on hand at July 1 will have been sold. Cost of goods sold will include the $500 price increase recognized in July.[14] The net impact of the holding gain on total replacement cost income can be summarized as follows:

Net increase in 19x1 income because of recognition of a holding gain:	$+500
Net decrease in 19x1 income because carrying value of goods sold is higher:	−500
Net change in 19x1 income as a consequence of inventory price rise:	$ 0

In contrast, the fixed asset will not be totally used up during 19x1. Although a holding gain of $10,000 will be recognized during 19x1, depreciation expense will be increased by only $500. The net impact of the fixed asset price rise on total replacement cost income will be:

Net increase in 19x1 income because of recognition of a holding gain:	$+10,000
Net decrease in 19x1 income because depreciation is higher:	− 500
Net change in 19x1 income as a consequence of fixed asset price rise:	$+ 9,500

Thus, it is apparent that the higher the turnover for a given asset category, the smaller the annual profit impact of a holding gain. Accord-

[14] The original entry for the increase would have been:

DR Inventory	$500	
CR Realizable Cost Savings		$500

ingly, the adverse consequences of a Type C price change are diminished with regard to inventory. Even if asset prices and future flows are moving in opposite directions, income will not be affected by the holding gain, per se. This means that the magnitude of disparate movements in income and operating flow potential will tend to be reduced. However, this relative stability of total replacement cost income in the face of inventory price changes introduces a potential problem where none previously existed. That is, if total replacement cost income tends toward stability in the face of inventory holding gains or losses, it will also be stable in the face of Type A price changes where an income change is desired. Fortunately, another characteristic of inventory price changes tends to offset this "problem" of stability and helps to maintain the correspondence between holding gains or losses and operating flow changes.

This other characteristic that tends to overcome the stability of income in the face of inventory price changes arises because inventory is divisible. Firms can purchase just enough inventory to meet reasonable short-term needs. Fixed assets are not generally divisible. Firms must buy a 10- or 20-year "supply" of asset services in the form of a single machine. Since inventory is usually purchased for near-term needs, input price changes often reflect anticipated near-term changes in output prices. That is, if an inventory price change is the result of some prospective change in the flows to be generated by sale of the inventory, then the change in the flows is likely to occur soon after the change in input prices. If this were not the case, higher priced inventory would have to be "stored" until the selling price increased in order to maintain profit margins. Thus, if a Type A inventory price increase occurs, the revenue impact is likely to be visible in the same period. This increase in revenues would maintain a loose correspondence between the recognition of a holding gain and the direction of change in operating flows. (But, a Type C change would still create a slight disparity; that is, a holding gain would be recognized in the same period that operating flows decline. However, the rapidity of inventory turnover reduces the magnitude of this disparate income effect.)

Thus, the characteristics of inventory—and inventory price changes —seemingly make adjustments in the face of Type B and Type C price changes relatively unimportant.

OTHER CONSIDERATIONS

Ending prices not in effect
throughout reporting period

Another means by which replacement cost income can conceivably generate information for predictions is the extrapolation method discussed in Chapter 5. There we examined prior writers' contentions that current operating profit has more predictive ability than alternative income constructs. Relative predictive ability is obviously an empirical issue; unfortunately, actual evidence in this area is sparse. Some theoretical issues must be resolved, however, before empirical testing becomes useful. For instance, what is the logical basis for ascribing predictive ability to current operating profit? Furthermore, what is the *object* that current operating profit supposedly better predicts?

The discussion of the predictive ability of current operating profit was directed to these theoretical issues. In Chapter 5 we developed the notion of current operating profit as an *ex ante* measure of the distributable operating flow of an enterprise. Given investors' concern with future dividend flows from an investment, distributable operating flow was suggested as an appropriate object of prediction. The reason is that distributable operating flow is itself a prime determinant of future dividends. Once this object of prediction is specified, the theoretical basis for the predictive advantages of current operating profit follow. As developed in Chapter 5, these are:

1. In the absence of contrary evidence, the actual current operating profit figure for any given year constitutes the best estimate of the current operating profit that will be realized in the succeeding year.
2. In turn, this estimate of the succeeding year's current operating profit is the best *ex ante* surrogate for the succeeding year's distributable operating flow.

Thus, one part of the theoretical basis for ascribing predictive significance to current operating profit rests on the belief that, under certain conditions, one year's current operating profit constitutes a valid estimate of the succeeding year's current operating profit. The purpose of this section is to examine the relationship among successive periods' current operating profits in greater depth.

In Chapter 3 current operating profit for a retailer was illustrated to develop the notion of distributable operating flow.[15] We assumed that the retailer bought refrigerators for $150 and sold them for $200. (For simplicity, costs of selling and administration were ignored.) We also assumed that after the retailer purchased one refrigerator for $150 its wholesale price rose to $175. If the refrigerator was subsequently sold for $200, the reported historical cost profit would be $50. But it was argued that the distributable profit on the sale was $25, not $50. That is, if the wholesale price of refrigerators is expected to remain at $175, subsequent inventory replenishment will entail an outflow of $175. If $50 of sales proceeds were distributed as a dividend, the remaining $150 would buy only 86

[15] See pp. 70–71n.

percent of a now higher-priced refrigerator. It was suggested that operating profit measured on a replacement cost basis provided a more accurate basis for projecting future operating flows. Comparative income statements illustrate this.

Historical Cost Basis		Replacement Cost Basis	
Sales revenue	$200	Sales revenue	$200
Historical cost of goods sold	150	Replacement cost of goods sold	175
Operating profit	$ 50	Current operating profit	$ 25
		Realized cost saving ($175 − 150)	25
		Total replacement cost income	$ 50

The presumption was that if purchasing and selling prices remained at their end of period levels, and if volume was constant, then current operating profit of the immediately past period would equal current operating profit of the succeeding period.

Unfortunately, this is an oversimplification. To see why, we will expand the retailer's volume from one to two refrigerator sales annually. Assume the same facts as above, except that one other refrigerator was purchased and sold *before* the wholesale price increased. Total current operating profit for the period would be $75, computed in the following fashion:

	1st Sale	2nd Sale	Total
Sales revenue	$200	$200	$400
Replacement cost of goods sold	150	175	325
Current operating profit	$ 50	$ 25	$ 75
Realized cost saving	—	25	25
Total replacement cost income	$ 50	$ 50	$100

Given the previously cited relationship between current operating profit and distributable operating flows, it should follow that if prices remain constant at their end-of-period levels and if expected sales volume in the following period is two refrigerators, then current operating profit (and thus distributable operating flow) should be $75. In fact, of course, this is not the case. Under the conditions cited, distributable flows will be $25 for each refrigerator sold. Total distributable flows in the succeeding period would thus be expected to total $50, not $75.

This anomalous result occurs because charges to cost of goods sold on a replacement cost basis are made at the level of costs that prevail at the time of sale. If replacement cost subsequently rises, no retroactive adjustment is made. Thus, unless end-of-period prices were in effect at the time of *each* sale during the period, simple extrapolations will mislead. Under these conditions, distributable operating flows cannot be estimated by merely extending current operating profit.

One means of overcoming this deficiency would involve an end of period adjustment to cost of goods sold. All costs would be adjusted to end-of-period price levels.[16] For the retailer, the adjusted statement might appear as follows:

Sales revenues (2 refrigerators)	$400
Replacement cost of goods sold, at year-end prices	350
Current operating profit	$ 50
Realized cost saving	25
Retroactive cost of goods sold adjustment	25
Total replacement cost income	$100

However, these end-of-period cost of goods sold adjustments may be unnecessary if Type A price changes predominate in the real world. For example, if the firm is a price *taker* in both input and output markets, Type A price changes would tend to predominate if input price changes vary directly with output price changes and volume is unaffected. If the firm is a price taker only in the input market, Type A price changes would tend to predominate as long as firms can maintain approximately stable profits in the face of cost changes. Under either circumstance, if we assume that the increase in the wholesale price of refrigerators is a Type A price change, then the second refrigerator might be sold for, say, $225, not $200. Replacement cost income (computed *without* an end-of-period cost of goods sold adjustment) would thus appear as follows:

	1st Sale	2nd Sale	Total
Sales revenue	$200	$225	$425
Replacement cost of goods sold	150	175	325
Current operating profit	$ 50	$ 50	$100
Realized cost saving	—	25	25
Total replacement cost income	$ 50	$ 75	$125

Thus, if the price change is of Type A, *and if output prices quickly adjust,* it is apparent that current operating profit may afford a basis for estimating future operating flows. That is, if volume is constant, and if no further price changes occur, then distributable operating flow in the succeeding period should total $100. (Obviously, the predictive basis provided by current operating profit is not necessarily precise. Nevertheless, a reasonable surrogate relationship may exist under certain circumstances, depending on the characteristics and timing of price changes.) [17]

16 Cf., L. S. Rosen, "Replacement-Value Accounting," *The Accounting Review,* 42 (January, 1967), 106–13.

17 As an indication of the theoretical predictive advantage of replacement costing, let us compute historical cost income under the same assumed conditions for the same period.

	1st Sale	2nd Sale	Total
Sales revenue	$200	$225	$425
Historical cost of goods sold	150	150	300
Historical cost operating margin	$ 50	$ 75	$125

Estimates of future distributable operating flows using historical cost margin will obviously be excessive and potentially misleading.

Thus, it appears that only Type B or Type C price changes would necessitate an adjustment to cost of goods sold in order to preserve the potential predictive ability of current operating profit.[18] This conclusion is important for two reasons. First, it tends to support our earlier generalization regarding the predictability of current operating profit under certain circumstances. But second, it underscores the potentially disruptive impact of Type B and Type C price changes. Until now, such changes were presumed to adversely influence only the holding gains component of replacement cost income. But as a result of our analysis in this section we now see that Type B and Type C price changes can also reduce the predictability of the current operating profit component of replacement cost income. Although this effect can theoretically be mitigated using end-of-period adjustments to cost of goods sold, such adjustments require an ability to differentiate among the various types of price changes.

When a long-lived asset price increase occurs—even if Type A—the situation is different. After adjustment, the replacement cost shown on the books is the current value of the asset in its present (used) condition. But the firm must eventually replace the asset (new) at its now higher price. To do this the firm must reduce the current dividend by the amount needed to compensate for past underdepreciation (given new asset price levels). This allows the firm to retain sufficient funds to replace the now higher-priced asset and increases owners' equity to the level that would have existed if the firm had perfect foreknowledge of the price increase. When multiplied by the prevailing normal rate of return, this equity figure will generate an estimate of future distributable operating flow. Thus, even long-lived asset price changes will seemingly not destroy the predictive ability of replacement costing if appropriate dividend policy is followed.

The impact of technological change

One subject that has not been specifically treated thus far is the impact of technological change on the determination of replacement cost income. This problem arises whenever assets still utilized in production have been superseded in the marketplace by newer models. How should the current market price of expired services be measured under such circumstances?

Edwards and Bell suggest that expired current costs be measured in terms of the prices that prevail for the actual fixed assets used in production. Their reasoning is straightforward. They contend that manage-

---

[18] For illustrative ease, the example presumes that the Type A change preserves absolute dollar operating profit. If, instead, *percentage* return is maintained, then the extrapolation basis provided by current operating profit is only an approximation.

ment requires a measure of the profitability of *existing* operations. That is, in order to evaluate the efficiency of current operations, management must be apprised of the real return generated by those assets in current use. Furthermore, they suggest that this information regarding the costs of employing current production techniques is necessary for evaluating replacement possibilities. Unless the current profitability of existing operations is known, proper replacement decisions cannot be made. Therefore, Edwards and Bell conclude, replacement cost income should reflect the current cost of using the fixed assets actually employed in production, irrespective of the availability of technologically improved alternatives.[19]

This view has been criticized because it seemingly ignores technological change. One such criticism is particularly interesting since it raises a provocative issue regarding predictive ability:

> The claim that "current operating profit" evaluates the existing mode of production remains valid, but the primary interest is in the long-run prospects of the firm, and there seems to be no particular reason why these long run prospects would be indicated by the prospects of the present mode of production, when it is becoming obsolete.[20]

The point raised, of course, is valid. It is possible that present current operating profit is an inadequate predictor of future current operating profit for a process that will eventually be replaced. But the issue is broader than mere technological change. Specifically, it is this: There may be general agreement that an accounting process ought to provide a basis for prediction. But should the resultant measurements be based on the premise that a firm adopts some production techniques different from those currently employed? Or should the method selected afford a basis for predictions under the assumption that existing processes are continued?

Edwards and Bell opt for the latter alternative. From a practical standpoint, this is a defensible position. The area of prediction is obviously filled with inherent difficulties. To generate accounting measurements based on some action that a firm has not yet taken (and may never take) introduces still greater difficulties. This approach would require someone to forecast what investment decisions a firm is likely to make in the future. Worse still, the costs of implementation and operation would also have to be estimated. In short, limiting the measurement model to the financial consequences of activities actually adopted by the firm is more in keeping with traditional thought regarding the appropriate role of accounting information.[21]

[19] Edwards and Bell, *Measurement of Business Income*, p. 186n.

[20] Kenneth W. Lemke, "Asset Valuation and Income Theory," *The Accounting Review*, 41 (January, 1966), 38.

[21] Edwards and Bell, *Measurement of Business Income*, p. 275.

Since, however, technological changes do occur, one might ask how such changes would affect the predictions generated by a replacement cost model that is based on a firm's *existing* activities. That is, can replacement cost income (which on the surface appears to ignore technological change) generate tolerably accurate predictions of future operating flows during a period of technological change?

To examine this issue, we adopt the following analytic approach. We assume the existence of a firm that owns and operates a single productive asset. A technological advance occurs and a new improved asset becomes available. However, this firm continues to use the older asset still in its possession. In order to examine the predictive ability of replacement cost income under these circumstances, we must examine some market effects that could affect the firm as a consequence of technological change. Of primary concern is the issue of who benefits from the technological change. For our purposes, four possibilities regarding the distribution of benefits from a technological advance will be considered:

1. The ultimate consumers of final output could be the sole beneficiaries of the technological change;
2. Capital equipment producers could receive all of the benefits from the technological advance;
3. Consumer goods manufacturers who adopt the technological change could gain all the benefits; or
4. Two or more of the preceding three groups could share the benefits in various proportions.

Our objective is to examine the effect of these technological-change possibilities on the predictive ability of replacement cost income. Which of the four basic possibilities prevails in a given situation is essentially a function of the competitive structure and supply-demand characteristics in the individual circumstances. While the benefits of technological change may often accrue to more than one group, analytically such results are merely some combination of the first three possibilities enumerated above. Thus, the analysis that follows will illustrate only the extreme points in the solution space, i.e., where all of the benefits of the change accrue to either (1) the ultimate consumer, (2) equipment producers, or (3) manufacturers who adopt the change. Aside from simplifying the analysis, there is a corollary advantage to limiting the analysis to the three extreme points. We will see that replacement cost income does not perform uniformly in each of these circumstances. By fragmenting the analysis into its simplest components, we will be able to identify those specific elements that adversely affect the performance of replacement costing. Were we to illustrate shared benefit cases, it would be impossible to specify which individual elements cause the observed results.

CONSUMERS OF FINAL OUTPUT
RECEIVE ALL BENEFITS

Consider the following illustrative situation in which the consumers of final output will be the beneficiaries of the technological change. Assume that the prevailing normal rate of return for the economy as a whole is 6 percent. An asset that costs $267.30, and has no expected salvage value, promises to generate net inflows of $100 per year for 3 years when operated at full capacity. Full capacity is 100 units of output. The expected net inflows are computed as follows:

Expected revenue per year (100 unit capacity × $2 per unit selling price)	$200
Expected production costs (100 unit capacity × $1 per unit production cost)	100
Expected net operating inflows per year	$100

The internal rate of return expected to be generated by this asset is 6 percent.[22]

Next assume that a technological advance results in the development of a new productive asset. This new asset is capable of producing 110 units of the same final product at no increase in cost. That is, the total cost of producing 110 units on the new machine is $100, which exactly equals the cost of producing 100 units on the old machine. Assume that the new machine will be priced to yield a 6 percent return to its users. If we further assume that this equilibrium price of the new machine is identical to the original price of the old machine (i.e., $267.30) and that the new machine also has a 3-year life, the unit selling price of the final product must fall to $1.82 in order to maintain a 6 percent rate of return. (It is this decline in the selling price that makes the consumers of final output the beneficiaries of the technological change.) At this unit price, net operating inflows for users of the *improved* equipment will continue to be $100; i.e.,

Expected revenue (110 units @ $1.82)	$200
Expected production costs, 110 units	100
Expected net operating inflows per year	$100

[22] We can verify that the internal rate of return is 6 percent by performing the following calculation:

	Year			
	1st	*2nd*	*3rd*	*Total*
Net operating inflows	$100.00	$100.00	$100.00	$300.00
Discount factor (@ 6%)	0.9434	0.8900	0.8396	2.6730
Net present value	$ 94.34	$ 89.00	$ 83.96	$267.30

The improved asset first becomes available on January 1, 19x2. The effect of this technological change on the replacement cost statements of a firm that continues to hold an old, technologically primitive asset will now be examined. Assume that this firm purchased the old asset on January 1, 19x1. If straight-line depreciation is used ($267.30 ÷ 3 = $89.10), the book value of the *old* asset on January 1, 19x2 is $178.20 ($267.30 − $89.10). If all equipment is priced to yield a 6 percent rate of return, the new market value of a 1-year-old unimproved asset should be $150.34. This price would be determined by discounting, at 6 percent, the new expected inflows [23] from operating the old machine over the remaining 2 years of its life. The computation is:

	19x2	19x3	Total
Sales revenue (100 units @ $1.82)	$182.00	$182.00	
Production costs (100 units @ $1.00)	100.00	100.00	
Net inflow	$ 82.00	$ 82.00	
Discount factor (at 6%)	0.9434	0.8900	
Present value	$ 77.36	$ 72.98	$150.34

If expectations are realized, replacement cost income for 19x2 and 19x3 would appear as follows for the firm that continues to use the old asset:

	19x2		19x3	
Sales revenues (100 units @ $1.82)		$182.00		$182.00
Replacement cost of goods sold:				
Production cost (100 units @ $1.00)	$100.00		$100.00	
Depreciation (straight-line,				
$150.34 ÷ 2)	75.17		75.17	
		175.17		175.17
Current operating profit		$ 6.83		$ 6.83
Realizable cost saving (loss):				
Book value, 1/1/x2	$178.20			
Market value, 1/1/x2	150.34			
		(27.86)		0
Total replacement cost income (loss)		$(21.03)		$ 6.83

As these statements illustrate, the technological change operated to the detriment of non-adopters. Whereas annual output could have previously been sold at $2 per unit, the new selling price falls to $1.82. In other words, the innovation reduces the future cash generating potential of non-adopters from $100 per year to $82 per year. And this is precisely what the replacement cost loss for 19x2 indicates. Total replacement cost income reflects both the 19x2 realized decline in operating flows and the anticipated 19x3 decline. Furthermore, after the change occurs, current

[23] Inflows have changed for non-adopters because we assume that the selling price of *all* units of final output has dropped to $1.82 per unit.

operating profit provides a good extrapolation basis for predicting future current operating profit (and thus, presumably, future distributable operating flow).

CAPITAL EQUIPMENT PRODUCER
RECEIVES ALL BENEFITS

Assume an independent situation similar to the previous example. Once again a technological improvement occurs. As before, the improved asset allows the manufacture of 110 units per year (as opposed to 100 using the unimproved asset) at a total cost of $100. Again, we assume that the new equipment is priced to yield a 6 percent return to its users. In contrast to the previous example, however, it is now assumed that the selling price of final output remains constant.[24] Therefore, the price of the improved asset must rise in order to reestablish the 6 percent yield at the new, higher level of net inflows. For adopters of the technological change, the new net inflows in each of the 3 years of asset life are expected to be:

Expected revenue (110 units @ $2.00)	$220
Expected production costs, 110 units	100
Expected net operating inflows per year	$120

The new equilibrium price of the asset, again assuming no salvage value, should be $320.76.[25] (We implicitly assume a monopolistic equipment manufacturer who gains the benefits of the technological change, in this specific example, by increasing the selling price of the new asset while its manufacturing cost is assumed constant.)

Since the selling price of final output is constant, the net inflows accruing to non-adopters is constant. Since there is no anticipated change in inflows, there ought to be no change in the market price of the unimproved asset. No holding gain would exist and replacement cost income

---

[24] The technological change could induce excess capacity at this price. For simplicity, assume that any excess is avoided by an eventual reduction in the total number of machines in use. Such behavior might be explained by a kink in the demand curve for the final product at the existing volume level which would require large price reductions to sell additional units.

[25] The computation is:

Year	Net Inflow	Discount Factor @ 6%	Present Value
1	$120	0.9434	$113.21
2	120	0.8900	106.80
3	120	0.8396	100.75
Market price of improved asset			$320.76

after the technological improvement would equal that which was recorded before the change. Once again, replacement cost income for non-adopters, which "ignores" the technological improvement, seems to correspond well to the impact on expected future inflows.

One conceivable problem could arise, however. In circumstances essentially similar to those described above, the market price for the old asset may be indeterminable. For example, the market for the unimproved asset may have dissipated. This, of course, makes it difficult to determine a replacement cost for the old asset. In the absence of an active market for the unimproved asset, specific price index adjustments might be used to approximate replacement cost. Unfortunately, the specific index number used would be based on market prices for the only such asset actively traded—the technologically improved one. Utilizing this index number would mean that the holder of an unimproved asset would recognize a holding gain. But we have seen that no change in future net flows is likely to accrue to non-adopters. Thus, the holding gain recognized by those who continue to use the old asset would be of Type B.

This problem, which was also discussed in Chapter 5,[26] can be avoided. First, to the extent that there is an active (and efficient) market for the unimproved asset, there is no problem. As illustrated above, there would be no price change for the old asset, no holding gain recognized, and no change in expected net inflows. Replacement cost income would seemingly correspond to operating flow potential.

Second, even if no market price is available for the unimproved asset, recognition of a misleading gain might be avoided. To the extent that indices can be developed that isolate the price impact of technological change, this element can be omitted from the price change recognized for unimproved assets. Admittedly, developing such indices is a difficult problem, but some progress in this direction has been made.[27] Furthermore, specific appraisals could also be employed for determining a replacement cost for the old asset. These appraisals would presumably isolate and omit the price effects of technological change.

CONSUMER GOODS MANUFACTURERS WHO
ADOPT THE CHANGE RECEIVE ALL BENEFITS

In our first illustration, the primary beneficiaries of the technological change were the consumers of final output because the selling price of the final output fell while equipment prices and rates of return were constant. In the second illustration, it was the equipment manu-

---

26 See p. 127n.

27 See, for example, Musgrave, "Price Changes in Construction."

facturer who benefited because the final output prices and rates of return were constant in the face of rising equipment prices. We will now consider a case in which the manufacturers of final output will themselves reap the benefits of the technological change.

If we assume that the selling price of final output remains constant at $2 per unit, and if we further assume that the cost of the technologically improved equipment equals the original cost of the unimproved equipment ($267.30), then the rate of return to users of the improved equipment rises to approximately 16.5 percent.[28] Under these circumstances, the replacement cost of the unimproved equipment should fall because this equipment, which previously sold new for $267.30, promises lower net cash inflows than does the improved equipment, which also sells for $267.30.

The change in the price of the unimproved asset is not accompanied by any change in the net flows expected to be generated by the asset. That is, the price change is of Type B. Firms that continue to use the unimproved asset will recognize a holding loss despite the fact that their expected operating flows are unchanged. Here, in contrast with the preceding two cases, the treatment of technological change in a replacement cost system does not seem to provide an adequate predictive basis.

Summary. Edwards and Bell suggest that replacement cost be measured by reference to those assets in current use rather than by reference to the replacement cost of technologically superior assets which provide equivalent services. We observed that technological change introduced difficulties into this replacement cost system under two circumstances. The first difficulty arises when there is no functioning market for the unimproved asset. In such circumstances, one might be

[28] Under these circumstances, net operating flows to adopters will be $120 (i.e., 110 units $\times$ $2 − $100). The expected rate of return would be determined as follows:

$$\frac{\$267.30}{\$120.00} = 2.227$$

Reference to a table of present values of an annuity for 3 years yields the following factors:

16%	2.246	2.246
		2.227
18%	2.174	
	0.072	0.019

Interpolation discloses that this rate of return is approximately 16.5%.

Here we assume that equipment prices are constant because of, say, intense competition among equipment manufacturers. Once again, the technological change could induce excess capacity. As before, assume that this is avoided by reducing the number of machines employed. To explain this behavior, we adopt the kinked demand curve assumption of footnote 24.

tempted to value the old asset by reference to the price of the new asset. However, this approach would tend to give misleading results if there is divergence between the expected flows from the old and new assets. The problem might be avoided if specific appraisals are used to determine the replacement cost of the old asset. Alternatively, one might use price indices that isolate the price effect attributable to technological change.

A second problem arises when a technological change precipitates an increase in the rate of return for those firms that employ the improved asset. The increased rate of return could affect the market price of the old asset despite the fact that cash flows emanating from that unimproved asset are unchanged. Recognizing this Type B price change in the income statements of non-adopters could diminish the predictive ability of such statements.

We examined only three extreme points regarding the distribution of benefits from technological change. Realistically, the entire gain from technological change will probably not accrue to any single group. Instead, these gains will often be distributed among equipment manufacturers, producers, and consumers. If these benefits are often shared, then insofar as the rate of return in the industry that employs the asset is increased, replacement cost measures could become misleading. Thus, the crucial question is this: When benefits are shared, how frequently might we expect a significant portion of the benefits to go to consumer goods manufacturers and thus appreciably raise their rate of return?

Obviously, the answer to this question is dependent on the specific circumstances confronting all industries and groups affected by the technological change. Relevant factors include the nature of the competitive structure in both the equipment manufacturing industry and the producing industry, and the elasticity of demand for production equipment and for the final product. Whether a given technological change would serve to change the rate of return in the producing industry would thus depend on the individual situation. We can, however, identify one characteristic, which if possessed by a given industry, would tend to lower its share of benefits from a technological change. Specifically, insofar as freedom of entry into the industry is high, competitive forces would limit the proportion of technological change benefits which accrue to producers and the industry rate of return would change little. This constancy would seemingly maintain an approximate correspondence between replacement cost information and future operating flows even for those firms that do not adopt the technological change. While empirical testing is necessary, our analysis does suggest that the difficulties that technological change introduces into a replacement cost system are not invariably as serious as previous criticisms suggest.

INTERDEPENDENCE BETWEEN OPERATING PROFIT AND COST SAVINGS

In Chapter 3 we described the traditional explanation for fragmenting total replacement cost income into current operating profit and cost savings components. In this view, each of these income components is intended to separately reflect a distinct category of income generating situations. That is, current operating profit supposedly pertains only to operating events, whereas the cost savings component is intended to reflect only holding activities. As we have already discussed, the theoretical advantage of this separation is that it would allow the user to evaluate management's operating effectiveness without having the results of price gains and losses commingled in the data. Furthermore, the realizable cost savings data should provide a means of gauging the net result of holding activities. However, the notion that current operating profit and realizable cost savings isolate and reflect only operating and holding activities, respectively, has been attacked by Drake and Dopuch.[29] Instead, these authors suggest that when a firm is actively speculating in prices changes, it is impossible to evaluate the success of such efforts through reference to the realizable cost savings component alone. Worse still, they believe that part of the costs attributable to speculative activity find their way into the current operating component, thereby confounding the analysis of operating activity. These observations are of sufficient importance to warrant examination at this point. We will discuss the case for inventory price changes and fixed asset price changes separately.

Inventory changes

Consider the case of a company that can accurately forecast its inventory demands as well as its cost of ordering, carrying, and running out of inventory. Using an available inventory model, this firm can determine both its optimal order quantity and its optimal order point. Although this situation is artificial, it will allow a full and readily comprehensible discussion of the observations of Drake and Dopuch.

In the absence of any expectations regarding future inventory price changes, or in the absence of any desire to speculate in inventory price changes, the firm will order that amount of inventory that its inventory model indicates to be optimal, and it will order that amount when in-

---

[29] David F. Drake and Nicholas Dopuch, "On the Case for Dichotomizing Income," *Journal of Accounting Research*, 3 (Autumn, 1965), 192–205. Much of the material that follows in this section is based on the comments of Drake and Dopuch.

ventory drops to a predetermined level. Let us designate the average inventory level that results from this policy as Q_1. Now, if the firm perceives the likelihood of inventory price increases, and if the firm is motivated to speculate in such increases, then it will hold more inventory than is required by the model. Call this quantity Q_2. By changing its inventory level, the firm has increased its total inventory costs beyond those that would be incurred at its optimal level. The rationale for doing so is based on the expectation that these increased costs will be more than offset by the avoided, larger cash outflow in later periods of higher inventory prices.

Now, assume that inventory prices do rise in ensuing periods. Whether the decision to speculate was a wise one must be determined by comparing the incremental costs of having departed from the optimal inventory strategy with the savings that resulted from above normal purchases. Only if the latter exceed the former was the decision to speculate profitable.

Drake and Dopuch contend, and rightly so, that the realizable cost savings data that are generated by replacement costing are inadequate as a basis for evaluating the effectiveness of management's speculative activities. Their argument proceeds as follows. First, the realizable cost savings figure overstates the savings from speculative activities. That is, holding gains are computed on all inventory units held by the firm. However, even in situations in which the firm does not anticipate price rises, it must still maintain a certain average inventory (Q_1) for operating purposes. Clearly, the firm has speculated only to the extent that, in anticipation of price rises, it raised its actual inventory level (Q_2) above normal levels (Q_1). The gains from speculation, then, must exclude those units that would have been held in any case. But realizable cost savings include gains on all units, not just on the $Q_2 - Q_1$ units that represent speculative activity. Second, not only are the savings overstated, but also the incremental costs of speculation will not appear in the realizable cost savings section. Instead, these carrying and purchasing costs on the extra speculative units will be buried in the current operating profit section.

From this it can be deduced that whenever a firm decides to speculate in inventory price changes, the replacement cost system will not generate data in a form that allows ready evaluation of the net result of such activity. More important still, the system will not isolate the costs incurred by having speculated. These incremental costs will instead be included in the current operating profit section. The statement reader could reasonably infer that such costs were the results of operating activities when, in fact, they are wholly attributable to speculative activities.

While the observations of Drake and Dopuch are correct for firms that actively speculate, a slightly different conclusion results if a firm is not speculating in price changes, a situation which we now examine. Assume that a certain firm expects inventory prices to rise in the future, but that this firm—as a matter of policy—refuses to speculate in such increases.[30] Under these circumstances the firm will continue to carry Q_1 inventory, the amount called for by its model, despite its expectation of future price increases. In this situation there is no need to evaluate management's speculative activities; as we are using the term, there were none.[31]

How will replacement costing perform in this situation, if we assume that the anticipated price increases did occur? Of primary concern is the reporting of operating activity—the only activity in which management chose to engage.

To be useful, current operating profit should facilitate evaluation of operating activities and exclude all non-operating events. This is precisely what will happen in this illustrative situation; gains attributable to having held assets in a period of rising prices will be segregated in the cost savings section of the report. Because the carrying value of the assets was increased as prices rose, cost expirations in the operating profit section will be shown at replacement value. Artificial dollar increases that are unavailable for dividend purposes without constricting the volume of future operating activities are omitted from operating profit. The reported current operating profit figure will reflect the success with which management utilized assets, given the current cost of these assets. Operating profit will not contain any costs attributable to speculative activity since management incurred no such costs.

Our purpose in developing this counter-example is to put the

---

[30] This policy need not be irrational. The firm may consider the impending price increases to be too small to warrant incurring the additional costs of speculation. Alternatively, spoilage and obsolescence may be an important factor.

[31] Strictly speaking, one could say that management's decision not to speculate was a speculative decision and, as such, merits analysis. The wisdom of such a decision must be evaluated on an opportunity cost basis. The opportunity cost of not having speculated would be equal to the price rise on that amount of extra inventory that the firm would have held had it chosen to speculate. The opportunity gain from not having speculated is equal to the incremental ordering and carrying costs that would have been paid if the firm had chosen to speculate. Thus, management's decision not to speculate would have been the correct one only if the latter savings exceed the former costs.

Obviously, the information necessary to make this evaluation will not be generated by the replacement cost system. It is probably unrealistic to expect an accounting system to generate opportunity cost data, since the alternative courses of action not chosen are endless. For instance, in the example above, how would one measure the opportunity cost of not having speculated when there is an infinite variety of inventory levels that the firm could have selected if it had decided to speculate?

observations of Drake and Dopuch in perspective. Obviously, replacement cost income is not a perfect measurement system, as the Drake and Dopuch example clearly illustrates. In an absolute sense, the dichotomization of profit components into operating and holding segments is not always as "clean" as proponents of replacement costing had contended. Specifically, it appears erroneous to equate cost savings with speculative acumen. Whenever a firm is actively engaged in speculation, it is generally not possible to evaluate the success of these activities by reference to the realizable cost savings figure alone. Worse still, some of the costs of such activity may "spill over" into the operating profit component.

On the other hand, if firms passively accept the inevitability of price changes without speculating—as in our counter-example—or if price changes are unanticipated, replacement costing does indeed separate operating and holding (not speculative) gains. Thus, it is clear that the Drake and Dopuch observation applies only to cases of active speculation. Furthermore, although their analysis discloses an *absolute* failing of replacement costing, we must bear in mind that despite the admitted inconsistency of the replacement cost dichotomization, it may still perform this separation *relatively* better than available alternative measurement systems.

Fixed asset changes

In similar fashion, Drake and Dopuch contend that the realizable cost savings component is an insufficient representation of the result of management speculation involving fixed assets. To demonstrate their point, they cite U. S. Steel's decision in 1952 to build the capital-intensive Fairless Steel Works.[32] From a strict rate of return point of view, using then prevailing prices for capital and labor, the investment could not be justified. However, the capital-intensive plant was felt to be economically justifiable given the increases in labor wage rates that were expected over the decade. "Apparently U. S. Steel determined that the incremental capital investment—the amount of investment in excess of that which could currently be justified—would produce future labor savings whose discounted present value was greater than the incremental cost of the capital investment." [33]

In retrospect, it turned out that U. S. Steel's forecasts were accurate. Labor rates did rise appreciably over the period, so much so that the capital-intensive plant was economically justified. Over this same period, the price of the capital assets employed also increased. In large measure,

[32] The example, and much of the following discussion, is taken from Drake and Dopuch, "Dichotomizing Income," 198–200.
[33] *Ibid.*, 199.

this increase was probably attributable to the savings generated by the substitution of capital for labor.[34]

How would U. S. Steel's decision to build and hold the Fairless Works have been reflected in a replacement cost report? A portion of the benefits would, of course, appear in the cost savings section as asset prices rose. However, the costs of this policy would be reflected in current operating profit. That is, the decision to build a capital-intensive plant at a time at which it was not warranted by prevailing wage rates had a cost to the firm. In relation to output, fixed costs were higher than they needed to have been. Furthermore, in later years, total operating costs were less than those that would have been incurred in a less mechanized plant. It is apparent once again that the *total* results of the speculative decision are not reflected in the cost savings account alone. In this situation

> . . . the company traded operating income in the period of acquisition and in the early periods of the life of the asset for higher operating income and some holding income in later periods. . . .

> In general, all investment decisions involve a series of trade-offs. . . . Holding gains (losses) only reflect the effects of changes in the prices of capital assets over time. The other effects of decisions to invest in a specific mix of input factors must be reported within the operating income statement. Very often it is not even possible to determine the total effects of the decision by merely adding the two components of income since the different trade-off effects could occur in different periods.[35]

We should emphasize in summarizing the position of Drake and Dopuch that these authors are not arguing for the rejection of replacement costing. Instead, they merely suggest that one of the reputed advantages of this measurement method may be illusory. Specifically, it is often contended that the dichotomization of income into operating and holding components is useful because it allows for the separate analysis of two types of management decisions—operating and speculative. The Drake and Dopuch examples illustrate that when a firm actively speculates, the two income components are so interdependent that data needed to evaluate such decisions will be found in both sections of the statement.

This discussion emphasizes the need for a careful definition of the purpose behind the dichotomization of replacement cost income. In light of the preceding analysis, it does seem apparent that the cost savings component is of limited utility as a reflection of speculative achieve-

34 *Ibid.*
35 *Ibid.*, 199–200.

ment. Therefore, let us reiterate an earlier alternative justification for separately reflecting holding gains.[36] In this alternative schema, cost savings are an adjunct; they are separately reflected only to eliminate their effect on operating profit. That is, when cost expirations are reflected in terms of replacement price (thereby necessitating the use of some sort of holding gain account), the operating margin will better measure the real change in net assets occasioned by operations. When firms do not expect price changes, or do not deem it worthwhile to speculate even if they do anticipate price changes, then, *ex post*, the operating profit component will reflect the results of operations in current price terms. The cost savings component will reflect the cumulative change in the prices of owned assets over the period. *Rather than a measure of managerial acumen or speculative ability, realizable cost savings are a reflection of the impact of random price changes on a passive entity. Thus, the integrity of operating performance data is the primary impetus for dichotomization, and cost savings data are a subordinate consequence of this objective.*

However, when a firm is not a passive observer of price changes, i.e., when it is an active speculator, some of the costs of speculation will find their way into the operating profit section, according to Drake and Dopuch. To the extent that these are technically non-operating, non-recurring costs, their inclusion in that section could diminish the usefulness of certain forecasts using replacement cost data. How serious this commingling of operating and speculative data is, is essentially an empirical issue. Specifically, we would first have to determine the prevalence of speculative activity on the part of business enterprises. Second, we would need to learn how frequently speculative activity generates costs that will be reflected in operating profit. Finally, we would need to discover how frequently the commingled costs of speculation will be sufficiently material to affect various forecasts.

SUMMARY

In this chapter we explored some additional issues that affect the predictive ability of replacement cost income. We first examined the impact of Type B and Type C price changes on forecasts of future operating flows. Our analysis indicated that the potentially disruptive effect of such price changes is stronger in the fixed asset area than in the inventory area. However, we suggested that a remedy is possible even if there is no covariance between fixed asset price changes and changes

---

[36] See p. 60.

in expected operating flows. By using economic depreciation in the computation of replacement cost income, one can maintain the correspondence between replacement cost income and economic income. However, from a practical point of view, this approach introduces serious measurement difficulties.

We next examined the theoretical accuracy of current operating profit extrapolations when end-of-period prices were not in effect throughout the reporting period. As a consequence of this analysis, it became apparent that the relationship between current operating profit and future distributable operating flow is likely to be only an approximate one. However, income measurement is a surrogation process. If a relationship is set forth between an accounting measure and some alternative concept, the link need not be precise. A reasonable surrogate relationship is adequate. In this case we observed that the nature and timing of those price changes which have occurred determines whether a reasonable surrogate relationship exists. This finding underscores the need for empirical research to determine the relative frequency and materiality of Type B and C price changes. No conclusions are possible until such evidence is available.

Another problem surveyed was the impact of technological change on replacement cost information for predictions. We concluded that when technological change alters the rate of return earned by manufacturers (i.e., equipment users are the beneficiaries of the technological change), total replacement cost income may not be a good lead indicator for the firm's operating flows. On the other hand, when consumers or equipment manufacturers gain the benefits of technological change, then the theoretical relationship between replacement cost income and future operating flows seemingly holds. Hopefully, this analysis of the effects of technological change provides the theoretical basis for gathering needed empirical evidence.

Finally, we examined the interdependence between replacement cost operating profit and holding gains. Here we discovered that the dichotomy between the two income components was not as sharp as replacement cost proponents had contended. That is, when firms are actively speculating in price changes, some of the costs of such speculation are likely to be reflected in the operating profit income component. This makes it difficult to separately evaluate the wisdom of the speculative decision. However, when firms are not actively speculating, this potential interdependence is not troublesome, and the dichotomization of replacement cost income serves its intended purpose.

CHAPTER SEVEN

Replacement
Cost Accounting
Ratios

The normative investor decision model that was developed in Chapter 2 requires information about the risk associated with future operating flows. Various accounting ratios have been shown to be good predictors of risk in other settings. For this reason we suggested that accounting ratios might also provide a useful basis for assessing the riskiness of the expected flows to investors. Accordingly, in order to evaluate the relevance of replacement cost information, one must examine the utility of the ratios that are prepared from replacement cost figures. This we will do here.

A complete analysis of replacement cost ratios will not be presented in this chapter. Such an analysis would require a detailed specification of those accounting ratios that are most useful to the investor in assessing risk. Unfortunately, this type of empirical evidence regarding replacement cost ratios is not yet available. Accordingly, our analysis must be limited to a brief treatment of certain basic issues. Our purpose is to explore some theoretical considerations regarding the utility of replacement cost ratios. Hopefully, this analysis will prove useful in formulating later empirical tests.

We will analyze replacement cost ratios using the following approach. First, we will specify the intended purpose of ratio analysis. For investors, this purpose is to use ratios in assessing the risk associated with future flows. Once the intended purpose of ratio analysis is specified, we must identify some specific ratios that are thought to be relevant to this objective. In Chapter 2 we suggested that ratios which reflect a firm's *liquidity-solvency position* and its *profit generating potential* are potentially useful in risk assessment. For liquidity-solvency, the specific ratios to be examined are the current ratio and the times interest earned ratio. For profit generating potential, the ratios are asset turnover, profit as a percentage of sales, and return on assets.[1]

Once we have selected a specific ratio and isolated its intended analytic purpose, we must examine the characteristics of the data that are used to compute the ratio. For example, a certain ratio may require a measurement of ending inventory. Since there are many methods for measuring ending inventory, one must analyze which method of inventory measurement best conforms to the intended purpose of the ratio. After performing many such analyses, one can specify those data that seem best suited to the analytic intent of various ratios. If a ratio is subsequently computed using those data that best conform to its intended purpose, the resultant index does in fact measure what it theoretically purports to measure. Ratios that possess this characteristic can be termed "theoretically valid." Thus, our first objective in this chapter is to determine the theoretical validity of the previously enumerated ratios when they are computed using replacement cost data.

But theoretical validity is only one aspect of ratio utility. In addition to the information content of the individual ratio, accounting ratios are also potentially useful because of the opportunities they afford for intertemporal comparisons for a single firm and relative comparisons between firms. As one author states: "The real significance in reported results . . . lies in trends and in intercorporate comparisons, not in the absolute numbers themselves." [2] Therefore, our second purpose in this chapter is to assess the usefulness of replacement cost ratios in making relative comparisons over time and among firms.

In evaluating the usefulness of replacement cost ratios, our interest is in how well these selected ratios perform in an absolute sense. From time to time, however, it will be helpful to compare the information

---

[1] We do not suggest that these five ratios are necessarily the best measures of liquidity-solvency and profit generating potential. Rather, these ratios were selected because they are frequently mentioned in various accounting texts. This frequency of reference makes such ratios familiar to most readers and provides a good basis for illustration. We should emphasize that our conclusions might differ if other ratios were selected. This observation underscores the tentative and limited nature of our analysis of replacement cost ratios.

[2] Andrew M. McCosh, "Accounting Consistency—Key to Stockholder Information," *The Accounting Review,* 42 (October, 1967), 697.

shown by a certain replacement cost ratio with the information that would be generated for the same ratio using historical cost accounting procedures. Although these comparisons may afford a readily visible means for demonstrating the *relative* performance of replacement costing, such procedures do not provide sufficient evidence about the absolute relevance of this measurement basis. In making such comparisons with historical costs, it must be remembered that any option—such as replacement costing—can be made to appear desirable in a relative sense if it is compared with a sufficiently undesirable alternative. Since our purpose is broader than the mere determination of whether replacement cost data are superior to their historical cost equivalents, we must be careful to avoid imputing relevance to replacement cost ratios just because they appear to be preferable to the corresponding historical cost ratios. Accordingly, in the development that follows, an attempt will be made to evaluate replacement cost ratios in their own right using normative standards as criteria, rather than in comparison to extant, generally accepted accounting procedures.

Before beginning the analysis, we must reiterate that there are differences between the appropriate measure of risk for (1) evaluating an individual security, and (2) considering that security for inclusion in a portfolio of many securities. Although this chapter is directed toward individual securities, it is quite possible that accounting ratios might be relevant for portfolio problems as well. That is, as long as there is some relationship between market determined risk measures and those individual firm characteristics incorporated in accounting ratios, then accounting ratios might also be relevant for assessing portfolio risk. However, such extensions must be quite tentative since the evidence in this area is still sparse.[3]

LIQUIDITY-SOLVENCY POSITION

Investors are concerned with information about a firm's liquidity-solvency position for one simple reason. If an enterprise has the capacity to meet its short- and intermediate-term obligations continuously, then its chances for realizing its long-term prospects are enhanced. Conversely, if a firm has a weak liquidity-solvency position, the risk associated with its future operating flows is great.

In the following sections, we will examine two of the more popular ratios that are used to represent liquidity-solvency. These are (1) the current ratio, and (2) the times interest earned ratio.

[3] For one related study, see Beaver, Kettler, and Scholes, "Market and Accounting Risk Measures."

Current ratio

Ideally, the current ratio should reflect the ability of a firm to meet its short-term obligations. A question immediately arises, however, with regard to the interpretation of this ratio. That is, does the calculation assume that firms will liquidate current obligations by using current assets in the normal operating cycle as they are successively transformed into cash? Or, alternatively, is the ratio intended to portray the ability of a firm to pay these debts under the most adverse conditions, i.e., by liquidating all current assets at their then present stage in the cycle? Although the issue is one of some importance, unfortunately there is seemingly no answer to this question.[4] In essence, this means there is no generally accepted definition of the purpose to be served by the current ratio. Instead, the meaning of this ratio is essentially a subjective one; what the ratio is intended to convey is essentially a function of the detailed uses to which it is put by the statement reader.[5] Because of the ambiguity surrounding the interpretation of the current ratio, any analysis of the usefulness of this ratio prepared from replacement cost data should consider both the normal operating cycle and the liquidation interpretations.

First, we will analyze the utility of the replacement cost current ratio when the normal operating cycle interpretation is employed. In arguing for this interpretation of the current ratio one author states:

> If . . . the amount of resources that will be provided [through operations] by the current assets were used in this computation, the usefulness of the working capital concept might be improved. This would lead to reflecting inventory on a present-value basis, i.e., net realizable value for purposes of working-capital analysis.[6]

Indeed, it seems reasonable to argue that if one adopted the normal operating cycle notion, *all* current assets should be valued at their net

---

4 Cf., Philip E. Fess, "The Working Capital Concept," *The Accounting Review,* 41 (April, 1966), 266–70. In this article, Fess argues in favor of the normal operating cycle notion.

5 Attempts to resolve the issue on a normative basis would likely prove fruitless. For instance, one could appeal to the going-concern concept in order to support the normal operating cycle notion of the current ratio. That is, since the continuity assumption is so pervasive in accounting theory, it might seem logical that the interpretation of the current ratio should also embrace this notion. If we adopt this view, then going-concern value should be used for the ratio components. But it is possible to counter this position as follows. Since the major purpose in computing the current ratio is to provide a basis for judging a firm's survival ability in the face of short-term financial crises, it seems somewhat self-defeating to blithely *assume* in constructing the ratio that the firm *will* survive. The argument is endless.

6 Fess, "The Working Capital Concept," 268.

realizable values for purposes of working capital analysis. Thus, in order to assess the relevance of the current ratio to those users who adopt the operating cycle notion, one must examine the correspondence between replacement cost asset values and the net realizable values of these same assets in the normal course of operations. We will now examine these correspondences.

Cash presents no difficulty since its replacement cost and net realizable value coincide. Receivables do pose a minor problem because the carrying values of these assets must be reduced by expected collection costs and discounted to their present worth in order to arrive at net realizable value. In many lines of business, collection costs are relatively insignificant and thus may be safely ignored. Furthermore, the preponderance of short-term receivables usually makes discounting unnecessary. However, if collection costs are material or if collection is delayed, replacement costing will tend to overstate the net realizable value of receivables.

Inventories are a more complex issue. Reproduced below as Figure 7–1 is a chart prepared by Professor George J. Staubus, depicting the relationship between the replacement cost of inventories and their net

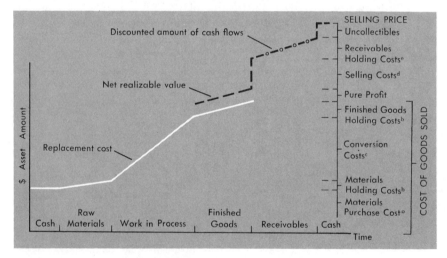

FIGURE 7–1

Relationship between net realizable value and replacement cost

a Including fringe acquisition costs such as transportation.
b Cost of capital, insurance, storage space, etc.
c Including holding costs during conversion.
d All costs are assumed to be allocable to one or more of the categories shown.
e Especially cost of capital.

Reproduced with the permission of Scholars Book Co. and the author.

realizable value.[7] The right-hand portion of the chart shows the cost and profit components which, when added together, constitute the eventual selling price of the inventory. Examination of the chart indicates that if the interest element of carrying costs is included in the computation of replacement cost (as it theoretically should be), then the replacement cost of inventory will differ from the net realizable value of inventory only by the amount of pure ("residual") profit. In general, then, one might conclude that replacement cost inventory value tends to *roughly* approximate the net realizable value of inventory. Staubus sums up the relationship in the following fashion:

> In the typical case, with the manufacturer earning a normal return on investment, the residual profit would be small. Under equilibrium conditions in an industry with a high degree of freedom of entry one might expect the residual income to be zero. The use of an interest rate not representing the economic cost of capital (such as a zero rate) in discounting the selling price or in accumulating carrying charges on the production costs would affect the reported residual profit. Absence of equilibrium conditions would also contribute to such a profit (or loss). Nevertheless, it is fair to say that replacement cost is related to net realizable value and to present values of future cash flows even though the relationship is likely to be sufficiently loose to lead us to prefer one of the latter measurement methods if it can be applied with acceptable objectivity.[8]

In a replacement cost system, liability carrying values will typically differ from their historical cost values only because of interest rate fluctuations. Since liabilities included in the working capital ratio have a short life, this adjustment will seldom be material.[9]

Although this analysis is unavoidably brief, nevertheless, it is apparent that there is some *general* relationship between working capital replacement costs and the net realizable values of these items in the normal course of operations. Empirical evidence is once again required in this area. If this evidence confirms our *a priori* analysis, then it seems reasonable to suggest that replacement costing will tend to generate output that should prove useful for investors' working capital and ratio analysis purposes when the intent of this analysis is to determine the ability of the firm to meet its current obligations through normal operating activities.

---

7 George J. Staubus, "The Relevance of Evidence of Cash Flows," in *Asset Valuation and Income Determination,* ed. Robert R. Sterling (Lawrence, Kan.: Scholars Book Co., 1971), p. 56.

8 Staubus, "Current Cash Equivalent for Assets," 655.

9 However, the adjustment needed to reflect long-term liabilities on a replacement cost basis may be material. For a discussion of these considerations see Edwards and Bell, *Measurement of Business Income,* pp. 203–7.

Next, we examine the usefulness of replacement cost current ratios when working capital analysis and the current ratio are used to determine the margin of safety in the face of near-term adversity. For this use the crucial issue is not what the assets will eventually realize through normal operation, but rather what the assets will command if financial difficulties necessitate their immediate conversion. If replacement cost data are to be relevant for this use, they must approximate the liquidation value of working capital items. As before, cash is cash, and therefore, presents no measurement difficulties. Receivables, on the other hand, do give rise to some problems since management's ability to accelerate the collection process, especially on short notice, is quite limited. Therefore, for short-term liquidation purposes, receivables must generally be assigned or sold at a sizable discount to compensate for risk and collection expenses. Replacement costing will thus generally overstate the liquidation value of receivables. Inventory values involve similar difficulties. It is doubtful whether a company could recover the full, current replacement cost of most inventory items. Although this is most evident for partially fabricated, in-process items (indeed, in many cases there may be *no* market for such goods), to a lesser extent the difficulty also exists for raw materials. Different prices may prevail in different markets (wholesale versus retail, etc.) and there may be sizable disposition costs. Therefore, a firm desirous of liquidating its inventories is likely to do so only at a net price that is below the current cost of these materials.

Thus it seems apparent that replacement costing will generate working capital values that are of less relevance to the liquidation-oriented reader than they are to the normal operating cycle reader. If liquidation value is relevant to users, this information must be obtained from other sources.

In analyzing the replacement cost current ratio, the issue of intertemporal comparisons, that is, the analysis of changes that occur in the current ratio from period to period, should also be discussed. Ideally, as the current ratio grows larger (smaller) over time, the liquidity position of the enterprise should be growing stronger (weaker). The issue of intertemporal validity, then, reduces to one simple question: Will the magnitude of the replacement cost current ratio tend to covary with the firm's liquidity position?

To answer this question, it must be recognized that the current ratio will grow larger for two possible reasons. First, during a period of stable prices, the magnitude of a firm's current assets could increase relative to its current liabilities. Second, over a period in which the *physical* magnitude of the assets relative to the liabilities is stable, the market value of the assets could rise proportionally more than the market value of the liabilities. (Additionally, of course, both types of changes could be occurring simultaneously.)

Traditionally, it is agreed that as the firm's current ratio grows larger because of the first circumstance, its liquidity and/or solvency position is simultaneously strengthened.[10] But what about the second type of change? Will the firm's liquidity and/or solvency position be enhanced because the replacement cost of its current assets rises relative to current liabilities? The answer to this question depends on whether there is covariance between movements in replacement costs and movements in (1) net realizable values, and (2) liquidation values. If net realizable values from operations and liquidation values both move in conjunction with replacement costs, then under both possible interpretations of the meaning of the current ratio, upward movements in the ratio would indeed reflect a strengthened working capital position.

In Chapters 4 and 6 we discussed the possibility that movements in replacement costs and future operating flows might diverge. Furthermore, because of market imperfections, replacement costs and liquidation values need not move in tandem either. Thus, it would seem premature to suggest that movements in replacement costs, realizable values, and liquidation values will be parallel. Empirical evidence is needed. If this evidence does disclose divergence among these quantities, then the usefulness of intertemporal comparisons using replacement cost current ratios would be impaired.

It has been suggested that interfirm ratio comparisons afford the statement reader an opportunity to make potentially valuable analyses of the relative investment potential of various companies. One of the reputed advantages of replacement costing is that its ratios facilitate more realistic interfirm comparisons. Replacement cost information is thought to be superior for interfirm comparisons because it is less prone to generating the artificial differences that frequently arise among firms when historical costing is used. To illustrate, consider the case of two firms that are identical in all respects. That is, each possesses the same physical quantities and types of assets and similar capital structures. Nevertheless, if both firms use historical cost accounting procedures,

---

[10] Although this is the prevalent view, it is well known that the current ratio *itself* is subject to certain deficiencies that might impair its intertemporal validity. Since these problems transcend the measurement basis by which the ratio components are derived, there is no need to discuss them here. For a discussion of these problems, the interested reader should see Kenneth W. Lemke, "The Evaluation of Liquidity: An Analytical Study," *Journal of Accounting Research*, 8 (Spring, 1970), 47–77.

Technically speaking, it is possible for the increase in the current ratio to be coupled with a shift in the proportional relationship among current asset categories. If the proportion of cash and receivables declines while the current ratio increases, liquidity could conceivably be diminished. Of course, the firm's solvency (i.e., its ability to meet its obligations in the intermediate term) would be increased.

differences in the accounting statements could exist. To cite a single example, one firm may choose to value its inventory on a LIFO basis whereas the other selects the FIFO basis. It is quite possible for the historical cost current ratios of these two firms to differ even though the physical quantities of the working capital items are identical.[11]

In contrast, replacement cost proponents contend that this measurement method gives rise to fewer such artificial divergences. With regard to the current ratio, our analysis in Chapter 3 tends to support this contention. There, in discussing the criterion of dispersion, we suggested that replacement cost ending inventory values would seemingly be less dispersed, on average, than their counterpart historical cost ending inventory values. That is, the use of market prices as a valuation device obviates the need to select an arbitrary inventory flow technique like LIFO or FIFO. By reducing the need for such arbitrary valuation techniques, we also reduce the possibility that two firms with similar physical inventories will report materially different balance sheet values for inventory. This means that the possibilities for divergence between physical asset levels and accounting valuations are substantially reduced following replacement costing.[12] Similar real asset positions will tend to be valued similarly; this is a relationship that may not occur when historical cost measurement methods are used. Because replacement cost current ratios reduce the possibilities for artificial valuation differences among firms, it seems plausible to suggest that this replacement cost ratio provides a more realistic basis for interfirm comparisons.

Times interest earned

From the point of view of the equity investor, the times interest earned computation is a rough indicator of the long-run solvency of the firm since it reflects the ability of the enterprise to meet its debt service cost out of current earnings. Solvency is jeopardized when the interest charge on fixed indebtedness is high relative to earnings. In such situ-

[11] It is possible that these artificial differences might be so large that *individual* investors could be misled. Indeed, the findings of one recent study bear this out. See Thomas R. Dyckman, "On the Effects of Earnings-trend, Size and Inventory Valuation Procedures in Evaluating a Business Firm," in *Research in Accounting Measurement*, ed. Jaedicke, *et al.*, pp. 175–85.

Although several such studies have shown that individual investors could be misled by artificial accounting differences, it does not necessarily follow that the market as a whole will be misled. This is a point of controversy between those who espouse "functional fixation," and those who believe in market efficiency. For an elaboration of this point, see Beaver, "The Behavior of Security Prices."

[12] Values for identical assets might still differ between two firms insofar as each buys its assets in different markets with different price structures. Of course, the very existence of alternative markets (and thus, alternative sources of supply) should tend to minimize such differences.

ations, little margin exists to protect the firm should it experience a protracted business downturn. The times interest earned ratio is often computed as follows:

$$\text{Times interest earned} = \frac{\text{pre-tax earnings} + \text{interest charges}}{\text{interest charges}}$$

Before examining the relevance of the replacement cost times interest earned ratio, a definitional issue must be solved. Specifically, should the earnings figure in the numerator be defined as total replacement cost income or should earnings be limited to just the current operating profit component?

Given the purpose of this ratio, it would appear that the latter earnings definition would be more appropriate. The intent of the ratio, of course, is to gauge the future solvency of the firm by comparing expected future operating flows with existing interest obligations. Ideally, to best serve this need, a series of ratios should be prepared, one for each year of the foreseeable future in which interest obligations must be met. Current earnings are used only as a proxy for this expected flow stream. It should be apparent that because we are seeking a proxy for future operating flows, the earnings measure used should be a recurring one. Total replacement cost income would not serve this need because the cost savings included therein cannot necessarily be expected to recur and, indeed, may be reversed in future periods. Furthermore, it is entirely possible that these cost savings may be of Type B or C and will not result in an operating inflow or a reduction in an outflow in later periods. Thus, for both of these reasons, in preparing a times interest earned computation using replacement cost data, earnings should be defined as current operating profit.

(A second definitional issue involves the denominator of this ratio, i.e., periodic interest charges. Edwards and Bell suggest that periodic interest charges be measured on a replacement cost basis using the actual market interest rate for similar securities during the period. This approach, like amortization of bond premium or discount, will cause reported interest expense to differ from actual interest payments. The question, then, is which of these two figures should be used in the denominator of the ratio? Once again, the answer relates to the intended purpose of the ratio. Since liquidity-solvency ratios are designed to portray the ability to meet near-term, actual obligations, it would appear that the interest outflow rather than some measure of reported interest expense would be preferable in the denominator.)

It must be emphasized that the solvency of a firm is highly dependent on the margin of safety, or spread, between net operating inflows and interest outflows. When interest obligations are constant while the operating level and/or profitability declines, then the firm's margin of safety diminishes. In this situation, a firm will be unable to maintain its pre-existing level of solvency at its pre-existing real level of operations. One or the other, or perhaps both, must suffer. Both of these possibilities increase the risk associated with future operating flows.

If historical cost income is used in the numerator of the times interest earned ratio, it is possible for this ratio to remain constant even though the real margin of safety is declining. For example, consider a situation where inventory prices have quickly risen while no corresponding adjustment in output price occurs. If inventory turnover is slow, it is possible that historical cost income will not immediately fall. Reported profit will be constant despite the fact that long-term profitability has been impaired. This reduction in profitability reduces the real margin of safety. But as long as reported historical cost profit does not change, the reported margin of safety will not decline.

If current operating profit is used to compute the times interest earned ratio, the situation is depicted differently. In this case, replacement cost income would decline because of the increases in replacement costs. The times interest earned ratio would also decline, of course. As a result, it would be evident that the real margin of safety has declined. That is, the spread between long-term profits and interest outflows has diminished.

For the purpose of intertemporal comparisons, the replacement cost times interest earned ratio seems to provide useful information. Changes in this ratio between years will reflect movements in the real margin of safety; existing computational procedures based on historical cost data will not necessarily reflect such movements. For example, consider a FIFO firm that experiences rising input costs but is precluded from adjusting selling prices for competitive reasons. Until lower priced stocks are exhausted, *reported* profit will continue at the previous high level despite the fall in long-term earnings. Although the real margin of safety has fallen in this situation, a comparison of historical cost ratios over time will not show this until reported profits decline.

Furthermore, interfirm ratio comparisons are probably improved by using the replacement cost times interest earned ratio. Two firms identical in all respects except for the timing of their asset purchases [13] will not necessarily display identical margins of safety in a period of changing prices if the ratio is computed using historical cost data. Replacement cost data, on the other hand, will tend to generate similar results for the two firms if indeed their real positions are identical.

[13] This issue is explored in greater detail in the following section.

PROFIT GENERATING POTENTIAL

The profitability of a firm is in large measure a reflection of the efficiency with which it is operated. By observing a firm's performance over time, one can assess the effectiveness of management's response to varying economic circumstances. High efficiency and proven success in adapting to a changing environment are reassuring indicators. They suggest continued growth if economic conditions are favorable and smaller reversals if conditions worsen. In short, profit potential ratios are theoretically related directly to the variability of the operating flow stream. The stronger is the operating base, the less is the expected variability of future flows. Accordingly, if the data inputs to these ratios effectively portray the underlying circumstances, then such ratios should be useful in evaluating the expected variability of future operating flows.

In the next sections, we will examine three of the more popular ratios that are employed to evaluate profit generating potential. These ratios are (1) asset turnover, (2) profit as a percentage of sales, and (3) return on assets.

Asset turnover

Asset turnover, which is the ratio of sales revenue to total assets, is one of two separate components that together comprise the return on assets measure. When the asset turnover is multiplied by the other component, i.e., profit as a percentage of sales, the product of this operation yields the return on assets employed.

Theoretically, asset turnover is a utilization ratio. That is, it is intended to reflect the intensity with which assets are employed within the enterprise. All other factors constant, the greater the intensity of utilization—i.e., the greater the amount of revenues generated by a given asset level—the greater the return on investment. The range of possible turnover levels is generally governed by the characteristics of the industry in which the firm is situated. But given this general boundary, the actual turnover level is a function of the efficiency with which management uses assets. Because it is a measure of past management efficiency, this ratio is thought to provide a reasonable basis for forecasting management's *future* efficiency. Such efficiency in asset utilization, of course, will be a prime determinant of the level of future flows accruing to the enterprise.

In order for the asset turnover ratio to present meaningful information, it is important as a practical matter that the computation be dimensionally sound.[14] Dimensional soundness means that the units in which the numerator and denominator are stated be such that, after division, the quotient has an unequivocal and meaningful interpretation.[15] This is a requirement, of course, that should be met by any ratio in order for the result to have operational significance. This concept is introduced now because the asset turnover ratio computed using historical cost data is *not* dimensionally sound. A simple examination of the components of the ratio discloses this. Notice that in the historical cost ratio the numerator, sales revenues, is in terms of dollars, as is the denomina-

---

[14] For a discussion of dimensional soundness, see David W. Miller and Martin K. Starr, *Executive Decisions and Operations Research* (2nd ed.) (Englewood Cliffs, N. J.: Prentice-Hall, Inc., 1969), pp. 159–62.

[15] This definition is best understood by means of an example. Take the case of the simple, deterministic, inventory reorder quantity model. When demand is known, and spread evenly over the period, the economic optimum order quantity (Q) is:

$$Q = \sqrt{\frac{2DK}{C}}$$

where: D = demand for the ordered part, in units, over some period of time
K = order cost stated in dollars
C = dollar cost per inventory unit per year
We know, furthermore, that Q, the optimum order quantity that results from the calculation, is stated in terms of units. In order to demonstrate the dimensional soundness of the formula, all the independent variables will be put in dimensional terms. Thus:

$$D = \frac{\text{units}}{\text{time}}$$
$$K = \$$$
$$C = \$/\text{units}/\text{time}$$

Inserting these dimensions into the formula yields:

$$\sqrt{\frac{2 \text{ units} \times \$}{\text{time}} \Big/ \$/\text{unit}/\text{time}}$$

Eliminating the pure number and dividing gives:

$$\sqrt{\frac{\$ \times \text{units}}{\text{time}} \times \frac{\text{time}}{\$/\text{units}}}$$

$$\sqrt{\$ \times \text{units} \times \frac{\text{units}}{\$}}$$

$$\sqrt{(\text{units})^2} = \text{units}$$

Thus we can observe that the *EOQ* formula is dimensionally sound since the dependent variable, Q, is in units, as we would expect it to be in order for it to have operational significance.

tor, average assets employed during the period. But the fact that both are in dollars is not enough. The ratio is intended to portray the asset dollar value that was needed to generate a given dollar volume of revenues. For the result to have a defensible meaning, the values in the numerator must relate to the same general time period as those in the denominator. Valuing assets by their historical cost violates this requirement. This is the case since the numerator is stated in terms of values that were received over the most recent operating period whereas the denominator is in terms of costs that were incurred in a series of prior periods.

In contrast, the asset turnover computed using replacement costs is dimensionally sound. The value shown for the assets employed in generating revenues is stated in terms of prices that prevailed over the past operating period. This is also true, of course, for the numerator, sales revenues. The resultant quotient (which, due to cancellation, is a pure number in this dimensionally sound ratio) shows how many times the market value received exceeded the market value that had to be tied up in order to generate those receipts. No similar unequivocal statement can be made to explain the meaning of the historical cost quotient.[16]

Intertemporal movements in the replacement cost asset turnover ratio also have an unequivocal interpretation. Consider a span of time over which there are increases in the prices of the factors used in production. In order to continue producing the same volume of output, the firm must now utilize more expensive inputs. If all other factors remain unchanged, these assets must now generate higher revenues in order to maintain a constant "real" turnover ratio. When input prices are rising, a profit maximizing firm should endeavor, at a minimum, to maintain its previous turnover ratio or if possible, to increase it. Valuing assets in the ratio at their current replacement cost will indicate whether or not the firm is accomplishing this objective. If it is not, a compensating adjustment in the markup must be made in order to avoid a decline in the real return on investment. This type of analysis is highly useful to the investor. It provides a basis for the development of a subjective assessment of management's ability to maintain a certain operating flow rate in the face of price adjustments. If product selling prices are at all sensitive to changes in input costs, historical cost turnover rates will tend to

[16] Technically, the replacement cost asset turnover ratio is strictly dimensionally sound only if (1) the average level of assets employed in the denominator is valued at the average market value of the period and (2) sales were spread evenly over the period. If these conditions are violated, then the ratio is still not strictly dimensionally sound. However, except for very extreme violations, we can still say that the ratio has a high degree of dimensional soundness because of the virtual overlap of the periods in the numerator and denominator; and this would certainly be the case over comparable periods relative to the historical cost-based ratio.

rise as input prices rise, since the numerator, revenue *flows,* will adjust more rapidly than the denominator, asset *stocks.* This rising turnover can occur even when the real turnover based on current prices is constant or falling. Analyses based on such data can easily precipitate erroneous expectations regarding future returns and their variability.

Interfirm turnover ratio comparisons are of limited utility unless they are confined to comparisons among firms in the same industry or among firms in different industries that have essentially similar production and marketing characteristics. If such interfirm comparisons are warranted, the replacement cost turnover ratio appears to provide potentially useful information.

We have already explained one facet of the reputed superiority of interfirm comparisons using replacement cost data. In discussing the current ratio, we pointed out that the use of market price data reduces the number of arbitrary accounting techniques required to prepare external reports. This, in turn, increases the likelihood that firms with similar assets will tend to value these assets similarly; the effect of this is to facilitate interfirm comparisons. However, there is yet another reason for suggesting that replacement cost ratios could improve interfirm comparability. Traditional accounting valuations are heavily influenced by the timing of assets purchases. This means that two firms with identical assets purchased at two different times will not report similar gross asset valuations *unless* the original historical purchase price was also identical at both points in time. In a replacement cost system, this discrepancy will not occur. If these hypothetical firms buy their assets in the same market,[17] then these assets would be valued similarly irrespective of the time of original purchase. Thus, interfirm asset turnover comparisons would tend to yield similar results for essentially similar firms. Historical cost turnover ratios do not possess this characteristic.

Profit as a percentage of sales

The other component of the return on investment calculation, profit as a percentage of sales, has a most obvious interpretation. It is intended to reflect the percentage profit contribution of each dollar of sales reve-

---

[17] If the firms buy their presumably identical assets in different markets, then different valuations might result. Such disparities would arise whenever prices differ among markets. In such situations, replacement costs would be determined by reference to the prevailing price in whatever market the firm customarily buys its assets. If prices do differ among markets, then despite the fact that two firms may employ identical assets and generate identical inflows, their respective positions are not identical. Whichever firm is in the higher-cost market is at a relative disadvantage vis-à-vis the other firm since it must pay more for the assets that generate its inflows. Replacement cost turnover ratios would be different for the two firms and this difference seems to correspond to the inherent positions of the two firms.

nues. The ratio has potential prognosticative utility insofar as management's ability to control past costs is a reasonable reflection of its ability to continue to do so in the future. Because this ratio deals with *operating* performance, and because it is intended to aid in assessing future performance potential, it seems appropriate, in the numerator of the ratio, to employ a profit concept that can theoretically be extrapolated. For purposes of this computation, it would therefore be necessary to define profit to equal current operating profit. Realizable cost savings would be excluded since these items reflect conditions that may or may not recur in future periods.

The use of replacement cost data in the preparation of this ratio seemingly facilitates interpretation of changes over time as well as comparisons among firms. Since cost expirations under replacement costing are always shown at the current value of the services consumed in generating revenues, the profitability ratio is not distorted by price changes. Furthermore, each period's ratio has the following interpretation: If no additional price changes occur in future periods, the percentage return on each dollar of sales can be expected to remain at its then current level—given constant management efficiency in the utilization of assets.[18]

Since price and efficiency changes can, and do, occur, examination of this ratio over time informs the reader of how those price changes that did occur have affected the firm and how successful management has been in maintaining, or increasing, the percentage return on sales. The resultant trend may thus be useful in providing a basis for forecasting the variability of future flows from operations.

Theoretically, interfirm comparisons are improved when the replacement cost profitability ratio is used. The reasoning is similar to that used in previous examples. That is, replacement costing is believed to necessitate fewer choices of arbitrary accounting techniques and tends to obliterate the artificial effects of timing differences in asset purchases. As a consequence, the resultant ratios are thought to provide a better basis for discerning the real differences among firms' results.

Return on investment

Since this ratio is equal to the product of the asset turnover and profitability percentage ratios, it is essentially a gauge of the overall

[18] This statement must be qualified somewhat whenever significant, non-offsetting price changes occurred throughout the past period. Since cost of goods sold will reflect the prices in effect at the time each sale was made, and since these prices may have changed further by the end of the period, current operating profit may not necessarily reflect future expectations even under *ceteris paribus* assumptions. This problem, which conceivably could be serious in certain circumstances, is diminished somewhat whenever input costs and operating flows move in tandem with no significant lags. This issue was discussed in Chapter 6.

operating efficiency of the enterprise. The percentage return that is shown using replacement cost data can be interpreted as that rate that would be earned from future operations if all prices and volume levels were to remain constant (subject to the caveat in footnote 18, *supra*). Since the characteristics of this measure have been treated in the discussion of its two component parts above, there is little need for further analysis.

SUMMARY

In this chapter we presented a brief evaluation of the theoretical characteristics of replacement cost financial ratios. Two essential features of these ratios were discussed. First, we suggested that the use of replacement cost data enhanced the theoretical validity of the specific ratios that we examined. That is, the replacement cost data seemed to conform well to the intended analytic purpose of these ratios. (The only exception related to the liquidation interpretation of the current ratio.) Second, replacement cost ratios theoretically provide an improved basis for intertemporal and interfirm comparisons because replacement costing reduces the need for arbitrary accounting allocations and dampens the effects of timing differences in asset purchases.

The specific ratios that we analyzed were selected only as a means for highlighting the reputed advantages of replacement cost ratios. Thus, our observations are intended to be exploratory and must be regarded as tentative. Our intention was to give direction to later empirical tests. A complete analysis would require an empirical determination of the specific ratios that are useful in risk assessment. After these ratios are identified, the theoretical propositions in this chapter would require empirical verification. If the evidence gathered by such empirical efforts supports our conclusions, then replacement cost financial ratios could improve investors' estimates of the risk associated with firms' expected operating flows.

CONCLUSION

This study was not designed to provide definitive answers to many of the issues surrounding replacement cost income. Answers require empirical evidence, a commodity that unfortunately is scarce in the replacement cost literature. Not only is empirical evidence scarce, but some of what does exist seems misdirected. In part, these misdirected studies can be explained by the absence of an adequate theory underlying replacement costing. Researchers require a theoretical structure to provide direction for their empirical efforts. Without a clear understanding of what are the purported advantages and objectives of replacement costing, research efforts are apt to be unrewarding.

This study aims to provide this absent theoretical structure in the replacement cost area. Our purpose has been to review the process by which replacement cost statements are generated, develop a normative structure that explains the potential relevance of replacement cost data, and to evaluate, logically, the ability of replacement costing to satisfy these normative objectives. Three major assumptions permeate this analysis. The first suggests that users' information needs may be diverse. Just as the objectives of various categories of users differ, so too may the information needed to accomplish these objectives. This implies that there is no universally "ideal" income measure. As a result, the utility of replacement cost reports must be examined in relation to some well-defined user objectives. Long-term external investors constitute the user group selected herein. This choice leads to the second basic assumption of this study. It is presumed that the primary information need of this investor group relates to the future dividend flows expected from an investment and the risk inherent to these flows. To be relevant to these needs, accounting data should facilitate such estimates. The final assumption is that simpler means for satisfying information requirements should be explored before more complicated, multidimensional reporting approaches are evaluated. As a consequence, this study examines the relevance of a single measurement method—replacement costing.

Various means were explored that explain how replacement cost reports could conceivably provide a basis for user projections of future flows. We suggested that replacement costing might provide users with *information for predictions*. The object of prediction would be future distributable operating flows—a prime determinant of future dividends. This information for predictions could be used either as a lead indicator for future flows or as a basis for extrapolating future flows.

We further suggested that ratio analysis might be useful in assessing the risk associated with future distributable operating flows. In order to evaluate the utility of replacement costs for this purpose, we briefly examined the characteristics of certain replacement cost ratios. Ratios regarding liquidity-solvency and profit generating potential were discussed.

In summary, our examination of the utility of replacement costing incorporated these steps. First, a theoretical structure for explaining how accounting data might aid a user in generating his own predictions of future events was developed. Second, replacement cost information was examined in light of these developed predictive alternatives. Normative criteria and analytical techniques were used extensively. Finally, available empirical evidence was incorporated into the developed framework wherever possible and avenues for future research approaches were explored.

Hopefully, this study provides some heretofore absent theoretical structure to the replacement cost area. This structure is useful in identifying the imbedded assumptions regarding the behavior of prices and other economic conditions which are necessary for replacement costing to perform as intended. Of course, the conditions necessary for the theory to generate precise forecasts are so restrictive that one would not expect them to be met precisely in practice. Realistically, then, the research issue is to discover how well these required conditions may approximate real-world conditions. If some approximate relationship does exist, then a replacement cost system may provide a basis by which one might generate tolerably accurate forecasts of future events. However, if the required conditions are greatly at variance with observed, real-world conditions, then a replacement cost system probably would not provide a useful predictive basis. Clearly, additional evidence is needed before such questions can be answered.

Portions of this book are likely to be controversial. Insofar as this controversy centers on the framework developed for explaining the relevance of replacement cost reports, critics should strive to develop some alternative framework or improve the one presented here. In this manner, the benefits of a theoretical structure in the replacement cost area will be realized. The structure that survives may be somewhat different from the structure developed in this study, but this is unimportant. What is important is that *some* theoretical framework be developed and accepted as a basis for guiding needed empirical research in the external reporting area.

Other areas of controversy may relate to certain of the normative objectives and resultant deductively derived conclusions within the overall theoretical structure. To effectively counter these conclusions, alternative propositions and relevant empirical evidence must be developed. To the extent that this study motivates such research efforts, it will hasten progress in the external reporting area and thus accomplish its basic purpose.

Index